The Super-Easy
Crock Pot Cookbook

2000+ Days of Hot Healthy and Amazing Homemade Recipes to Discover the Deliciousness of Slow Cooking | with Easy-to-Follow Instructions for Beginners

Florence D. Prince

Contents

Chapter 3: Lunch Recipes 33

Chapter 4: Dinner Recipes 46

Chapter 5: Vegetable and Vegetarian Recipes 60

Chapter 6: Sides & Appetiser Recipes 72

Chapter 7: Soup & Stews 84

Chapter 8: Fish and Seafood 94

Chapter 9: Beef, Pork and Lamb Recipes 106

Chapter 10: Dessert Recipes 118

Introduction

Welcome to the world of hassle-free, delicious home-cooked meals! In this comprehensive guide, we embark on a culinary journey exploring the wonders of Crock Pot cooking. Whether you're a seasoned chef or a kitchen novice, this book is your gateway to mastering the art of slow cooking. Discover the convenience of preparing mouthwatering dishes with minimal effort and maximum flavour. From hearty stews simmered to perfection to decadent desserts that melt in your mouth, our book is packed with a diverse array of recipes tailored to tantalise your taste buds. Learn the secrets of balancing flavours, experimenting with ingredients, and transforming simple ingredients into extraordinary culinary creations. So, dust off your Crock Pot, roll up your sleeves, and let's embark on a culinary adventure that will redefine your approach to home cooking. Get ready to savour the aroma of slow-cooked goodness and delight your senses with every dish. Let's cook up a storm!

What Can You Cook In A Crock Pot?

The beauty of a crock pot lies in its versatility. It's not merely a kitchen appliance; it's a culinary wizard that can conjure a vast array of dishes, satisfying every palate and dietary preference. So, what exactly can you cook in a crock pot? The answer: almost anything your heart desires.

Hearty Stews and Soups
Crock pots excel at creating hearty and soul-warming stews and soups. Imagine tender chunks of meat, vibrant vegetables, and aromatic herbs simmering together for hours, infusing the broth with rich flavours. From classic beef stew to exotic Moroccan lentil soup, your crock pot can turn simple ingredients into a bowl of comfort.

Succulent Roasts
One of the crock pot's most celebrated talents is turning tough cuts of meat into succulent, melt-in-your-mouth roasts. Whether it's a pork shoulder, beef brisket, or whole chicken, the slow and low cooking method transforms them into tender masterpieces, perfect for family dinners or gatherings.

Flavourful Curries
Spice enthusiasts rejoice! Crock pots are excellent at coaxing out the intricate flavours of spices, making them ideal for cooking curries. From creamy butter chicken to fiery Thai red curry, your crock pot can handle a myriad of spice combinations, creating restaurant-quality curries in the comfort of your home.

Pasta Bakes and Casseroles
Who doesn't love a bubbling, cheesy pasta bake? Your crock pot can effortlessly prepare pasta dishes, from classic lasagna to innovative mac and cheese variations. Layer your favourite ingredients, set the timer, and return to a piping hot, perfectly baked pasta masterpiece.

Healthy Vegetarian and Vegan Dishes
Vegetarians and vegans, rejoice! The crock pot is a treasure trove for plant-based cooking. Think creamy coconut chickpea curry, hearty lentil stews, or vegetable-packed ratatouille. With the gentle heat of the crock pot, vegetables and legumes transform into delectable, satisfying meals.

Delectable Desserts
Yes, you read that right – desserts! Crock pots are not limited to savoury dishes. They can whip up mouthwatering desserts like bread pudding, fruit cobblers, and even cheesecake. The slow cooking process ensures that flavours meld together perfectly, creating desserts that are as convenient as they are delicious.

Breakfast Delights
Your crock pot can even simplify your breakfast routine. Prepare overnight oats, breakfast casseroles, or even yoghurt right in the crock pot. Wake up to the enticing aroma of a fully cooked breakfast, ready to be enjoyed without any morning rush.

Infused Beverages
Beyond food, crock pots can be used to infuse beverages. Create mulled wine, cider, or spiced syrups for cocktails. The low heat gently extracts flavours, resulting in beverages that are rich, aromatic, and perfect for entertaining.

In essence, a crock pot is a gateway to a world of culinary possibilities. It's not just a time-saving device; it's a tool that empowers you to experiment, innovate, and create meals that delight the senses. So, whether you're a busy professional, a home cook with a passion for flavours, or someone looking to simplify their cooking journey, the crock pot is your steadfast companion, ready to transform ordinary ingredients into extraordinary gastronomic delights.

What Is A Crock Pot?

In the bustling realm of modern kitchens, where time is a precious commodity and flavour is non-negotiable, the humble crock pot stands as an unsung hero. Also known as a slow cooker, this ingenious device has revolutionised the way we prepare meals, turning everyday ingredients into culinary masterpieces with minimal effort.

At its core, a crock pot is a countertop electrical appliance designed to simmer food at low temperatures for an extended period. The magic lies in its simplicity. A durable ceramic or porcelain pot sits nestled within an electric heating element. This pot, often referred to as the crock, is where the culinary alchemy happens.

How Does It Work?
The crock pot operates on a principle of prolonged, low-temperature cooking. Unlike conventional stovetop cooking, where high heat is applied quickly, the crock

pot simmers ingredients slowly over several hours. This gentle and consistent heat allows flavours to meld together, transforming even the toughest cuts of meat into tender, succulent delights.

Key Components:

- Heating Element: The heating element, usually located at the base of the appliance, provides the necessary heat to cook the food. It's designed to maintain a constant, low temperature, ensuring slow and even cooking.
- Crock: The crock, made from durable materials like ceramic or porcelain, is where the ingredients are placed. Its heat distribution and heat retention properties are crucial for the slow cooking process. The crock is removable, making it easy to clean and serve meals directly from it.
- Lid: The crock pot is always covered with a fitted lid during cooking. The lid traps moisture and heat, creating a sealed environment that enhances the flavours and ensures the ingredients remain juicy and tender.

Why Choose a Crock Pot?

- Convenience: Crock pots are a busy cook's best friend. With minimal preparation, you can toss ingredients into the pot, set the temperature, and go about your day. Return hours later to a perfectly cooked meal, ready to be enjoyed.
- Versatility: From soups and stews to roasts and desserts, a crock pot can prepare a wide variety of dishes. It accommodates everything from breakfast to dinner and even beverages, making it a versatile addition to any kitchen.
- Health Benefits: The slow cooking process retains more nutrients in the food compared to high-heat methods. It also allows for leaner cuts of meat to become tender without added fats, promoting healthier eating habits.
- Economical: Crock pots are incredibly energy-efficient. Their low wattage means they consume minimal electricity, making them an economical choice for cooking.

Overall, a crock pot is more than a kitchen appliance; it's a culinary companion that simplifies meal preparation while elevating the taste and texture of your dishes. It embodies the essence of slow and mindful cooking, bringing warmth, aroma, and exceptional flavours to your table with every meal. Whether you're a novice cook or a seasoned chef, a crock pot is an indispensable tool that transforms ordinary ingredients into extraordinary feasts, one slow-cooked dish at a time.

Benefits Of Using A Crock Pot

Beyond its apparent convenience, using a crock pot offers a plethora of benefits that cater to both the novice cook and the seasoned chef, making it an indispensable kitchen companion. Here are the remarkable advantages of incorporating a crock pot into your culinary repertoire:

Time Efficiency

The primary allure of a crock pot lies in its time-saving prowess. With our lives becoming busier by the day, the crock pot allows you to prepare delicious, homemade meals with minimal hands-on time. Once the ingredients are in the pot and the timer is set, you can carry on with your day while the crock pot works its magic, slow-cooking your meal to perfection.

Effortless Preparation

Crock pot recipes often involve minimal preparation. No need for intricate knife skills or constant supervision; simply chop your ingredients, toss them into the pot, and let the slow cooker do the rest. This simplicity makes it ideal for busy professionals, parents, or anyone looking to simplify their cooking routine.

Enhanced Flavours

Slow cooking is synonymous with intensified flavours. The gentle, prolonged cooking process allows spices and seasonings to meld seamlessly, resulting in dishes that are rich, aromatic, and deeply flavorful. Tough cuts of meat tenderise, and the natural juices of the ingredients are retained, creating mouthwatering, succulent meals.

Nutrient Preservation

Unlike high-heat cooking methods that can deplete food of essential nutrients, the low and steady heat of a crock pot preserves vitamins, minerals, and antioxidants in your ingredients. Vegetables retain their vibrant colours and nutritional value, ensuring that your meals are as healthy as they are tasty.

Versatility

Crock pots are incredibly versatile. From hearty stews and soups to tender roasts, casseroles, desserts, and even beverages, there's almost nothing a crock pot can't prepare. Its adaptability makes it suitable for a wide range of cuisines and culinary preferences, making experimenting with different recipes a delight.

Energy Efficiency

Crock pots are designed to be energy-efficient. Their low wattage means they consume minimal electricity, making them an eco-friendly choice compared to conventional ovens or stovetop cooking methods. Slow cooking over several hours also reduces the need for constant reheating, further saving energy.

Economical

Using a crock pot can save you money. It allows you to transform budget-friendly ingredients, such as affordable cuts of meat and seasonal produce, into delectable meals. The slow-cooking process tenderises less expensive cuts of meat, making them as palatable as pricier options.

Stress-Free Entertaining

Crock pots are invaluable when hosting gatherings or dinner parties. They enable you to prepare large quantities of food in advance, ensuring that your guests are treated to freshly cooked, restaurant-quality meals without the stress and chaos of last-minute preparations.

In conclusion, the crock pot is not merely a kitchen appliance; it is a time-saving, flavour-enhancing, and nutrition-preserving marvel that empowers you to create wholesome, delightful meals effortlessly. Its benefits extend far beyond the realm of convenience, making it a kitchen essential that elevates your cooking experience while accommodating your modern, fast-paced lifestyle.

How To Use A Crock Pot?

Mastering the art of using a crock pot is akin to discovering a secret doorway to effortless, flavorful meals. Whether you're a beginner or a seasoned cook, understanding how to utilise this kitchen marvel can elevate your culinary skills to new heights. Here's a comprehensive guide on how to make the most of your crock pot:

Familiarise Yourself With Your Crock Pot

- Every crock pot is unique. Before you begin, read the user manual to understand its specific features, settings, and safety instructions.
- Take note of the pot's size and capacity. Overfilling or under-filling can affect cooking times and results.

Choose the Right Recipe

- Opt for recipes specifically designed for slow cookers. These recipes are tailored to the slow-cooking process, ensuring the best results.
- Consider the cooking time. Some dishes, like soups and stews, benefit from long, slow cooking, while others, like seafood, require shorter durations to avoid overcooking.

Preparation is Key

- Prep your ingredients beforehand. Chop vegetables, trim meats, and measure seasonings in advance. This makes assembly a breeze and allows for a smoother cooking process.
- If a recipe calls for searing meat or sautéing vegetables, do so in a separate pan before adding them to the crock pot. This step enhances flavours.

Layering Matters

- Proper layering ensures even cooking. Place dense, slow-cooking vegetables like potatoes and carrots at the bottom, followed by meats and lighter vegetables. Liquids and seasonings should be poured over the top.

Mind the Liquid

- Liquids do not evaporate as they do with conventional cooking methods. Reduce the amount of liquid in the recipe, especially if you're adapting a stovetop or oven recipe for the crock pot.
- For soups and stews, add just enough liquid to cover the ingredients. Remember, the ingredients will release their own juices during cooking.

Resist the Urge to Peek

- Each time you lift the lid, heat and moisture escape, extending the cooking time. Trust the process and resist the temptation to check on your dish frequently.

Timing Is Everything

- Follow the recipe's recommended cooking time closely. Slow cookers are designed to maintain a low, steady heat, so overcooking is less likely to occur.
- If you need to leave the dish cooking for longer than the recipe suggests, consider using a timer. Many crock pots have timers that switch to a 'warm' setting after the cooking time is complete.

Experiment and Have Fun

- Once you're comfortable with basic recipes, don't hesitate to experiment. Crock pots are versatile and can accommodate various cuisines and ingredients.
- Keep a culinary journal. Note down successful recipes, modifications, and cooking times. This helps you refine your skills and tailor recipes to your preferences.

By mastering these steps, you'll unlock the full potential of your crock pot, transforming everyday ingredients into delectable, comforting meals with minimal effort. As you gain confidence, you'll find that your crock pot becomes an indispensable tool, allowing you to explore the vast world of slow-cooked delights.

Tips And Tricks For Using Your Crock Pot

Using a crock pot can be a game-changer in your kitchen, simplifying your cooking routine and enhancing the flavours of your meals. Here are some expert tips and tricks to help you make the most out of your crock pot experience:

Choose the Right Cut of Meat

For succulent, tender results, opt for tougher cuts of meat like chuck roast, brisket, or pork shoulder. These cuts benefit from the slow-cooking process, becoming incredibly tender and flavorful.

Brown Your Meat First

While it's not necessary, browning meat before adding it to the crock pot enhances the depth of flavour. Searing the meat in a hot pan creates a caramelised crust, adding richness to your dishes.

Layer Ingredients Wisely

As a general rule, place root vegetables at the bottom of the crock pot, followed by meat, and then softer vegetables and liquids on top. This arrangement ensures even cooking and prevents certain ingredients from becoming mushy.

Mind the Liquid

Slow cookers require less liquid than traditional cooking methods. Liquids don't evaporate as much, so reduce the amount of broth, sauces, or water in your recipes to avoid overly watery dishes.

Harness the Power of Herbs and Spices

Dried herbs and spices can lose their potency over long cooking times. Add them at the beginning for a subtle infusion of flavours. Fresh herbs, however, should be added towards the end of the cooking process to maintain their vibrancy.

Don't Overfill

Fill your crock pot to at least half full for best results, but avoid overfilling. Overcrowding can lead to uneven cooking and may result in undercooked food.

Avoid the Temptation to Stir

Unlike stovetop cooking, stirring isn't necessary in a crock pot. The ingredients cook evenly without intervention. Resist the urge to lift the lid and stir, as this can prolong the cooking time.

Add Dairy Products Towards the End

Dairy products, such as milk, cream, or cheese, have a tendency to curdle or separate when subjected to prolonged heat. Add these ingredients during the last hour or so of cooking to prevent this from happening.

Utilise Slow Cooker Liners

Slow cooker liners are a convenient way to make clean-up easier. These disposable liners fit into your crock pot and prevent food from sticking, making the washing-up process a breeze.

Experiment with Desserts and Breakfast Dishes

Slow cookers aren't just for savoury meals. Explore dessert options like puddings, cobblers, and cakes, as well as breakfast dishes like oatmeal and frittatas. Your crock pot can create delightful sweet and savoury treats with minimal effort.

With these tips in mind, you'll be well-equipped to create a variety of delicious dishes using your crock pot. Whether you're a busy professional, a parent, or someone who simply loves flavorful, home-cooked meals, your crock pot will become your most valued kitchen companion. Happy slow cooking!

The Functions Of A Crock Pot

A crock pot, also known as a slow cooker, is a versatile kitchen appliance designed to simplify the cooking process and enhance the flavours of your meals. Its functions extend far beyond basic simmering. Here's a comprehensive look at what a crock pot can do:

Low and Slow Cooking

The primary function of a crock pot is to cook food slowly at low temperatures over an extended period. This gentle cooking method tenderise tough cuts of meat, allowing them to become succulent and flavorful. It's ideal for braises, stews, soups, and chilis.

One-Pot Meals

Crock pots are perfect for creating one-pot meals. You can combine various ingredients such as meat, vegetables, grains, and spices in the pot, and let them cook together to develop complex flavours. This makes meal preparation incredibly convenient, requiring minimal hands-on time.

Meal Prepping

Crock pots are a game-changer for meal prepping. You can prepare large batches of your favourite recipes and portion them into containers for the week. This not only saves time but also ensures you have delicious, homemade meals ready to enjoy whenever you need them.

Desserts and Baked Goods

Beyond savoury dishes, crock pots are excellent for making desserts and baked goods. You can prepare moist and flavorful cakes, puddings, cobblers, and even cheesecakes. The slow, even heat ensures that these sweets turn out perfectly every time.

Infusion of Flavors

Crock pots are exceptional at infusing flavours into your dishes. Herbs, spices, and aromatics have ample time to mingle and develop, resulting in rich, aromatic meals. This slow infusion process can transform ordinary ingredients into extraordinary culinary creations.

Hands-Off Cooking

One of the greatest benefits of a crock pot is its hands-off cooking nature. Once you've loaded the ingredients, set the temperature, and timer, you can leave it unattended. This makes it an excellent appliance for busy individuals or families, allowing you to return home to a hot, home-cooked meal.

Keep Warm Function

Most modern crock pots come with a "keep warm" function, which keeps your food at a safe serving temperature after it has finished cooking. This feature ensures your meal is ready to enjoy whenever you are, without the risk of overcooking.

Yoghurt Making

Some crock pots have a low-temperature setting ideal for making yoghurt. With the right ingredients and a bit of patience, you can create creamy, homemade yoghurt without the need for a specialised yoghurt maker.

Understanding these functions opens up a world of culinary possibilities. Whether you're a novice cook or a seasoned chef, a crock pot can become your secret weapon in the kitchen, helping you prepare delicious and satisfying meals with minimal effort. Explore the diverse functions of your crock pot, and you'll discover the joy of easy, flavorful cooking.

Quick Start Guide

This Quick Start Guide will help you familiarise yourself with the basics, ensuring you get the most out of your appliance from day one. Here's how to dive right into slow-cooking success:

Unboxing and Inspection

Carefully unpack your crock pot and inspect it for any visible damage. Make sure all components, such as the ceramic pot, lid, and heating base, are present and intact.

Cleaning and Preparation

Wash the ceramic pot, lid, and other accessories with warm, soapy water before your first use. Dry them thoroughly. This step ensures your crock pot is clean and ready for cooking.

Understanding the Controls

Familiarise yourself with the control panel. Most crock pots have settings such as Low, High, and Warm. Low and High refer to the cooking temperatures, while Warm is for keeping your food at a safe serving temperature.

Simple Recipes for Beginners

Start with easy recipes. Soups, stews, and chilli are great beginner options. They usually involve combining ingredients in the pot, setting the temperature, and letting the crock pot work its magic.

Proper Ingredient Preparation

Ensure ingredients are cut into uniform sizes to ensure even cooking. Meats, vegetables, and other components should be appropriately sized according to the recipe instructions.

Layering for Best Results

For layered recipes, such as casseroles, start with dense, slow-cooking ingredients like potatoes at the bottom. Add meats and other ingredients, ending with softer vegetables and liquids on top. This layering technique promotes even cooking.

Avoid Overfilling

Do not overfill your crock pot. Most models have a recommended fill line. Overfilling can prevent proper cooking and might lead to spills. Follow the guidelines in your user manual.

Understanding Cooking Times

Familiarise yourself with the suggested cooking times for various recipes. Cooking times can vary based on the temperature setting and the type of dish you're preparing.

Experimenting and Customization

Once you're comfortable with basic recipes, don't be afraid to experiment. Modify recipes to suit your taste preferences, and don't hesitate to try out new dishes. Crock pot cooking is versatile and allows for creativity.

Safety First

Always follow safety instructions provided in your user manual. Use pot holders or oven mitts when handling hot components, and keep the crock pot on a stable surface away from the edge of the counter.

By following this Quick Start Guide, you'll be well on your way to mastering the art of crock pot cooking. With a bit of practice, you'll soon be creating delicious, home-cooked meals with minimal effort. Enjoy the journey of discovering the endless possibilities your crock pot has to offer!

What's Included In Crock Pot Cuisine?

Crock pot cuisine is a world of flavour and convenience waiting to be explored. In this section, we'll delve into the diverse array of dishes and cuisines you can create using your crock pot. From hearty soups to mouthwatering roasts, the possibilities are endless.

Soups and Stews

Crock pots are renowned for producing rich, flavorful soups and stews. Whether you're making a classic chicken noodle soup, a hearty beef stew, or a spicy chilli, your crock pot will infuse every spoonful with mouthwatering goodness. The slow and steady cooking process allows flavours to meld, resulting in a comforting bowl of warmth.

Roasts and Braised Meats

Achieving perfectly tender and succulent roasts and braised meats is effortless with a crock pot. From pot roasts to pulled pork, the low and slow cooking method transforms tougher cuts of meat into melt-in-your-mouth masterpieces. Marinades, herbs, and spices work their magic over time, resulting in a symphony of flavours.

Casseroles and One-Pot Wonders

Simplify your meal preparation with crock pot casseroles and one-pot wonders. Layered dishes like lasagna, cheesy potatoes, and pasta bakes come together effortlessly in your crock pot. With minimal effort and a single pot to clean, you'll have a satisfying meal ready in no time.

Curries and Ethnic Delights

Explore the world of international cuisines by preparing curries, tagines, and ethnic dishes in your crock pot. Whether it's a fragrant Indian curry, a Moroccan tagine, or a Mexican mole, your crock pot can handle a wide range of spices and ingredients to transport your taste buds.

Breakfast and Brunch

Your crock pot isn't just for dinner. Wake up to the aroma of a slow-cooked breakfast or brunch. Prepare dishes like overnight oats, breakfast casseroles, and even cinnamon rolls. Your morning routine just got a whole lot tastier and easier.

Desserts and Sweets

Don't forget about dessert! Crock pots are versatile enough to whip up delightful sweet treats like bread pudding, lava cakes, and fruit cobblers. The gentle heat ensures your desserts are perfectly cooked without the risk of burning.

Vegetarian and Vegan Options

Vegetarians and vegans can also enjoy the benefits of crock pot cooking. Create plant-based soups, vegetable curries, and protein-packed legume dishes that are as flavorful as they are nutritious.

Dips and Appetisers

Hosting a gathering? Crock pots are ideal for keeping dips and appetisers warm and ready for dipping. From cheesy dips to meatball appetisers, your crock pot will be the life of the party.

Beverages and Mulled Delights

Extend your crock pot's usefulness to beverages. Make mulled wine, spiced cider, or hot chocolate for a crowd during colder months. Your guests will appreciate the comforting and aromatic drinks.

Leftover Makeovers

Don't let leftovers go to waste. Repurpose last night's meal into something new and exciting. Transform roast chicken into tacos, or beef stew into a savoury pie filling.

In the world of crock pot cuisine, your imagination is the only limit. With a little creativity and experimentation, you can craft a wide variety of dishes and culinary delights, all while enjoying the ease and convenience of slow cooking. So, roll up your sleeves, gather your ingredients, and let your crock pot take you on a flavorful journey through the world of delicious cuisine.

Things To Consider Before Using Your Crock Pot

Before you embark on your culinary journey with your crock pot, there are a few essential considerations to ensure that your cooking experience is safe, efficient, and enjoyable.

Selecting the Right Size
Consider the size of your crock pot in relation to the quantity of food you plan to prepare. Crock pots come in various sizes, so choose one that suits your family's needs. A smaller pot is ideal for dips and sauces, while larger ones can accommodate roasts and soups for a crowd.

Prepping Ingredients
Preparing ingredients properly is crucial for successful crock pot meals. Chop vegetables uniformly to ensure even cooking, and trim excess fat from meats to avoid an oily residue in your dishes. Browning meats before placing them in the crock pot can enhance flavours and texture.

Understanding Cooking Times
Different recipes require varying cooking times and temperature settings. Familiarise yourself with your crock pot's low, medium, and high settings. Most recipes provide guidelines, but experimenting and keeping track of cooking times can help you perfect your favourite dishes.

Layering Ingredients
Layering ingredients strategically can impact the final taste and texture of your meal. Place root vegetables and dense meats at the bottom, where they'll benefit from direct heat. Delicate ingredients like seafood and quick-cooking vegetables should be added later in the cooking process to prevent overcooking.

Liquid Levels
The amount of liquid in your crock pot can significantly influence the outcome of your dish. Ingredients release moisture during cooking, so be cautious about adding too much liquid initially. You can always adjust the consistency later in the cooking process if necessary.

Avoiding Recipe Overcrowding
While it might be tempting to maximise your crock pot's capacity, overcrowding ingredients can lead to uneven cooking. Leave some space between ingredients to allow hot air to circulate, ensuring that everything cooks evenly.

Safety First
Always prioritise safety when using your crock pot. Avoid sudden temperature changes, such as placing a hot pot on a cold surface, to prevent cracking. Use pot holders and handle your crock pot with care, especially when it's hot. Also, avoid lifting the lid unnecessarily, as this can significantly extend the cooking time.

Care and Maintenance
Regular cleaning and proper storage are vital for your crock pot's longevity. Follow the manufacturer's instructions for cleaning, and store your crock pot in a cool, dry place. Be mindful of the electrical components, and never immerse the base in water.

By keeping these considerations in mind, you'll be well-equipped to make the most out of your crock pot cooking adventures. With a little attention to detail and a dash of creativity, you'll soon be preparing delicious, hassle-free meals that will delight your taste buds and simplify your busy life.

The Difference Between A Slow Cooker And A Crock Pot

The terms "slow cooker" and "crock pot" are often used interchangeably, but there are some subtle differences between the two. Understanding these differences can help you make an informed choice when selecting the right appliance for your cooking needs.

Origin and Branding
"Crock Pot" is a specific brand of slow cooker, and it's become synonymous with the appliance itself. The name "crock pot" is often used colloquially to refer to any type of slow cooker. Slow cookers, on the other hand, are a broader category of appliances that include various brands and models, each with its own features and designs.

Heating Elements
Both slow cookers and crock pots function on the same principle: they use low heat and a long cooking time to prepare meals. However, different brands might employ slightly different heating elements and technologies, leading to variations in cooking times and temperatures. It's essential to refer to the specific instructions for your appliance to achieve the best results.

Construction and Material
Crock pots, being a specific brand, have their unique design and construction features. They often have a stoneware or ceramic inner pot that sits inside an electric heating element. Some slow cookers have metal pots, while others feature stoneware. The choice of material can affect the way heat is distributed and retained, influencing the cooking process.

Features and Controls
Slow cookers come in a wide range of models with various features. Some have programmable timers, allowing you to set precise cooking durations and switch to a warming mode afterward. Others have manual controls with low, medium, and high heat settings. Crock pots may offer specific features unique to the brand, but many slow cookers also come with similar functionalities.

Availability and Price
Slow cookers are widely available from different manufacturers and retailers. Crock pots, being a specific brand, might have a distinct price point associated with their reputation and features. When choosing between the two, consider your budget and the specific features you need for your cooking endeavours.

In summary, while "crock pot" is a brand name that has

become synonymous with slow cookers, the market offers various slow cooker models from different brands. When selecting an appliance, focus on its features, construction, and controls to ensure it aligns with your cooking requirements. Whether you choose a renowned crock pot or another reputable slow cooker brand, both can help you create delicious, convenient, and perfectly cooked meals with minimal effort.

What To Consider When Buying A Crock Pot?

Purchasing a crock pot is an investment in convenient and flavorful cooking, but with numerous options available, it's essential to consider several factors before making a decision. Here's a comprehensive guide to help you choose the perfect crock pot for your culinary needs:

Size and Capacity
Consider the size of your household and the number of people you usually cook for. Crock pots come in various sizes, ranging from compact 1.5-quart models suitable for singles or couples, to larger 8-quart options ideal for families or entertaining guests. Choose a size that matches your typical batch sizes to prevent overfilling or underutilizing the appliance.

Programmable vs. Manual
Decide whether you prefer a crock pot with programmable features or a manual one. Programmable models allow you to set specific cooking times and temperature levels, ensuring your meals are perfectly cooked without the risk of overcooking. Manual crock pots come with basic settings like low, medium, and high, offering simplicity for those who prefer more control over the cooking process.

Shape and Design
Crock pots come in oval and round shapes. Oval pots are great for cooking large cuts of meat or whole chickens, while round pots are ideal for soups, stews, and casseroles. Consider the types of dishes you plan to prepare and choose the shape that accommodates your recipes best.

Material and Durability
Crock pots typically feature a stoneware or ceramic inner pot, which retains and distributes heat evenly. Ensure the material is durable, easy to clean, and safe for dishwasher use. The outer casing is usually made of stainless steel or other heat-resistant materials. Opt for a crock pot with sturdy construction that can withstand long hours of cooking.

Lid Seal and Ventilation
Look for a crock pot with a well-fitting lid that creates a tight seal. A secure seal retains moisture and flavour, ensuring your dishes remain succulent. Some lids have a vent to release excess steam, preventing pressure buildup. This feature is particularly useful when preparing recipes that generate a lot of steam.

Heat Settings and Warming Function
Consider the number of heat settings the crock pot offers. Most models have at least three settings: low, medium, and high. Some advanced crock pots have additional settings like sauté and sear. A warming function is essential for keeping your meals hot and ready to serve after cooking. Ensure the warming feature operates automatically or can be manually activated to avoid overcooking your food.

Portability
If you plan to take your crock pot to potlucks, gatherings, or picnics, consider a model with locking lids and secure handles. Portability features make it easier to transport your dishes without the risk of spills or accidents.

Budget
Set a budget for your crock pot purchase. While there are various models available at different price points, remember that investing in a higher-quality crock pot often translates to better durability and performance. Consider your budget constraints and choose the best crock pot within your financial range.

Brand Reputation and Reviews
Research different brands and read customer reviews to gauge the reputation and reliability of the crock pots you're considering. Reputable brands often provide better customer support and warranty options, ensuring your investment is protected.

Additional Features
Some crock pots come with additional features such as delay start timers, temperature probes for checking meat doneness, and cooking accessories. Evaluate these extras based on your cooking style and preferences.

By carefully considering these factors, you can select a crock pot that aligns with your cooking habits, making meal preparation a breeze while enhancing the flavours of your favourite recipes.

Crock Pot Kitchen Equipment And Tools

Preparing meals with a crock pot involves more than just the appliance itself; having the right kitchen equipment and tools can greatly enhance your cooking experience. Here's a detailed guide to the essential kitchen equipment and tools you'll need to make the most out of your crock pot cooking adventures:

Crock Pot
Of course, the first and most crucial item is the crock pot itself. Choose a size and features that suit your cooking needs, as discussed in the previous section.

Cutting Board and Knives
A durable cutting board and sharp knives are essential for preparing ingredients. Invest in a good-quality cutting board to chop vegetables, meat, and other components of your recipes safely and efficiently.

Measuring Cups and Spoons
Accurate measurements are vital for successful crock pot cooking. Invest in both liquid and dry measuring cups, as well as a set of measuring spoons. This ensures precise quantities of ingredients, especially for recipes that require specific ratios of liquids and solids.

Sauté Pan or Skillet

While some crock pots have sauté functions, having a separate sauté pan or skillet is handy for recipes that require browning meat or caramelising onions before transferring them to the crock pot. Choose a non-stick or stainless steel pan for versatile and efficient cooking.

Wooden Spoon or Silicone Spatula

Wooden spoons or silicone spatulas are perfect for stirring ingredients in both the sauté pan and the crock pot. They're gentle on the crock pot's non-stick surface and help in evenly distributing flavours.

Tongs

Tongs are useful for turning and flipping meat when browning it in a sauté pan. They provide a secure grip and prevent accidents while handling hot ingredients.

Slow Cooker Liners

Slow cooker liners are convenient disposable bags that fit inside your crock pot. They make cleanup a breeze by preventing food from sticking to the pot's surface. Using liners can save you time and effort in washing up.

Aluminium Foil

Aluminium foil is versatile and can be used to create a barrier between layers of ingredients in the crock pot, preventing them from overcooking. It's also handy for making foil packets for individual servings.

Instant-Read Thermometer

An instant-read thermometer is invaluable for checking the internal temperature of meat, ensuring it's cooked to the proper doneness and safe to eat. This tool is especially useful for recipes requiring precise meat temperatures.

Crock Pot Recipe Books

While not a physical tool, having a collection of crock pot recipe books or access to reliable online recipes broadens your culinary horizons. Experiment with various cuisines and cooking techniques to keep your meals diverse and exciting.

Storage Containers

Proper storage is essential for leftovers. Invest in a set of airtight storage containers in various sizes to store your crock pot creations safely. Glass or BPA-free plastic containers are excellent options.

Timer or Alarm Clock

Many crock pot recipes require specific cooking times. While programmable crock pots have built-in timers, having an external timer or setting an alarm clock ensures you don't miss any crucial steps in your recipes.

By having these essential kitchen tools and equipment on hand, you can approach crock pot cooking with confidence, knowing you have everything you need to create delicious and wholesome meals for yourself and your family. Happy cooking!

Crock Pot Cleaning And Maintenance

Crock pots are wonderful appliances that simplify meal preparation, but to ensure their longevity and the quality of your dishes, proper cleaning and maintenance are essential. Follow these guidelines to keep your crock pot in excellent condition:

Cool Down Before Cleaning

Always allow your crock pot to cool down completely before attempting to clean it. Placing hot ceramic parts in cold water can cause them to crack, ruining the pot.

Removable Parts

Most modern crock pots have removable stoneware inserts and lids. Remove these parts carefully after use and wash them separately. These components are usually dishwasher-safe, making cleanup easier. If you prefer handwashing, use warm, soapy water and a soft sponge to avoid scratching the surface.

Non-Removable Parts

Some crock pots have non-removable parts like the base and heating element. To clean these, unplug the appliance and use a damp cloth to wipe the exterior. Avoid getting any moisture inside the base, as it can damage the electrical components.

Tough Stains and Residue

For stubborn stains or residue in the stoneware insert, create a paste of baking soda and water. Apply the paste to the stained areas and let it sit for a few hours. Then, scrub gently with a soft brush or sponge. Rinse thoroughly to remove any residue.

Avoid Abrasive Cleaners

Avoid using abrasive cleaners or scouring pads on your crock pot, as they can scratch the surface and damage the non-stick coating. Opt for soft brushes, sponges, or cloths to maintain the pot's integrity.

Handle with Care

Be gentle with the stoneware insert, especially when washing or storing it. Avoid drastic temperature changes, as this can cause the ceramic to crack.

Lid Care

Clean the crock pot's lid thoroughly after each use. If there are food particles stuck in the vent holes, use a toothpick or a soft brush to remove them. Make sure the lid is completely dry before storing it to prevent odours or mould growth.

Regular Maintenance

Check the cord and plug for any signs of wear or damage. If you notice any issues, contact the manufacturer or a qualified technician for repairs. Regularly inspect the crock pot for signs of wear and tear, and address any problems promptly to avoid further damage.

Storage

Store your crock pot and its components separately to prevent scratches and breakage. If possible, keep the original packaging for safe storage when the crock pot is not in use.

By following these cleaning and maintenance practices, you can ensure that your crock pot remains in excellent condition, allowing you to continue preparing delicious, hassle-free meals for years to come.

Chapter 1: Breakfast Recipes

Full English Breakfast Casserole

Serves: 6 Prep time: 15 minutes / Cook time: 6 hours on low heat

Ingredients:
- 400g diced potatoes
- 200g diced bacon
- 200g pork sausages, sliced
- 150g sliced mushrooms
- 100g cherry tomatoes, halved
- 400g canned baked beans
- 6 large eggs
- 250ml whole milk
- Salt and black pepper, to taste
- 100g shredded cheddar cheese

Preparation instructions:
1. In the crock pot, layer the diced potatoes, diced bacon, sliced pork sausages, sliced mushrooms, and halved cherry tomatoes.
2. Pour the canned baked beans over the layered Ingredients.
3. In a separate bowl, whisk together eggs, whole milk, salt, and black pepper.
4. Pour the egg mixture evenly over the layered Ingredients in the crock pot.
5. Sprinkle shredded cheddar cheese on top.
6. Cover and cook on low heat for 6 hours or until the eggs are set and the potatoes are tender.
7. Serve hot, portioning out the casserole for a traditional Full English Breakfast experience.

Slow Cooker Porridge

Serves: 4 Prep time: 5 minutes / Cook time: 8 hours on low heat

Ingredients:
- 200g steel-cut oats
- 800ml water
- 400ml whole milk
- 2 tbsp honey or maple syrup
- 1/2 tsp ground cinnamon
- 1/2 tsp vanilla extract
- Fresh berries and nuts for topping

Preparation instructions:
1. Combine steel-cut oats, water, whole milk, honey, cinnamon, and vanilla extract in the crock pot.
2. Stir well and cover. Cook on low heat for 8 hours, or overnight.
3. Stir the porridge before serving, adding more milk if necessary.
4. Serve hot, topped with fresh berries and nuts.

Crockpot Breakfast Burritos

Serves: 4 Prep time: 15 minutes / Cook time: 3 hours on low heat

Ingredients:
- 4 large flour tortillas
- 400g cooked breakfast sausages, crumbled
- 200g shredded cheddar cheese
- 6 large eggs, scrambled
- 1 green pepper, diced
- 1 red onion, finely chopped
- 1/2 tsp chilli powder
- Salt and black pepper, to taste
- Fresh oregano, chopped, for garnish

Preparation instructions:
1. In a mixing bowl, combine crumbled sausages, shredded cheese, scrambled eggs, diced pepper, chopped red onion, chilli powder, salt, and black pepper.
2. Lay out a tortilla and spoon the mixture in the centre. Roll the tortilla into a burrito, tucking in the ends.
3. Place the burritos seam-side down in the crock pot.
4. Cover and cook on low heat for 3 hours, until the burritos are heated through and the cheese is melted.
5. Serve hot, garnished with fresh oregano.

English Breakfast Beans

Serves: 4 Prep time: 10 minutes / Cook time: 2 hours on low heat

Ingredients:
- 400g canned baked beans
- 1 tbsp tomato paste
- 1 tbsp brown sugar
- 1/2 tsp mustard powder
- 1/2 tsp Worcestershire sauce
- Salt and black pepper, to taste

Preparation instructions:
1. In the crock pot, combine baked beans, tomato paste, brown sugar, mustard powder, Worcestershire sauce, salt, and black pepper.
2. Stir well to combine all the Ingredients.
3. Cover and cook on low heat for 2 hours, stirring occasionally, until the beans are heated through and the flavours meld together.
4. Serve hot as a side dish to your breakfast.

Slow Cooker Bacon and Egg Casserole

Serves: 4 Prep time: 15 minutes / Cook time: 4 hours on low heat

Ingredients:
- 200g bacon, chopped
- 8 large eggs
- 250ml whole milk
- 100g shredded cheddar cheese
- 1/2 tsp garlic powder
- 1/2 tsp onion powder
- Salt and black pepper, to taste
- Fresh parsley, chopped, for garnish

Preparation instructions:
1. In a skillet, cook the chopped bacon until crispy. Drain excess fat and set aside.
2. In a bowl, whisk together eggs, whole milk, garlic powder, onion powder, salt, and black pepper.
3. Grease the crock pot with butter or non-stick spray.
4. Layer cooked bacon in the bottom of the crock pot. Pour the egg mixture over the bacon.
5. Sprinkle shredded cheddar cheese on top.

5. Cover and cook on low heat for 4 hours, until the eggs are set.
6. Garnish with fresh chopped parsley before serving.

Vegetarian Breakfast Hash

Serves: 4 Prep time: 10 minutes / Cook time: 4 hours on low heat

Ingredients:
- 400g diced potatoes
- 200g diced peppers (assorted colours)
- 200g diced red onion   • 200g sliced mushrooms
- 2 tbsp olive oil   • 1/2 tsp paprika
- 1/2 tsp cumin powder
- Salt and black pepper, to taste
- Fresh parsley, chopped, for garnish

Preparation instructions:
1. In a large bowl, toss diced potatoes, peppers, red onion, and sliced mushrooms with olive oil, paprika, cumin powder, salt, and black pepper.
2. Transfer the seasoned vegetables to the crock pot.
3. Cover and cook on low heat for 4 hours, stirring occasionally, until the potatoes are tender and golden brown.
4. Garnish with fresh chopped parsley before serving.

Slow Cooker Black Pudding

Serves: 4 Prep time: 10 minutes / Cook time: 3 hours on low heat

Ingredients:
- 400g black pudding, sliced into rounds
- 2 tbsp vegetable oil
- 400g sliced mushrooms
- 1 red onion, finely chopped
- 2 cloves garlic, minced
- 1/2 tsp dried thyme
- Salt and black pepper, to taste

Preparation instructions:
1. Heat vegetable oil in a skillet over medium heat. Add black pudding rounds and cook until browned on both sides. Remove from the skillet and set aside.
2. In the same skillet, add sliced mushrooms, chopped red onion, minced garlic, dried thyme, salt, and black pepper. Cook until the mushrooms are tender and the onions are translucent.
3. Transfer the mushroom mixture to the crock pot. Arrange the cooked black pudding rounds on top.
4. Cover and cook on low heat for 3 hours, allowing the flavours to meld together.
5. Serve hot as a hearty breakfast dish.

Crockpot Sausage and Mushroom Omelette

Serves: 4 Prep time: 10 minutes / Cook time: 2 hours on low heat

Ingredients:
- 200g cooked breakfast sausages, sliced
- 200g sliced mushrooms
- 1 red pepper, diced
- 1 green pepper, diced
- 1/2 red onion, finely chopped
- 8 large eggs
- 250ml whole milk
- Salt and black pepper, to taste
- Fresh parsley, chopped, for garnish

Preparation instructions:
1. In the crock pot, layer sliced breakfast sausages, sliced mushrooms, diced red and green peppers, and chopped red onion.
2. In a bowl, whisk together eggs, whole milk, salt, and black pepper.
3. Pour the egg mixture over the layered Ingredients in the crock pot.
4. Cover and cook on low heat for 2 hours, until the eggs are set.
5. Garnish with fresh chopped parsley before serving.

Overnight Crockpot Breakfast Casserole

Serves: 6 Prep time: 15 minutes / Cook time: 6-8 hours on low heat

Ingredients:
- 400g diced potatoes   • 200g diced bacon
- 200g cooked breakfast sausages, crumbled
- 1 red pepper, diced   • 1 green pepper, diced
- 1/2 red onion, finely chopped
- 150g shredded cheddar cheese
- 8 large eggs   • 300ml whole milk
- 1/2 tsp garlic powder   • 1/2 tsp onion powder
- Salt and black pepper, to taste
- Fresh parsley, chopped, for garnish

Preparation instructions:
1. Grease the crockpot with butter or non-stick spray.
2. Layer diced potatoes, diced bacon, crumbled breakfast sausages, diced red and green peppers, chopped red onion, and shredded cheddar cheese in the crockpot.
3. In a bowl, whisk together eggs, whole milk, garlic powder, onion powder, salt, and black pepper.
4. Pour the egg mixture evenly over the layered Ingredients in the crockpot.
5. Cover and refrigerate overnight.
6. In the morning, set the crockpot to low heat and cook for 6-8 hours.
7. Garnish with fresh chopped parsley before serving. Enjoy your hearty breakfast casserole!

Slow Cooker Bubble and Squeak

Serves: 4 Prep time: 15 minutes / Cook time: 2-3 hours on low heat

Ingredients:
- 400g potatoes, boiled and mashed
- 200g cabbage, finely chopped
- 200g cooked Brussels sprouts, mashed
- 1 red onion, finely chopped
- 2 tbsp butter
- Salt and black pepper, to taste
- 100g shredded cheddar cheese
- Fresh chives, chopped, for garnish

Preparation instructions:

1. In a skillet, sauté the finely chopped red onion in butter until translucent.
2. In a large bowl, combine boiled and mashed potatoes, finely chopped cabbage, mashed Brussels sprouts, sautéed red onion, salt, and black pepper. Mix well.
3. Grease the crockpot with butter or non-stick spray.
4. Transfer the vegetable mixture to the crockpot, pressing it down gently.
5. Cook on low heat for 2-3 hours, allowing the flavours to meld together.
6. Sprinkle shredded cheddar cheese on top and cover until the cheese melts.
7. Garnish with fresh chopped chives before serving. Enjoy your comforting Bubble and Squeak straight from the crockpot!

Crockpot Veggie Full English

Serves: 4 Prep time: 15 minutes / Cook time: 4 hours on low heat

Ingredients:

- 400g diced potatoes
- 200g button mushrooms, sliced
- 200g cherry tomatoes, halved
- 150g canned baked beans
- 4 large eggs
- 250ml whole milk
- 1 tbsp vegetable oil
- Salt and black pepper, to taste
- Fresh parsley, chopped, for garnish

Preparation instructions:

1. In a skillet, heat vegetable oil over medium heat. Add diced potatoes and cook until golden brown and crispy. Transfer the potatoes to the crockpot.
2. Layer sliced button mushrooms and halved cherry tomatoes on top of the potatoes.
3. Pour the canned baked beans over the vegetables.
4. In a bowl, whisk together eggs, whole milk, salt, and black pepper. Pour the egg mixture evenly over the layered Ingredients in the crockpot.
5. Cover and cook on low heat for 4 hours, until the eggs are set and the vegetables are tender.
6. Garnish with fresh chopped parsley before serving. Enjoy your vegetarian version of the classic Full English breakfast!

Slow Cooker Scottish Oats

Serves: 4 Prep time: 5 minutes / Cook time: 6 hours on low heat

Ingredients:

- 200g steel-cut oats
- 800ml water
- 400ml whole milk
- 2 tbsp honey or maple syrup
- 1/2 tsp ground cinnamon
- 1/2 tsp vanilla extract
- Fresh berries and nuts for topping

Preparation instructions:

1. Combine steel-cut oats, water, whole milk, honey, cinnamon, and vanilla extract in the crockpot.
2. Stir well and cover. Cook on low heat for 6 hours, or overnight.
3. Stir the oats before serving, adding more milk if necessary.
4. Serve hot, topped with fresh berries and nuts. Enjoy a hearty and nutritious Scottish breakfast straight from the crockpot!

English Breakfast Quinoa

Serves: 4 Prep time: 10 minutes / Cook time: 3 hours on low heat

Ingredients:

- 200g quinoa, rinsed and drained
- 400ml vegetable broth
- 200g cherry tomatoes, halved
- 1 red pepper, diced
- 1 green pepper, diced
- 1 red onion, finely chopped
- 2 tbsp olive oil
- 1/2 tsp paprika
- 1/2 tsp cumin powder
- Salt and black pepper, to taste
- Fresh parsley, chopped, for garnish

Preparation instructions:

1. In the crockpot, combine rinsed quinoa and vegetable broth.
2. In a skillet, heat olive oil over medium heat. Add diced red pepper, diced green pepper, and finely chopped red onion. Cook until vegetables are tender.
3. Add the cooked vegetables, halved cherry tomatoes, paprika, cumin powder, salt, and black pepper to the crockpot. Stir well to combine.
4. Cover and cook on low heat for 3 hours, until the quinoa is cooked and the flavours are melded together.
5. Garnish with fresh chopped parsley before serving. Enjoy a wholesome and flavorful English Breakfast Quinoa made effortlessly in the crockpot!

Crockpot Breakfast Frittata

Serves: 4 Prep time: 15 minutes / Cook time: 2 hours on low heat

Ingredients:

- 200g diced potatoes
- 100g diced peppers (assorted colours)
- 100g diced red onion
- 100g diced mushrooms
- 6 large eggs
- 250ml whole milk
- 100g shredded cheddar cheese
- Salt and black pepper, to taste
- Fresh chives, chopped, for garnish

Preparation instructions:

1. In the crockpot, layer diced potatoes, diced peppers, diced red onion, and diced mushrooms.
2. In a bowl, whisk together eggs, whole milk, salt, and black

pepper. Pour the egg mixture evenly over the layered Ingredients in the crockpot.
3. Sprinkle shredded cheddar cheese on top.
4. Cover and cook on low heat for 2 hours, until the eggs are set and the vegetables are tender.
5. Garnish with fresh chopped chives before serving. Enjoy your delightful Breakfast Frittata straight from the crockpot!

Slow Cooker Breakfast Enchiladas

Serves: 4 Prep time: 20 minutes / Cook time: 4 hours on low heat

Ingredients:
- 8 small flour tortillas
- 400g cooked breakfast sausage, crumbled
- 200g diced peppers (assorted colours)
- 200g diced red onion
- 200g shredded cheddar cheese
- 400ml enchilada sauce
- Salt and black pepper, to taste
- Fresh oregano, chopped, for garnish
- Sour cream, for serving

Preparation instructions:
1. In a bowl, mix together cooked breakfast sausage, diced peppers, diced red onion, and half of the shredded cheddar cheese.
2. Spread a portion of the mixture onto each tortilla, roll them up, and place them seam-side down in the crockpot.
3. Pour enchilada sauce over the rolled tortillas.
4. Sprinkle the remaining shredded cheddar cheese on top.
5. Cover and cook on low heat for 4 hours, until the enchiladas are heated through and the cheese is melted.
6. Garnish with fresh chopped oregano and serve with sour cream. Enjoy your flavorful Breakfast Enchiladas!

Crockpot Baked Beans on Toast

Serves: 4 Prep time: 10 minutes / Cook time: 2-3 hours on low heat

Ingredients:
- 400g canned baked beans
- 1 tbsp tomato paste
- 1 tbsp brown sugar
- 1/2 tsp mustard powder
- 1/2 tsp Worcestershire sauce
- 4 slices of your favourite bread, toasted
- Butter, for spreading
- Salt and black pepper, to taste
- Fresh parsley, chopped, for garnish

Preparation instructions:
1. In the crockpot, combine baked beans, tomato paste, brown sugar, mustard powder, and Worcestershire sauce. Stir well to combine all the Ingredients.
2. Cover and cook on low heat for 2-3 hours, stirring occasionally, until the beans are heated through and the flavours meld together.
3. Toast the slices of bread and spread butter on each slice.
4. Spoon the baked beans over the buttered toast.

5. Season with salt and black pepper to taste.
6. Garnish with fresh chopped parsley before serving. Enjoy your comforting Crockpot Baked Beans on Toast!

Slow Cooker Veggie Omelette

Serves: 4 Prep time: 15 minutes / Cook time: 2 hours on low heat

Ingredients:
- 200g mushrooms, sliced
- 100g baby spinach leaves
- 1 red pepper, diced
- 1 green pepper, diced
- 1 small red onion, finely chopped
- 6 large eggs
- 250ml whole milk
- Salt and black pepper, to taste
- 100g shredded cheddar cheese
- Fresh chives, chopped, for garnish

Preparation instructions:
1. In the crockpot, layer sliced mushrooms, baby spinach leaves, diced red and green peppers, and finely chopped red onion.
2. In a bowl, whisk together eggs, whole milk, salt, and black pepper. Pour the egg mixture evenly over the layered vegetables in the crockpot.
3. Sprinkle shredded cheddar cheese on top.
4. Cover and cook on low heat for 2 hours, until the eggs are set and the vegetables are tender.
5. Garnish with fresh chopped chives before serving. Enjoy your wholesome Slow Cooker Veggie Omelette!

Crockpot Breakfast Potatoes

Serves: 4 Prep time: 15 minutes / Cook time: 3 hours on low heat

Ingredients:
- 500g potatoes, peeled and diced
- 1 red onion, finely chopped
- 2 cloves garlic, minced
- 2 tbsp olive oil
- 1/2 tsp paprika
- 1/2 tsp dried thyme
- Salt and black pepper, to taste
- Fresh parsley, chopped, for garnish

Preparation instructions:
1. In the crockpot, combine diced potatoes, finely chopped red onion, and minced garlic.
2. Drizzle olive oil over the potatoes and toss to coat evenly.
3. Season with paprika, dried thyme, salt, and black pepper. Stir well to combine.
4. Cover and cook on low heat for 3 hours, stirring occasionally, until the potatoes are golden brown and tender.
5. Garnish with fresh chopped parsley before serving. Enjoy your flavorful Crockpot Breakfast Potatoes!

Slow Cooker Mushroom and Spinach Breakfast Casserole

Serves: 4 Prep time: 20 minutes / Cook time: 3 hours on low heat

Ingredients:
- 200g mushrooms, sliced • 200g baby spinach leaves
- 1 small red onion, finely chopped
- 6 large eggs • 250ml whole milk
- 100g shredded cheddar cheese
- 1/2 tsp dried thyme
- Salt and black pepper, to taste
- Fresh chives, chopped, for garnish

Preparation instructions:
1. In the crockpot, layer sliced mushrooms, baby spinach leaves, and finely chopped red onion.
2. In a bowl, whisk together eggs, whole milk, dried thyme, salt, and black pepper. Pour the egg mixture evenly over the layered vegetables in the crockpot.
3. Sprinkle shredded cheddar cheese on top.
4. Cover and cook on low heat for 3 hours, until the eggs are set and the vegetables are tender.
5. Garnish with fresh chopped chives before serving. Enjoy your delicious Slow Cooker Mushroom and Spinach Breakfast Casserole!

Crockpot Breakfast Quesadillas

Serves: 4 Prep time: 15 minutes / Cook time: 2 hours on low heat

Ingredients:
- 200g vegetarian sausages, crumbled
- 100g cherry tomatoes, diced
- 1 small red onion, finely chopped
- 1 green chilli, finely chopped (optional)
- 100g grated cheddar cheese
- 4 large flour tortillas
- Salt and black pepper, to taste
- Fresh coriander, chopped, for garnish
- Sour cream and salsa, for serving

Preparation instructions:
1. In a skillet, cook crumbled vegetarian sausages until browned. Add diced cherry tomatoes, finely chopped red onion, and green chilli (if using). Cook until the vegetables are tender. Remove from heat.
2. Place a tortilla on a flat surface. Spread a portion of the sausage and vegetable mixture on one half of the tortilla. Sprinkle grated cheddar cheese on top. Fold the tortilla in half to create a quesadilla.
3. Repeat with the remaining tortillas and filling mixture.
4. Grease the crockpot lightly. Place the quesadillas inside.
5. Cover and cook on low heat for 2 hours, until the quesadillas are heated through and the cheese is melted.
6. Cut into wedges, garnish with fresh chopped coriander, and serve hot with sour cream and salsa.

Slow Cooker Breakfast Stuffed Peppers

Serves: 4 Prep time: 20 minutes / Cook time: 3 hours on low heat

Ingredients:
- 4 large peppers, any colour
- 200g cooked breakfast sausage, crumbled
- 100g cooked quinoa
- 1 small red onion, finely chopped
- 1 garlic clove, minced
- 200g canned diced tomatoes
- 100g grated cheddar cheese
- Salt and black pepper, to taste
- Fresh parsley, chopped, for garnish

Preparation instructions:
1. Cut the tops off the peppers and remove the seeds and membranes.
2. In a bowl, mix together crumbled cooked breakfast sausage, cooked quinoa, finely chopped red onion, minced garlic, and canned diced tomatoes. Season with salt and black pepper.
3. Stuff the peppers with the sausage and quinoa mixture.
4. Place the stuffed peppers in the crockpot.
5. Cover and cook on low heat for 3 hours, until the peppers are tender.
6. Sprinkle grated cheddar cheese on top of each pepper, cover, and cook for an additional 15 minutes, or until the cheese is melted.
7. Garnish with fresh chopped parsley before serving. Enjoy your hearty Breakfast Stuffed Peppers!

Crockpot Veggie Sausage Casserole

Serves: 4 Prep time: 15 minutes / Cook time: 4 hours on low heat

Ingredients:
- 200g vegetarian sausages, sliced
- 400g canned cannellini beans, drained and rinsed
- 1 red pepper, diced
- 1 yellow pepper, diced
- 1 small red onion, finely chopped
- 2 cloves garlic, minced
- 200g canned diced tomatoes
- 250ml vegetable broth
- 1 tsp dried mixed herbs
- Salt and black pepper, to taste
- Fresh basil, chopped, for garnish

Preparation instructions:
1. In the crockpot, combine sliced vegetarian sausages, cannellini beans, diced red and yellow peppers, finely chopped red onion, minced garlic, canned diced tomatoes, vegetable broth, dried mixed herbs, salt, and black pepper.
2. Stir well to combine all the Ingredients.
3. Cover and cook on low heat for 4 hours, allowing the flavours to meld together.
4. Garnish with fresh chopped basil before serving. Enjoy your comforting Veggie Sausage Casserole straight from the crockpot!

Slow Cooker Breakfast Polenta

Serves: 4 Prep time: 10 minutes / Cook time: 4 hours on low heat

Ingredients:
- 200g cornmeal • 800ml water
- 250ml whole milk • 100g shredded cheddar cheese

- 1 tbsp butter
- Salt and black pepper, to taste
- Fresh chives, chopped, for garnish

Preparation instructions:

1. In the crockpot, combine cornmeal, water, whole milk, shredded cheddar cheese, butter, salt, and black pepper.
2. Stir well to combine all the Ingredients.
3. Cover and cook on low heat for 4 hours, stirring occasionally, until the polenta is creamy and thick.
4. Garnish with fresh chopped chives before serving. Enjoy your comforting Slow Cooker Breakfast Polenta straight from the crockpot!

Crockpot Tomato and Egg Breakfast

Serves: 4 Prep time: 15 minutes / Cook time: 3 hours on low heat

Ingredients:

- 400g canned diced tomatoes
- 1 small red onion, finely chopped
- 2 cloves garlic, minced
- 1 tsp olive oil
- 1/2 tsp paprika
- 1/2 tsp dried oregano
- 4 large eggs
- Salt and black pepper, to taste
- Fresh parsley, chopped, for garnish

Preparation instructions:

1. In a skillet, heat olive oil over medium heat. Add finely chopped red onion and minced garlic. Cook until translucent.
2. Add canned diced tomatoes, paprika, and dried oregano to the skillet. Cook for a few minutes until the mixture thickens slightly.
3. Grease the crockpot lightly. Transfer the tomato mixture into the crockpot.
4. Create wells in the tomato mixture and carefully crack eggs into the wells.
5. Cover and cook on low heat for 3 hours, until the eggs are set.
6. Season with salt and black pepper.
7. Garnish with fresh chopped parsley before serving. Enjoy your wholesome Crockpot Tomato and Egg Breakfast!

Slow Cooker Avocado Breakfast

Serves: 4 Prep time: 15 minutes / Cook time: 2 hours on low heat

Ingredients:

- 2 ripe avocados, peeled, pitted, and mashed
- 1 small red onion, finely chopped
- 1 small tomato, diced
- 1 green chilli, finely chopped (optional)
- 2 tbsp fresh lime juice
- Salt and black pepper, to taste
- 4 large eggs
- Fresh coriander, chopped, for garnish

Preparation instructions:

1. In a bowl, combine mashed avocados, finely chopped red onion, diced tomato, green chilli (if using), fresh lime juice, salt, and black pepper.
2. Grease the crockpot lightly. Spread the avocado mixture evenly on the bottom.
3. Create wells in the avocado mixture and carefully crack eggs into the wells.
4. Cover and cook on low heat for 2 hours, until the eggs are set and the avocado mixture is heated through.
5. Garnish with fresh chopped coriander before serving. Enjoy your delightful Slow Cooker Avocado Breakfast!

Crockpot Breakfast Strata

Serves: 4 Prep time: 15 minutes / Cook time: 3 hours on low heat

Ingredients:

- 400g bread, cut into cubes
- 200g cooked breakfast sausage, crumbled
- 100g shredded cheddar cheese
- 1 small red onion, finely chopped
- 1 red pepper, diced
- 6 large eggs
- 300ml whole milk
- 1 tsp Dijon mustard
- Salt and black pepper, to taste
- Fresh parsley, chopped, for garnish

Preparation instructions:

1. In the crockpot, layer bread cubes, crumbled cooked breakfast sausage, shredded cheddar cheese, finely chopped red onion, and diced red pepper.
2. In a bowl, whisk together eggs, whole milk, Dijon mustard, salt, and black pepper. Pour the egg mixture evenly over the layered Ingredients in the crockpot.
3. Cover and refrigerate for at least 2 hours or overnight, allowing the bread to soak up the egg mixture.
4. Cook on low heat for 3 hours, until the strata is set and the top is golden brown.
5. Garnish with fresh chopped parsley before serving. Enjoy your hearty Crockpot Breakfast Strata!

Slow Cooker Breakfast Pizza

Serves: 4 Prep time: 15 minutes / Cook time: 2 hours on low heat

Ingredients:

- 1 ready-made pizza dough (about 400g)
- 200g cooked breakfast sausage, crumbled
- 100g cherry tomatoes, halved
- 1 small red onion, thinly sliced
- 150g shredded mozzarella cheese
- 4 large eggs
- 60ml whole milk
- Salt and black pepper, to taste
- Fresh basil leaves, for garnish

Preparation instructions:

1. Roll out the pizza dough and fit it into the bottom of the greased crockpot.
2. Layer crumbled cooked breakfast sausage, halved cherry tomatoes, thinly sliced red onion, and shredded mozzarella cheese over the pizza dough.
3. In a bowl, whisk together eggs, whole milk, salt, and black pepper. Pour the egg mixture evenly over the pizza

toppings in the crockpot.

4.Cover and cook on low heat for 2 hours, until the eggs are set and the pizza crust is golden brown.

5.Garnish with fresh basil leaves before serving. Enjoy your delicious Slow Cooker Breakfast Pizza!

Crockpot Spinach and Cheese Breakfast Casserole

Serves: 4 Prep time: 15 minutes / Cook time: 3 hours on low heat

Ingredients:

- 200g fresh spinach leaves, chopped
- 100g shredded cheddar cheese
- 100g feta cheese, crumbled
- 1 small red onion, finely chopped
- 6 large eggs
- 250ml whole milk
- 1/2 tsp dried thyme
- Salt and black pepper, to taste
- Fresh dill, chopped, for garnish

Preparation instructions:

1.In the crockpot, layer chopped fresh spinach leaves, shredded cheddar cheese, crumbled feta cheese, and finely chopped red onion.

2.In a bowl, whisk together eggs, whole milk, dried thyme, salt, and black pepper. Pour the egg mixture evenly over the layered Ingredients in the crockpot.

3.Cover and cook on low heat for 3 hours, until the casserole is set and the cheese is melted.

4.Garnish with fresh chopped dill before serving. Enjoy your delightful Crockpot Spinach and Cheese Breakfast Casserole!

Slow Cooker Breakfast Tacos

Serves: 4 Prep time: 15 minutes / Cook time: 3 hours on low heat

Ingredients:

- 400g cooked breakfast sausages, chopped
- 200g canned black beans, drained and rinsed
- 1 small red onion, finely chopped
- 1 red pepper, diced
- 1 green chilli, finely chopped (optional)
- 1/2 tsp ground cumin
- 1/4 tsp chilli powder
- Salt and black pepper, to taste
- 8 small corn or flour tortillas
- 100g shredded cheddar cheese
- Fresh coriander, chopped, for garnish
- Sour cream and salsa, for serving

Preparation instructions:

1.In the crockpot, combine chopped cooked breakfast sausages, black beans, finely chopped red onion, diced red pepper, and green chilli (if using).

2.Add ground cumin, chilli powder, salt, and black pepper. Stir well to combine all the Ingredients.

3.Cover and cook on low heat for 3 hours, allowing the flavours to meld together.

4.Warm the tortillas according to the package instructions.

5.Spoon the sausage and bean mixture onto each warm tortilla. Top with shredded cheddar cheese.

6.Garnish with fresh chopped coriander. Serve hot with sour cream and salsa. Enjoy your delicious Slow Cooker Breakfast Tacos!

Crockpot Breakfast Couscous

Serves: 4 Prep time: 10 minutes / Cook time: 2 hours on low heat

Ingredients:

- 200g couscous
- 250ml boiling water
- 200ml whole milk
- 50g dried apricots, chopped
- 50g almonds, chopped
- 1 tbsp honey
- 1/2 tsp ground cinnamon
- 1/4 tsp vanilla extract
- Fresh mint leaves, chopped, for garnish

Preparation instructions:

1.In the crockpot, combine couscous, boiling water, whole milk, chopped dried apricots, chopped almonds, honey, ground cinnamon, and vanilla extract.

2.Stir well to combine all the Ingredients.

3.Cover and cook on low heat for 2 hours, fluffing the couscous with a fork halfway through the cooking time.

4.Garnish with fresh chopped mint leaves before serving. Enjoy your warm and comforting Crockpot Breakfast Couscous!

Slow Cooker Breakfast Stuffed Mushrooms

Serves: 4 Prep time: 15 minutes / Cook time: 2 hours on low heat

Ingredients:

- 8 large mushrooms, stems removed and finely chopped
- 100g cooked breakfast sausages, crumbled
- 50g breadcrumbs
- 50g shredded cheddar cheese
- 2 tbsp fresh parsley, chopped
- 1 garlic clove, minced
- Salt and black pepper, to taste
- 2 tbsp olive oil

Preparation instructions:

1.In a bowl, combine finely chopped mushroom stems, crumbled cooked breakfast sausages, breadcrumbs, shredded cheddar cheese, chopped fresh parsley, minced garlic, salt, and black pepper.

2.Stuff each mushroom cap with the sausage mixture.

3.Grease the crockpot lightly with olive oil. Place the stuffed mushrooms inside.

4.Cover and cook on low heat for 2 hours, until the mushrooms are tender and the filling is heated through.

5.Serve hot, garnished with additional fresh parsley if desired. Enjoy your flavorful Slow Cooker Breakfast Stuffed Mushrooms!

Crockpot Breakfast Ratatouille

Serves: 4 Prep time: 15 minutes / Cook time: 3 hours on low heat

Ingredients:
- 400g aubergine, diced • 300g courgette, diced
- 200g peppers, diced (mixed colours)
- 200g tomatoes, diced
- 1 small red onion, finely chopped
- 2 cloves garlic, minced
- 2 tbsp olive oil
- 1/2 tsp dried thyme
- 1/2 tsp dried basil
- Salt and black pepper, to taste
- 4 large eggs
- Fresh parsley, chopped, for garnish

Preparation instructions:
1. In the crockpot, combine diced aubergine, courgette, peppers, tomatoes, finely chopped red onion, and minced garlic.
2. Add olive oil, dried thyme, dried basil, salt, and black pepper. Stir well to combine all the Ingredients.
3. Cover and cook on low heat for 3 hours, allowing the vegetables to soften and the flavours to meld together.
4. Create wells in the ratatouille mixture and carefully crack eggs into the wells.
5. Cover and cook for an additional 15-20 minutes, or until the eggs are set to your preference.
6. Garnish with fresh chopped parsley before serving. Enjoy your delightful Crockpot Breakfast Ratatouille!

Slow Cooker Breakfast Skewers

Serves: 4 Prep time: 20 minutes / Cook time: 2 hours on low heat

Ingredients:
- 400g cooked breakfast sausages
- 200g cherry tomatoes
- 200g button mushrooms
- 1 small red onion, cut into chunks
- 1 red pepper, cut into chunks
- 2 tbsp olive oil
- 1/2 tsp dried oregano
- 1/4 tsp garlic powder
- Salt and black pepper, to taste

Preparation instructions:
1. In a bowl, mix together cooked breakfast sausages, cherry tomatoes, button mushrooms, red onion chunks, and red pepper chunks.
2. Add olive oil, dried oregano, garlic powder, salt, and black pepper. Toss to coat the Ingredients evenly.
3. Thread the sausage and vegetable mixture onto skewers, alternating the Ingredients.
4. Grease the crockpot lightly. Place the skewers inside.
5. Cover and cook on low heat for 2 hours, until the vegetables are tender and the sausages are heated through.
6. Serve hot and enjoy your tasty Slow Cooker Breakfast Skewers!

Crockpot Breakfast Flatbreads

Serves: 4 Prep time: 15 minutes / Cook time: 2 hours on low heat

Ingredients:
- 400g flatbreads (such as naan or pita)
- 200g cooked breakfast bacon, chopped
- 150g shredded mozzarella cheese
- 100g cherry tomatoes, halved
- 1 small red onion, thinly sliced
- 1 tbsp olive oil
- 1/2 tsp dried basil
- 1/4 tsp red chilli flakes (optional)
- Salt and black pepper, to taste
- Fresh basil leaves, for garnish

Preparation instructions:
1. Brush flatbreads with olive oil and sprinkle with dried basil, red chilli flakes (if using), salt, and black pepper.
2. Top the flatbreads with chopped cooked breakfast bacon, shredded mozzarella cheese, halved cherry tomatoes, and thinly sliced red onion.
3. Grease the crockpot lightly. Place the prepared flatbreads inside.
4. Cover and cook on low heat for 2 hours, until the cheese is melted and bubbly.
5. Garnish with fresh basil leaves before serving. Enjoy your flavorful Crockpot Breakfast Flatbreads!

Slow Cooker Breakfast Samosas

Serves: 4 Prep time: 20 minutes / Cook time: 3 hours on low heat

Ingredients:
- 400g potatoes, peeled and diced
- 200g cooked breakfast sausages, crumbled
- 100g frozen peas
- 1 small onion, finely chopped
- 2 cloves garlic, minced
- 1 tsp curry powder
- 1/2 tsp ground turmeric
- 1/2 tsp ground cumin
- Salt and black pepper, to taste
- 8 sheets of filo pastry
- 60ml olive oil

Preparation instructions:
1. In the crockpot, combine diced potatoes, crumbled cooked breakfast sausages, frozen peas, finely chopped onion, minced garlic, curry powder, ground turmeric, ground cumin, salt, and black pepper. Stir well to combine all the Ingredients.
2. Cover and cook on low heat for 3 hours, allowing the filling to cook and the flavours to meld together.
3. Preheat the crockpot to 190°C for 5 minutes.
4. Lay out a sheet of filo pastry, brush it with olive oil, and place a spoonful of the filling at one corner. Fold the pastry diagonally to form a triangle, sealing the edges with a bit of olive oil.

5. Repeat with the remaining filo pastry sheets and filling.
6. Place the samosas in the crockpot and cook at 190°C for 15-20 minutes, until they are golden and crispy.
7. Once cooked, remove from the crockpot and let cool for a few minutes before serving. Enjoy your delicious Slow Cooker Breakfast Samosas!

Crockpot Breakfast Crepes

Serves: 4 Prep time: 15 minutes / Cook time: 2 hours on low heat

Ingredients:
- 200g plain flour
- 2 eggs
- 500ml whole milk
- 1/4 tsp salt
- 200g cooked breakfast bacon, chopped
- 100g shredded cheddar cheese
- 100g mushrooms, sliced
- 1 small red onion, thinly sliced
- 1 tbsp olive oil
- Fresh chives, chopped, for garnish

Preparation instructions:
1. In a bowl, whisk together plain flour, eggs, whole milk, and salt to make the crepe batter. Let it rest for 10 minutes.
2. In a frying pan, heat olive oil over medium heat. Add sliced mushrooms and red onion. Sauté until tender.
3. Grease the crockpot lightly. Pour a small amount of crepe batter into the crockpot and tilt to spread it thinly. Cook for a minute or until the edges start to lift. Repeat with the remaining batter.
4. Fill each crepe with cooked breakfast bacon, shredded cheddar cheese, and sautéed mushrooms and red onion.
5. Fold the crepes into quarters and place them back in the crockpot. Cover and cook on low heat for 2 hours.
6. Garnish with fresh chopped chives before serving. Enjoy your delightful Crockpot Breakfast Crepes!

Slow Cooker Breakfast Pudding

Serves: 4 Prep time: 15 minutes / Cook time: 2 hours on low heat

Ingredients:
- 200g white bread, cut into cubes
- 500ml whole milk
- 3 eggs
- 75g granulated sugar
- 1 tsp vanilla extract
- 1/2 tsp ground cinnamon
- 1/4 tsp ground nutmeg
- 50g raisins
- 25g unsalted butter, melted
- 1 tbsp demerara sugar

Preparation instructions:
1. In a bowl, combine white bread cubes and whole milk. Let it soak for 10 minutes.
2. In another bowl, whisk together eggs, granulated sugar, vanilla extract, ground cinnamon, and ground nutmeg.
3. Stir the egg mixture into the soaked bread along with raisins and melted unsalted butter.
4. Grease the crockpot lightly. Pour the pudding mixture into the crockpot. Sprinkle the top with demerara sugar.

5. Cover and cook on low heat for 2 hours, until the pudding is set and golden brown on top.
6. Serve warm, optionally with a dollop of custard or cream. Enjoy your comforting Slow Cooker Breakfast Pudding!

Crockpot Breakfast Empanadas

Serves: 4 Prep time: 20 minutes / Cook time: 2.5 hours on low heat

Ingredients:
- 400g puff pastry, thawed
- 200g cooked breakfast sausages, crumbled
- 100g shredded cheddar cheese
- 1 small red onion, finely chopped
- 1 green pepper, finely chopped
- 2 tbsp olive oil
- 1/2 tsp paprika
- Salt and black pepper, to taste
- 1 egg, beaten, for egg wash

Preparation instructions:
1. In a frying pan, heat olive oil over medium heat. Add chopped red onion and green pepper. Sauté until tender. Add crumbled cooked breakfast sausages, paprika, salt, and black pepper. Cook until well combined. Remove from heat and let it cool.
2. Preheat the crockpot to 190°C for 5 minutes.
3. Roll out the puff pastry and cut it into circles, approximately 10 cm in diameter.
4. Place a spoonful of the sausage mixture onto each pastry circle. Sprinkle shredded cheddar cheese over the filling.
5. Fold the pastry over the filling, forming a half-moon shape. Press the edges to seal. Use a fork to create a decorative pattern around the edges.
6. Place the empanadas in the crockpot. Brush the tops with beaten egg for a golden finish.
7. Cover and cook on low heat for 2.5 hours, or until the empanadas are golden and crispy.
8. Once cooked, remove from the crockpot and let cool for a few minutes before serving. Enjoy your delicious Crockpot Breakfast Empanadas!

Slow Cooker Breakfast Scones

Serves: 4 Prep time: 15 minutes / Cook time: 2 hours on low heat

Ingredients:
- 300g self-raising flour
- 75g unsalted butter, cold and cubed
- 50g granulated sugar
- 150ml milk
- 1 tsp vanilla extract
- 100g mixed dried fruits (such as raisins and currants)
- 1 tbsp demerara sugar, for sprinkling

Preparation instructions:
1. In a large bowl, rub the cold cubed butter into the self-raising flour until the mixture resembles breadcrumbs. Stir in granulated sugar.
2. Gradually add milk and vanilla extract, mixing to form a

soft dough. Gently fold in the mixed dried fruits.

3. Shape the dough into a circle, approximately 2 cm thick. Cut out scones using a round cutter.
4. Grease the crockpot lightly. Place the scones inside, slightly touching each other.
5. Sprinkle the tops of the scones with demerara sugar.
6. Cover and cook on low heat for 2 hours, or until the scones are cooked through and golden brown on top.
7. Serve warm with butter, jam, or clotted cream. Enjoy your delightful Slow Cooker Breakfast Scones!

Crockpot Breakfast Galette

Serves: 4 Prep time: 20 minutes / Cook time: 2.5 hours on low heat

Ingredients:

- 400g puff pastry, thawed
- 200g cooked breakfast bacon, chopped
- 150g crumbled feta cheese
- 1 small red onion, thinly sliced
- 1 tbsp olive oil
- 1 tbsp balsamic vinegar
- Fresh basil leaves, for garnish
- Salt and black pepper, to taste

Preparation instructions:

1. In a frying pan, heat olive oil over medium heat. Add thinly sliced red onion and sauté until caramelised. Stir in balsamic vinegar and cook for another minute. Remove from heat and let it cool.
2. Preheat the crockpot to 190°C for 5 minutes.
3. Roll out the puff pastry into a circle, approximately 25 cm in diameter.
4. Transfer the pastry to the crockpot.
5. Spread the caramelised red onions over the pastry, leaving a border around the edges.
6. Scatter chopped cooked breakfast bacon and crumbled feta cheese over the onions.
7. Fold the edges of the pastry over the filling, creating a rustic galette shape.
8. Cover and cook on low heat for 2.5 hours, or until the pastry is golden and the filling is heated through.
9. Garnish with fresh basil leaves before serving. Enjoy your delicious Crockpot Breakfast Galette!

Slow Cooker Breakfast Burrito Bowls

Serves: 4 Prep time: 15 minutes / Cook time: 3 hours on low heat

Ingredients:

- 400g cooked quinoa
- 8 cooked breakfast sausages, sliced
- 200g black beans, drained and rinsed
- 1 avocado, diced
- 200g cherry tomatoes, halved
- 100g sweetcorn kernels
- 100g shredded cheddar cheese
- Fresh oregano, chopped, for garnish
- Salt and black pepper, to taste

Preparation instructions:

1. In the crockpot, layer cooked quinoa, sliced cooked breakfast sausages, black beans, diced avocado, cherry tomatoes, and sweetcorn kernels.
2. Season with salt and black pepper.
3. Sprinkle shredded cheddar cheese over the top.
4. Cover and cook on low heat for 3 hours, allowing the flavours to meld together.
5. Once cooked, gently stir the mixture to combine the Ingredients.
6. Serve the burrito bowls hot, garnished with fresh chopped oregano. Enjoy your delicious Slow Cooker Breakfast Burrito Bowls!

Crockpot Breakfast Bruschetta

Serves: 4 Prep time: 15 minutes / Cook time: 2 hours on low heat

Ingredients:

- 400g cherry tomatoes, diced
- 1 small red onion, finely chopped
- 2 cloves garlic, minced
- 2 tbsp balsamic vinegar
- 1 tbsp olive oil
- Salt and black pepper, to taste
- 4 slices of crusty bread, toasted
- 4 large eggs
- Fresh basil leaves, for garnish

Preparation instructions:

1. In the crockpot, combine diced cherry tomatoes, finely chopped red onion, minced garlic, balsamic vinegar, olive oil, salt, and black pepper. Stir well to combine.
2. Cover and cook on low heat for 2 hours, allowing the flavours to meld together.
3. While the bruschetta mixture is cooking, toast the slices of crusty bread.
4. Just before serving, poach the eggs.
5. Spoon the bruschetta mixture onto the toasted bread slices.
6. Top each bruschetta with a poached egg.
7. Garnish with fresh basil leaves before serving. Enjoy your delightful Crockpot Breakfast Bruschetta!

Slow Cooker Breakfast Soufflé

Serves: 4 Prep time: 20 minutes / Cook time: 3 hours on low heat

Ingredients:

- 6 large eggs
- 200ml whole milk
- 100g shredded cheddar cheese
- 100g baby spinach, chopped
- 1 small red pepper, finely chopped
- 1 small red onion, finely chopped
- Salt and black pepper, to taste
- Fresh chives, chopped, for garnish

Preparation instructions:

1. In a bowl, whisk together eggs and whole milk.
2. Stir in shredded cheddar cheese, chopped baby spinach, finely chopped red pepper, and finely chopped red onion.

Season with salt and black pepper.

3. Grease the crockpot lightly.
4. Pour the egg mixture into the crockpot.
5. Cover and cook on low heat for 3 hours, allowing the soufflé to rise and set.
6. Once cooked, sprinkle fresh chopped chives over the top.
7. Serve the breakfast soufflé hot. Enjoy your scrumptious Slow Cooker Breakfast Soufflé!

Crockpot Breakfast BLT Wraps

Serves: 4 Prep time: 15 minutes / Cook time: 2 hours on low heat

Ingredients:
- 400g cherry tomatoes, halved
- 200g cooked bacon, chopped
- 4 large eggs, beaten
- 60ml whole milk
- Salt and black pepper, to taste
- 4 large lettuce leaves
- 4 large tortilla wraps
- 60g mayonnaise
- 1 avocado, sliced

Preparation instructions:
1. In the crockpot, combine cherry tomatoes and chopped cooked bacon.
2. In a bowl, whisk together beaten eggs, whole milk, salt, and black pepper. Pour the egg mixture over the tomatoes and bacon in the crockpot.
3. Cover and cook on low heat for 2 hours, stirring occasionally, until the eggs are set.
4. While the eggs are cooking, spread mayonnaise over each tortilla wrap.
5. Once the eggs are cooked, spoon the egg mixture onto the tortilla wraps.
6. Top with avocado slices and lettuce leaves.
7. Roll up the wraps tightly and serve. Enjoy your tasty Crockpot Breakfast BLT Wraps!

Slow Cooker Breakfast Spring Rolls

Serves: 4 Prep time: 20 minutes / Cook time: 2 hours on low heat

Ingredients:
- 200g cooked breakfast sausages, sliced
- 100g cooked bacon, chopped
- 100g cooked vermicelli noodles
- 1 carrot, julienned
- 1 cucumber, julienned
- 4 large spring roll wrappers
- 60ml hoisin sauce
- 30ml soy sauce
- 1 tbsp rice vinegar
- 1 tbsp honey
- Sesame seeds, for garnish
- Fresh oregano leaves, for garnish

Preparation instructions:
1. In a bowl, combine sliced cooked breakfast sausages, chopped cooked bacon, cooked vermicelli noodles, julienned carrot, and julienned cucumber.
2. In another bowl, whisk together hoisin sauce, soy sauce, rice vinegar, and honey. Pour the sauce over the sausage mixture and toss to coat.
3. Dip a spring roll wrapper in warm water for a few seconds to soften it.
4. Place a portion of the sausage mixture onto the softened wrapper and roll it up tightly, folding in the sides as you go.
5. Repeat with the remaining Ingredients to make more spring rolls.
6. Place the spring rolls in the crockpot, seam side down.
7. Cover and cook on low heat for 2 hours.
8. Once cooked, sprinkle sesame seeds and fresh oregano leaves over the top before serving. Enjoy your delightful Slow Cooker Breakfast Spring Rolls!

Crockpot Breakfast Tarts

Serves: 4 Prep time: 15 minutes / Cook time: 2 hours on low heat

Ingredients:
- 1 sheet ready-made puff pastry, thawed
- 200g cooked breakfast sausages, crumbled
- 100g shredded cheddar cheese
- 4 large eggs
- 60ml whole milk
- Salt and black pepper, to taste
- Fresh parsley, chopped, for garnish

Preparation instructions:
1. Preheat the crockpot to 190°C for 5 minutes.
2. Cut the puff pastry sheet into 4 equal squares.
3. Press each square of pastry into the bottom and up the sides of 4 silicone tart moulds.
4. In a bowl, combine crumbled cooked breakfast sausages and shredded cheddar cheese. Divide the mixture evenly among the pastry-lined tart moulds.
5. In another bowl, whisk together eggs, whole milk, salt, and black pepper. Pour the egg mixture into each tart mould.
6. Place the tart moulds in the crockpot.
7. Cover and cook on low heat for 2 hours, or until the tarts are set and golden brown.
8. Garnish with chopped fresh parsley before serving. Enjoy your delicious Crockpot Breakfast Tarts!

Slow Cooker Breakfast Calzone

Serves: 4 Prep time: 15 minutes / Cook time: 2 hours on low heat

Ingredients:
- 400g pizza dough
- 200g cooked breakfast sausages, chopped
- 100g shredded cheddar cheese
- 4 large eggs
- 60ml whole milk
- 1/4 tsp garlic powder
- 1/4 tsp onion powder
- Salt and black pepper, to taste

- 1 tbsp olive oil
- 30g tomato sauce
- Fresh basil leaves, for garnish

Preparation instructions:
1. Roll out the pizza dough on a floured surface to form a large circle.
2. In a bowl, combine chopped cooked breakfast sausages, shredded cheddar cheese, garlic powder, onion powder, salt, and black pepper.
3. In another bowl, whisk together eggs and whole milk.
4. Spread the sausage and cheese mixture over half of the pizza dough circle, leaving a border around the edge.
5. Pour the egg mixture over the sausage and cheese layer.
6. Fold the other half of the dough over the filling, creating a half-moon shape. Press the edges to seal.
7. Carefully transfer the calzone into the preheated crockpot.
8. Brush the top of the calzone with olive oil and spread tomato sauce over the top.
9. Cover and cook on low heat for 2 hours, or until the calzone is golden brown and cooked through.
10. Garnish with fresh basil leaves before serving. Enjoy your delightful Slow Cooker Breakfast Calzone!

Crockpot Breakfast Croissants

Serves: 4 Prep time: 15 minutes / Cook time: 2 hours on low heat

Ingredients:
- 4 large croissants
- 200g cooked bacon, sliced
- 100g cooked breakfast sausages, chopped
- 4 large eggs
- 60ml whole milk
- 1/4 tsp garlic powder
- 1/4 tsp onion powder
- Salt and black pepper, to taste
- 100g shredded mozzarella cheese
- Fresh chives, chopped, for garnish

Preparation instructions:
1. Cut the croissants in half horizontally, creating a top and bottom half.
2. In a bowl, combine sliced cooked bacon, chopped cooked breakfast sausages, garlic powder, onion powder, salt, and black pepper.
3. Spread the bacon and sausage mixture evenly over the bottom half of each croissant.
4. In another bowl, whisk together eggs and whole milk. Pour the egg mixture over the bacon and sausage layer.
5. Sprinkle shredded mozzarella cheese over the egg mixture.
6. Place the top half of the croissants over the filling, pressing down gently.
7. Carefully place the croissants in the crockpot.
8. Cover and cook on low heat for 2 hours, or until the croissants are warm and the filling is set.
9. Garnish with chopped fresh chives before serving. Enjoy your scrumptious Crockpot Breakfast Croissants!

Slow Cooker Breakfast Waffles

Serves: 4 Prep time: 15 minutes / Cook time: 2 hours on low heat

Ingredients:
- 400g waffle batter (prepared according to package instructions)
- 200g cooked breakfast sausages, sliced
- 100g cooked bacon, chopped
- 60ml maple syrup
- 1/4 tsp garlic powder
- 1/4 tsp onion powder
- Salt and black pepper, to taste
- Fresh parsley, chopped, for garnish

Preparation instructions:
1. Preheat the waffle iron and cook the waffles according to the package instructions. Keep the waffles warm.
2. In a bowl, combine sliced cooked breakfast sausages, chopped cooked bacon, garlic powder, onion powder, salt, and black pepper.
3. In the crockpot, layer the cooked waffles with the sausage and bacon mixture, creating a stack.
4. Drizzle maple syrup over the waffles and sausage-bacon layers.
5. Cover and cook on low heat for 2 hours, allowing the flavours to meld together.
6. Garnish with chopped fresh parsley before serving. Enjoy your delightful Slow Cooker Breakfast Waffles!

Crockpot Breakfast Bagels

Serves: 4 Prep time: 15 minutes / Cook time: 2 hours on low heat

Ingredients:
- 4 large bagels, halved and toasted
- 200g cooked breakfast sausages, sliced
- 100g cream cheese, softened
- 1 avocado, sliced
- 1 tomato, sliced
- Salt and black pepper, to taste
- Fresh dill, for garnish

Preparation instructions:
1. Spread a generous layer of softened cream cheese on the cut sides of each toasted bagel half.
2. On the bottom half of each bagel, layer sliced cooked breakfast sausages, avocado slices, and tomato slices.
3. Sprinkle it with salt and black pepper to taste.
4. Place the top half of the bagels over the filling, creating sandwiches.
5. Carefully place the bagel sandwiches in the crockpot.
6. Cover and cook on low heat for 2 hours, allowing the flavours to meld together.
7. Garnish with fresh dill before serving. Enjoy your delicious Crockpot Breakfast Bagels!

Chapter 2: Snacks

Slow Cooker Spiced Nuts

Serves: 4 Prep time: 5 minutes / Cook time: 2 hours on low heat

Ingredients:
- 200g mixed nuts (such as almonds, cashews, and walnuts)
- 30g unsalted butter, melted
- 30ml maple syrup
- 1/2 tsp ground cinnamon
- 1/4 tsp ground ginger
- 1/4 tsp ground nutmeg
- 1/4 tsp ground cloves
- 1/4 tsp salt

Preparation instructions:
1. In a bowl, combine mixed nuts with melted butter, maple syrup, ground cinnamon, ground ginger, ground nutmeg, ground cloves, and salt. Toss until the nuts are well coated.
2. Transfer the nut mixture into the crockpot.
3. Cover and cook on low heat for 2 hours, stirring occasionally to ensure even coating of the spices.
4. After 2 hours, spread the spiced nuts on a parchment-lined tray to cool and crisp up.
5. Once cooled, store in an airtight container. Enjoy your delicious Slow Cooker Spiced Nuts as a tasty snack or party treat!

Crockpot Cheese Fondue

Serves: 4 Prep time: 10 minutes / Cook time: 1 hour on low heat

Ingredients:
- 200g Gruyere cheese, grated
- 200g Emmental cheese, grated
- 1 clove garlic, halved
- 200ml dry white wine
- 1 tbsp lemon juice
- 1/2 tsp Dijon mustard
- 1/4 tsp ground white pepper
- 1/4 tsp nutmeg
- 1 tbsp cornstarch
- 30ml kirsch (cherry brandy)
- Bread cubes, vegetables, and apples for dipping

Preparation instructions:
1. Rub the inside of the crockpot with the halved garlic clove.
2. In the crockpot, combine grated Gruyere cheese, grated Emmental cheese, dry white wine, lemon juice, Dijon mustard, ground white pepper, and nutmeg. Stir well to combine.
3. Cover and cook on low heat for 1 hour, stirring occasionally until the cheese is melted and smooth.
4. In a small bowl, mix cornstarch with kirsch to create a smooth paste. Stir the cornstarch mixture into the cheese mixture in the crockpot.
5. Continue cooking for an additional 15 minutes, or until the fondue thickens.
6. Serve the cheese fondue in the crockpot, alongside bread cubes, vegetables, and apple slices for dipping. Enjoy your delightful Crockpot Cheese Fondue!

Slow Cooker English Tea Sandwiches

Serves: 4 Prep time: 15 minutes

Ingredients:
- 8 slices white bread, crusts removed
- 100g cream cheese, softened
- 1 cucumber, thinly sliced
- 4 slices smoked salmon
- Fresh dill, for garnish
- Salt and black pepper, to taste

Preparation instructions:
1. Spread a thin layer of softened cream cheese evenly on one side of each bread slice.
2. For cucumber sandwiches: Arrange thinly sliced cucumber on 4 bread slices. Sprinkle with a pinch of salt and black pepper. Top with the remaining bread slices.
3. For smoked salmon sandwiches: Arrange a slice of smoked salmon on 4 bread slices. Garnish with fresh dill. Top with the remaining bread slices.
4. Gently press the sandwiches together to meld the flavours.
5. Wrap the prepared sandwiches in foil and place them in a slow cooker on the warm setting for about 15-20 minutes to allow the flavours to meld and the sandwiches to warm slightly.
6. Arrange the warm sandwiches on a serving platter and serve immediately. Alternatively, cover with a damp cloth and keep warm in the slow cooker until serving time. Enjoy your classic Slow Cooker English Tea Sandwiches!

Slow Cooker Garlic Parmesan Pretzels

Serves: 4 Prep time: 10 minutes / Cook time: 18 minutes

Ingredients:
- 200g pretzels
- 100g grated Parmesan cheese
- 60g unsalted butter, melted
- 2 cloves garlic, minced
- 1/4 tsp onion powder
- Salt and black pepper, to taste
- Fresh parsley, chopped, for garnish

Preparation instructions:
1. In a mixing bowl, combine the pretzels, grated Parmesan cheese, melted butter, minced garlic, onion powder, salt, and black pepper. Toss until the pretzels are evenly coated with the mixture.
2. Divide the seasoned pretzels evenly among 4 silicone muffin cups, pressing them down gently.
3. Place the muffin cups in the preheated crock pot.
4. Cover and cook on low heat for 18 minutes or until the

pretzels are golden brown and crispy.

5. Once cooked, remove from the crock pot and let cool for a few minutes before serving.

6. Garnish with chopped fresh parsley and serve warm. Enjoy your Slow Cooker Garlic Parmesan Pretzels!

Crockpot Sticky Toffee Pudding Bites

Serves: 4 Prep time: 10 minutes / Cook time: 18 minutes

Ingredients:

* 200g dates, pitted and chopped
* 200ml boiling water
* 1 tsp vanilla extract
* 150g self-raising flour
* 1/2 tsp baking soda
* 1/2 tsp ground cinnamon
* 100g unsalted butter, softened
* 100g brown sugar
* 2 large eggs
* 60ml milk
* Toffee Sauce:
* 100g unsalted butter
* 100g brown sugar
* 150ml double cream

Preparation instructions:

1. In a bowl, combine the chopped dates, boiling water, and vanilla extract. Let it sit for 10 minutes to soften the dates.

2. In another bowl, whisk together the self-raising flour, baking soda, and ground cinnamon.

3. In a separate large mixing bowl, cream together the softened butter and brown sugar. Add the eggs, one at a time, beating well after each addition.

4. Gradually add the flour mixture to the wet Ingredients, alternating with the milk, and mix until well combined.

5. Fold in the soaked dates into the batter.

6. Divide the batter evenly among 4 silicone muffin cups.

7. In a small saucepan, combine the toffee sauce Ingredients (butter, brown sugar, and double cream) over low heat. Stir continuously until the sauce thickens.

8. Pour the toffee sauce over the pudding batter in the muffin cups.

9. Place the muffin cups in the preheated crock pot.

10. Cover and cook on low heat for 18 minutes or until the pudding is cooked through and the toffee sauce is gooey.

11. Once cooked, remove from the crock pot and let cool for a few minutes before serving.

12. Serve the sticky toffee pudding bites warm, drizzled with extra toffee sauce if desired. Enjoy!

Slow Cooker Cheese and Bacon Dip

Serves: 4 Prep time: 10 minutes / Cook time: 18 minutes

Ingredients:

* 200g cream cheese, softened
* 100g shredded cheddar cheese
* 100g cooked bacon, crumbled
* 60ml sour cream
* 1/4 tsp garlic powder

* 1/4 tsp onion powder
* Salt and black pepper, to taste
* Fresh chives, chopped, for garnish
* Tortilla chips, for serving

Preparation instructions:

1. In a bowl, combine the softened cream cheese, shredded cheddar cheese, crumbled bacon, sour cream, garlic powder, onion powder, salt, and black pepper. Mix until well combined.

2. Divide the cheese and bacon mixture evenly among 4 silicone muffin cups.

3. Place the muffin cups in the preheated crock pot.

4. Cover and cook on low heat for 18 minutes or until the dip is hot and bubbly.

5. Once cooked, remove from the crock pot and let cool for a few minutes before serving.

6. Garnish with chopped fresh chives.

7. Serve the cheese and bacon dip warm with tortilla chips. Enjoy your Slow Cooker Cheese and Bacon Dip!

Crockpot Mini Sausage Rolls

Serves: 4 Prep time: 10 minutes / Cook time: 18 minutes

Ingredients:

* 300g puff pastry, rolled out
* 8 cooked breakfast sausage links, chopped
* 1 egg, beaten (for egg wash)

Preparation instructions:

1. Preheat the crock pot to 190°C for 5 minutes.

2. Roll out the puff pastry and cut it into small rectangles.

3. Place a portion of chopped breakfast sausage links in the centre of each pastry rectangle.

4. Fold the pastry over the sausage filling, sealing the edges to form mini sausage rolls.

5. Brush the tops of the rolls with beaten egg for a golden finish.

6. Arrange the sausage rolls in the preheated crock pot.

7. Cover and cook at 190°C for 18 minutes or until the pastry is golden brown and crispy.

8. Once cooked, remove from the crock pot and let cool for a few minutes before serving. Enjoy your Crock Pot Mini Sausage Rolls!

Slow Cooker Lemon Drizzle Cake Bars

Serves: 4 Prep time: 10 minutes / Cook time: 18 minutes

Ingredients:

* 200g self-raising flour
* 150g unsalted butter, softened
* 150g granulated sugar
* 2 large eggs
* Zest of 1 lemon
* 60ml freshly squeezed lemon juice
* 100g icing sugar (for the drizzle)

Preparation instructions:

1. In a mixing bowl, cream together the softened butter and granulated sugar until light and fluffy.

2. Beat in the eggs, one at a time, until well incorporated.
3. Stir in the self-raising flour and lemon zest, mixing until a smooth batter forms.
4. Grease and line a baking tray with parchment paper, then spread the batter evenly in the tray.
5. Cook in the preheated crock pot at 190°C for 18 minutes or until a toothpick inserted into the centre comes out clean.
6. While the cake is still warm, prepare the drizzle by mixing the freshly squeezed lemon juice with icing sugar until smooth.
7. Prick the warm cake with a fork and pour the lemon drizzle over the top, allowing it to soak into the cake.
8. Let the cake cool in the tray before slicing into bars. Enjoy your Slow Cooker Lemon Drizzle Cake Bars!

Crockpot Cheddar and Chive Biscuits

Serves: 4 Prep time: 10 minutes / Cook time: 18 minutes

Ingredients:
- 250g self-raising flour
- 1/2 tsp baking powder
- 1/2 tsp salt
- 100g unsalted butter, chilled and cubed
- 150g grated cheddar cheese
- 2 tbsp fresh chives, chopped
- 180ml milk

Preparation instructions:
1. In a large mixing bowl, combine the self-raising flour, baking powder, and salt.
2. Rub in the chilled butter cubes until the mixture resembles breadcrumbs.
3. Stir in the grated cheddar cheese and chopped chives.
4. Gradually add the milk, stirring until a soft dough forms.
5. Drop spoonfuls of the dough onto the bottom of the greased crock pot, creating individual biscuits.
6. Cover and cook at 190°C for 18 minutes or until the biscuits are golden brown on top.
7. Once cooked, remove from the crock pot and let cool for a few minutes before serving. Enjoy your Crockpot Cheddar and Chive Biscuits!

Slow Cooker Welsh Rarebit

Serves: 4 Prep time: 10 minutes / Cook time: 18 minutes

Ingredients:
- 200g grated cheddar cheese
- 60ml stout or dark beer
- 1 tbsp Worcestershire sauce
- 1/2 tsp mustard powder
- Salt and black pepper, to taste
- 4 slices of thick bread

Preparation instructions:
1. In a mixing bowl, combine the grated cheddar cheese, stout or dark beer, Worcestershire sauce, mustard powder, salt, and black pepper. Mix until well combined.
2. Toast the slices of thick bread lightly and place them on the bottom of the greased crock pot.
3. Spread the cheese mixture evenly over the toasted bread slices.
4. Cover and cook in the preheated crock pot at 190°C for 18 minutes or until the cheese mixture is melted and bubbling.
5. Once cooked, remove from the crock pot and let cool for a few minutes before serving. Enjoy your Slow Cooker Welsh Rarebit!

Crockpot Mini Cornish Pasties

Serves: 4 Prep time: 10 minutes / Cook time: 18 minutes

Ingredients:
- 300g shortcrust pastry, rolled out
- 200g beef steak, diced
- 1 potato, peeled and diced
- 1 onion, finely chopped
- 1 carrot, peeled and diced
- Salt and black pepper, to taste
- 1 egg, beaten (for egg wash)

Preparation instructions:
1. Preheat the crock pot to 190°C for 5 minutes.
2. Cut the rolled-out shortcrust pastry into small circles.
3. In a mixing bowl, combine the diced beef steak, potato, onion, carrot, salt, and black pepper.
4. Place a portion of the mixture onto each pastry circle, then fold the pastry over the filling, sealing the edges to form mini Cornish pasties.
5. Brush the tops of the pasties with beaten egg for a golden finish.
6. Arrange the pasties in the preheated crock pot.
7. Cover and cook at 190°C for 18 minutes or until the pastry is golden brown and cooked through.
8. Once cooked, remove from the crock pot and let cool for a few minutes before serving. Enjoy your Crockpot Mini Cornish Pasties!

Slow Cooker Apple Cinnamon Chips

Serves: 4 Prep time: 10 minutes / Cook time: 18 minutes

Ingredients:
- 4 apples, cored and thinly sliced
- 1 tbsp lemon juice
- 1 tbsp ground cinnamon
- 2 tbsp granulated sugar

Preparation instructions:
1. In a large bowl, toss the thinly sliced apples with lemon juice to prevent browning.
2. In a separate bowl, mix together the ground cinnamon and granulated sugar.
3. Dip each apple slice into the cinnamon-sugar mixture, coating both sides evenly.
4. Arrange the coated apple slices on the bottom of the greased crock pot.
5. Cover and cook at 190°C for 18 minutes or until the apple slices are dehydrated and crispy.
6. Once cooked, remove from the crock pot and let cool for

a few minutes before serving. Enjoy your Slow Cooker Apple Cinnamon Chips!

Crockpot Cheese and Onion Scones

Serves: 4 Prep time: 10 minutes / Cook time: 18 minutes

Ingredients:
- 200g self-raising flour
- 50g unsalted butter, cold and diced
- 100g grated cheddar cheese
- 1 small onion, finely chopped
- 120ml whole milk
- Salt and black pepper, to taste

Preparation instructions:
1. In a large bowl, combine the self-raising flour and diced cold butter. Rub the mixture with your fingertips until it resembles breadcrumbs.
2. Stir in the grated cheddar cheese and finely chopped onion.
3. Gradually add the whole milk, mixing until the dough comes together. Season with salt and black pepper to taste.
4. Divide the dough into 4 equal portions and shape each portion into a round scone.
5. Place the scones in the greased crock pot.
6. Cover and cook at 190°C for 18 minutes or until the scones are golden brown and cooked through.
7. Once cooked, remove from the crock pot and let cool for a few minutes before serving. Enjoy your Crockpot Cheese and Onion Scones!

Slow Cooker Stuffed Mushrooms

Serves: 4 Prep time: 10 minutes / Cook time: 18 minutes

Ingredients:
- 16 large mushrooms, stems removed and finely chopped
- 1 small onion, finely chopped
- 50g breadcrumbs
- 50g grated Parmesan cheese
- 1 tbsp fresh parsley, chopped
- 2 tbsp olive oil
- Salt and black pepper, to taste

Preparation instructions:
1. In a bowl, combine the chopped mushroom stems, finely chopped onion, breadcrumbs, grated Parmesan cheese, and fresh parsley. Mix well.
2. Stuff each mushroom cap with the prepared mixture.
3. Drizzle the stuffed mushrooms with olive oil and season with salt and black pepper.
4. Place the stuffed mushrooms in the greased crock pot.
5. Cover and cook at 190°C for 18 minutes or until the mushrooms are tender and the filling is golden brown.
6. Once cooked, remove from the crock pot and let cool for a few minutes before serving. Enjoy your Slow Cooker Stuffed Mushrooms!

Crockpot Chocolate Fondue

Serves: 4 Prep time: 10 minutes / Cook time: 18 minutes

Ingredients:
- 200g dark chocolate, chopped
- 120ml double cream
- 1 tsp vanilla extract
- Assorted fruits, marshmallows, and biscuits for dipping

Preparation instructions:
1. In a heatproof bowl, combine the chopped dark chocolate, double cream, and vanilla extract.
2. Place the bowl in the crock pot and fill the crock pot with water until it reaches halfway up the sides of the bowl.
3. Cover and cook at 190°C for 18 minutes or until the chocolate is melted and smooth, stirring occasionally.
4. Once the chocolate fondue is ready, serve it with assorted fruits, marshmallows, and biscuits for dipping.
5. Enjoy your indulgent Crockpot Chocolate Fondue!

Slow Cooker Rosemary Roasted Almonds

Serves: 4 Prep time: 10 minutes / Cook time: 18 minutes

Ingredients:
- 200g raw almonds
- 1 tbsp olive oil
- 1 tbsp fresh rosemary, finely chopped
- 1/2 tsp salt
- 1/4 tsp black pepper

Preparation instructions:
1. In a bowl, toss the raw almonds with olive oil, fresh rosemary, salt, and black pepper until well coated.
2. Place the seasoned almonds in the slow cooker.
3. Cover and cook on low heat for 18 minutes, stirring occasionally, until the almonds are roasted and fragrant.
4. Once roasted, remove from the slow cooker and let cool for a few minutes before serving. Enjoy your Slow Cooker Rosemary Roasted Almonds!

Crockpot Mini Scotch Eggs

Serves: 4 Prep time: 10 minutes / Cook time: 18 minutes

Ingredients:
- 4 large eggs
- 400g sausage meat
- 50g breadcrumbs
- 1 tbsp fresh parsley, finely chopped
- Salt and black pepper, to taste
- Vegetable oil, for frying

Preparation instructions:
1. Place the eggs in a saucepan and cover with water. Bring to a boil and cook for 6-7 minutes for hard-boiled eggs. Remove from heat, cool under cold water, and peel the shells.
2. In a bowl, combine the sausage meat, breadcrumbs, fresh parsley, salt, and black pepper. Mix well.
3. Divide the sausage mixture into 4 equal portions.
4. Flatten each portion in your hand, place a peeled boiled egg in the centre, and wrap the sausage mixture around the egg, ensuring it's fully covered.
5. Heat vegetable oil in a frying pan over medium heat. Fry

the Scotch eggs until golden brown on all sides.

6. Transfer the fried Scotch eggs to the slow cooker.

7. Cover and cook on low heat for 18 minutes or until the sausage is cooked through and browned.

8. Once cooked, remove from the slow cooker and let cool for a few minutes before serving. Enjoy your Crockpot Mini Scotch Eggs!

Slow Cooker Fruit Compote

Serves: 4 Prep time: 10 minutes / Cook time: 18 minutes

Ingredients:

- 400g mixed fruits (such as apples, pears, and berries), peeled, cored, and chopped
- 60g granulated sugar
- 1/2 tsp ground cinnamon
- 1/4 tsp vanilla extract
- 60ml water

Preparation instructions:

1. In the slow cooker, combine the mixed fruits, granulated sugar, ground cinnamon, vanilla extract, and water.

2. Stir well to combine all the Ingredients.

3. Cover and cook on low heat for 18 minutes or until the fruits are soft and tender.

4. Once cooked, remove from the slow cooker and let cool for a few minutes before serving. Enjoy your Slow Cooker Fruit Compote!

Crockpot Lemon Curd

Serves: 4 Prep time: 10 minutes / Cook time: 18 minutes

Ingredients:

- 4 large eggs
- 150g granulated sugar
- Zest of 2 lemons
- 120ml fresh lemon juice
- 60g unsalted butter, cubed

Preparation instructions:

1. In a heatproof bowl, whisk together the eggs and granulated sugar until well combined.

2. Stir in the lemon zest, fresh lemon juice, and cubed unsalted butter.

3. Place the bowl in the slow cooker and fill the crock pot with water until it reaches halfway up the sides of the bowl.

4. Cover and cook on low heat for 18 minutes, stirring occasionally, until the lemon curd thickens.

5. Once thickened, remove the bowl from the slow cooker and let cool for a few minutes before transferring to jars. Seal the jars and refrigerate until ready to use. Enjoy your Crockpot Lemon Curd!

Slow Cooker Herbed Popcorn

Serves: 4 Prep time: 10 minutes / Cook time: 18 minutes

Ingredients:

- 80g popcorn kernels
- 60g unsalted butter, melted

- 1 tbsp dried mixed herbs (such as thyme, rosemary, and oregano)
- Salt and black pepper, to taste

Preparation instructions:

1. Place the popcorn kernels in the slow cooker.

2. Drizzle the melted unsalted butter over the popcorn kernels, ensuring they are well coated.

3. Sprinkle the dried mixed herbs, salt, and black pepper over the popcorn.

4. Cover and cook on low heat for 18 minutes, stirring occasionally, until the popcorn is crispy and infused with the herbed butter.

5. Once cooked, remove from the slow cooker and let cool for a few minutes before serving. Enjoy your Slow Cooker Herbed Popcorn!

Crockpot Caramelized Onion Dip

Serves: 4 Prep time: 10 minutes / Cook time: 18 minutes

Ingredients:

- 500g onions, thinly sliced
- 60g unsalted butter
- 1 tbsp olive oil
- 200g sour cream
- 100g cream cheese, softened
- Salt and black pepper, to taste
- Fresh chives, chopped, for garnish

Preparation instructions:

1. In a pan, heat the unsalted butter and olive oil over medium heat. Add the thinly sliced onions and cook, stirring occasionally, until caramelised and golden brown, about 15 minutes.

2. In the slow cooker, combine the caramelised onions, sour cream, and softened cream cheese. Stir well to combine all the Ingredients.

3. Cover and cook on low heat for 18 minutes, stirring occasionally, until the dip is heated through and creamy.

4. Season with salt and black pepper to taste.

5. Once cooked, transfer the dip to a serving bowl, garnish with fresh chives, and serve warm with your favourite chips or crackers. Enjoy your Crockpot Caramelized Onion Dip!

Slow Cooker Mini Yorkshire Puddings

Serves: 4 Prep time: 10 minutes / Cook time: 18 minutes

Ingredients:

- 100g plain flour
- 2 large eggs
- 150ml whole milk
- 1/4 tsp salt
- 1/4 tsp black pepper
- 2 tbsp vegetable oil

Preparation instructions:

1. In a mixing bowl, whisk together the plain flour, eggs, whole milk, salt, and black pepper until a smooth batter forms.

2. Grease the wells of the silicone muffin cups with vegetable oil.
3. Pour the batter into the muffin cups until they are 3/4 full.
4. Place the muffin cups in the preheated crock pot.
5. Cover and cook on high heat for 18 minutes or until the Yorkshire puddings are puffed up and golden brown.
6. Once cooked, remove from the crock pot and let cool for a few minutes before serving. Enjoy your Slow Cooker Mini Yorkshire Puddings!

Crockpot Raspberry Jam

Makes: Approximately 400g Prep time: 10 minutes / Cook time: 3 hours

Ingredients:
- 500g fresh raspberries
- 250g granulated sugar
- Juice of 1 lemon

Preparation instructions:
1. In the crock pot, combine the fresh raspberries, granulated sugar, and lemon juice.
2. Stir well to combine the Ingredients.
3. Cover and cook on low heat for 3 hours, stirring occasionally, until the raspberries break down and the mixture thickens to jam consistency.
4. Using a potato masher, mash any remaining raspberry pieces to desired consistency.
5. Transfer the jam into sterilised jars while it's still hot. Seal the jars and let cool completely before storing in the refrigerator. Enjoy your Crockpot Raspberry Jam!

Slow Cooker Coconut Macaroons

Makes: Approximately 12 macaroons Prep time: 10 minutes / Cook time: 2 hours

Ingredients:
- 200g desiccated coconut
- 200ml sweetened condensed milk
- 1 tsp vanilla extract
- 2 large egg whites
- Pinch of salt

Preparation instructions:
1. In a mixing bowl, combine the desiccated coconut, sweetened condensed milk, and vanilla extract. Mix well.
2. In a separate bowl, whisk the egg whites with a pinch of salt until stiff peaks form.
3. Gently fold the whipped egg whites into the coconut mixture until well combined.
4. Grease the wells of the silicone muffin cups.
5. Scoop the coconut mixture into the muffin cups, filling each cup almost to the top.
6. Place the muffin cups in the crock pot.
7. Cover and cook on low heat for 2 hours or until the coconut macaroons are set and lightly golden on top.
8. Once cooked, remove from the crock pot and let cool for a few minutes before serving. Enjoy your Slow Cooker Coconut Macaroons!

Crockpot Baked Camembert with Cranberries

Serves: 4 Prep time: 10 minutes / Cook time: 1 hour

Ingredients:
- 250g Camembert cheese
- 100g fresh cranberries
- 30ml honey
- 50g chopped almonds
- Fresh rosemary sprigs, for garnish
- 200g assorted crackers or bread, for dipping

Preparation instructions:
1. Preheat the crock pot to low heat.
2. Remove the Camembert cheese from its packaging and place it in a small heatproof dish.
3. In a bowl, combine the fresh cranberries and honey. Mix well.
4. Spread the cranberry mixture over the Camembert cheese.
5. Sprinkle the chopped almonds on top.
6. Place the dish in the crock pot and cover. Cook on low heat for 1 hour or until the cheese is gooey and the cranberries are soft.
7. Garnish with fresh rosemary sprigs.
8. Serve the baked Camembert with assorted crackers or bread for dipping. Enjoy your Crockpot Baked Camembert with Cranberries!

Slow Cooker Chilli Cheese Nachos

Serves: 4 Prep time: 10 minutes / Cook time: 2 hours

Ingredients:
- 200g tortilla chips
- 200g grated cheddar cheese
- 1 can (400g) black beans, drained and rinsed
- 1 small red onion, finely chopped
- 1 jalapeño pepper, sliced (optional)
- 200g sour cream
- Fresh coriander leaves, for garnish

Preparation instructions:
1. Arrange half of the tortilla chips in the bottom of the crock pot.
2. Sprinkle half of the grated cheddar cheese over the chips.
3. Layer half of the black beans, chopped red onion, and jalapeño slices (if using) on top.
4. Repeat the layers with the remaining tortilla chips, cheddar cheese, black beans, red onion, and jalapeño slices.
5. Cover and cook on low heat for 2 hours or until the cheese is melted and bubbly.
6. Dollop spoonfuls of sour cream over the nachos.
7. Garnish with fresh coriander leaves.
8. Serve the chilli cheese nachos directly from the crock pot. Enjoy your Slow Cooker Chilli Cheese Nachos!

Crockpot Apricot and Almond Bars

Makes: Approximately 12 bars Prep time: 10 minutes / Cook time: 3 hours

Ingredients:

- 200g dried apricots, chopped
- 100g almonds, chopped
- 100g oats
- 50g desiccated coconut
- 100g honey
- 50g almond butter
- 50g coconut oil, melted
- 1/2 tsp vanilla extract

Preparation instructions:

1. In a large mixing bowl, combine the chopped dried apricots, almonds, oats, and desiccated coconut.
2. In a separate microwave-safe bowl, heat the honey, almond butter, melted coconut oil, and vanilla extract until well combined and slightly runny.
3. Pour the wet mixture over the dry Ingredients. Mix well until everything is evenly coated.
4. Line a baking dish that fits into the crock pot with parchment paper, leaving some overhang for easy removal.
5. Press the mixture firmly into the prepared dish.
6. Place the dish in the crock pot, cover, and cook on low heat for 3 hours.
7. Remove the dish from the crock pot and let it cool completely.
8. Once cooled, cut the mixture into bars.
9. Store the apricot and almond bars in an airtight container. Enjoy your Crockpot Apricot and Almond Bars!

Slow Cooker Garlic Herb Breadsticks

Serves: 4 Prep time: 10 minutes / Cook time: 2 hours

Ingredients:

- 250g all-purpose flour
- 7g instant yeast
- 5g salt
- 1/2 tsp sugar
- 150ml warm water
- 30ml olive oil
- 2 cloves garlic, minced
- 1 tsp dried mixed herbs (such as basil, oregano, and thyme)
- 30g grated Parmesan cheese

Preparation instructions:

1. In a bowl, combine the flour, instant yeast, salt, and sugar.
2. Gradually add warm water and olive oil to the dry Ingredients, stirring continuously until a dough forms.
3. Knead the dough on a lightly floured surface until smooth and elastic.
4. Divide the dough into 8 equal portions and roll each portion into a long, thin rope.
5. In a small bowl, mix minced garlic and dried herbs.
6. Brush each breadstick with the garlic-herb mixture and sprinkle with grated Parmesan cheese.
7. Place the breadsticks in the slow cooker, cover, and cook on low heat for 2 hours or until the breadsticks are cooked through and lightly browned.
8. Serve the garlic herb breadsticks warm from the slow

cooker. Enjoy your Slow Cooker Garlic Herb Breadsticks!

Crockpot Spinach and Artichoke Dip

Serves: 4 Prep time: 10 minutes / Cook time: 2 hours

Ingredients:

- 200g frozen spinach, thawed and drained
- 200g canned artichoke hearts, drained and chopped
- 200g cream cheese, softened
- 100g sour cream
- 100g mayonnaise
- 1 garlic clove, minced
- 100g shredded mozzarella cheese
- 50g grated Parmesan cheese
- Salt and black pepper, to taste

Preparation instructions:

1. In a medium bowl, combine the thawed and drained spinach, chopped artichoke hearts, softened cream cheese, sour cream, mayonnaise, and minced garlic.
2. Stir in the shredded mozzarella cheese and grated Parmesan cheese. Season with salt and black pepper to taste.
3. Transfer the mixture into the crockpot.
4. Cover and cook on low heat for 2 hours or until the dip is hot and bubbly.
5. Stir the dip well before serving.
6. Serve the spinach and artichoke dip with breadsticks, crackers, or vegetable sticks. Enjoy your Crockpot Spinach and Artichoke Dip!

Slow Cooker Mini Beef Wellingtons

Serves: 4 Prep time: 15 minutes / Cook time: 2.5 hours

Ingredients:

- 500g beef tenderloin fillet, cut into 8 equal portions
- Salt and black pepper, to taste
- 30ml olive oil
- 200g mushrooms, finely chopped
- 2 cloves garlic, minced
- 1 tbsp fresh parsley, chopped
- 200g puff pastry, thawed if frozen
- 1 egg, beaten (for egg wash)

Preparation instructions:

1. Season the beef fillet portions with salt and black pepper.
2. Heat olive oil in a pan over medium-high heat. Sear the beef fillet portions on all sides until browned. Remove from heat and let them cool.
3. In the same pan, sauté the chopped mushrooms and minced garlic until the mushrooms release their moisture and become golden brown. Stir in fresh parsley and remove from heat.
4. Roll out the puff pastry on a floured surface and cut into 8 equal rectangles.
5. Place a spoonful of the mushroom mixture on each pastry rectangle and top with a seared beef fillet portion.
6. Brush the edges of the pastry with beaten egg and fold the pastry over the beef, sealing the edges to form mini

Wellingtons.

7. Place the mini Beef Wellingtons in the slow cooker.

8. Cover and cook on low heat for 2.5 hours or until the pastry is golden brown and the beef is cooked to your desired doneness.

9. Serve the mini Beef Wellingtons hot from the slow cooker. Enjoy your Slow Cooker Mini Beef Wellingtons!

Crockpot Mulled Wine

Serves: 4 Prep time: 5 minutes / Cook time: 1.5 hours

Ingredients:

- 750ml red wine
- 60g caster sugar
- 1 orange, thinly sliced
- 1 lemon, thinly sliced
- 6 cloves
- 2 cinnamon sticks
- 1 star anise
- 1/4 tsp ground nutmeg

Preparation instructions:

1. In the crockpot, combine the red wine, caster sugar, thinly sliced orange, thinly sliced lemon, cloves, cinnamon sticks, star anise, and ground nutmeg.

2. Stir well to dissolve the sugar.

3. Cover and cook on low heat for 1.5 hours, allowing the flavours to meld and the wine to warm up.

4. After 1.5 hours, ladle the mulled wine into mugs or heatproof glasses, ensuring to strain out the spices and fruit slices.

5. Serve the warm mulled wine garnished with a slice of orange or lemon. Enjoy your Crockpot Mulled Wine!

Slow Cooker BBQ Meatballs

Serves: 4 Prep time: 10 minutes / Cook time: 2 hours

Ingredients:

- 500g beef or pork meatballs
- 200ml barbecue sauce
- 60g brown sugar
- 60ml apple cider vinegar
- 1/2 tsp garlic powder
- 1/2 tsp onion powder
- Salt and black pepper, to taste
- Fresh parsley, chopped (for garnish)

Preparation instructions:

1. In the crockpot, combine the meatballs, barbecue sauce, brown sugar, apple cider vinegar, garlic powder, onion powder, salt, and black pepper.

2. Stir gently to coat the meatballs evenly with the sauce.

3. Cover and cook on low heat for 2 hours, allowing the meatballs to absorb the flavours of the sauce.

4. Once cooked, garnish the meatballs with chopped fresh parsley.

5. Serve the BBQ meatballs hot from the slow cooker, either as an appetiser or with rice or mashed potatoes. Enjoy your Slow Cooker BBQ Meatballs!

Crockpot Stuffed Peppers

Serves: 4 Prep time: 20 minutes / Cook time: 3 hours

Ingredients:

- 4 large peppers, any colour
- 200g cooked rice
- 400g lean ground beef
- 1 onion, finely chopped
- 2 cloves garlic, minced
- 1 can (400g) diced tomatoes
- 1 tsp dried basil
- 1 tsp dried oregano
- Salt and black pepper, to taste
- 100g shredded mozzarella cheese

Preparation instructions:

1. Cut the tops off the peppers and remove the seeds and membranes. Set aside.

2. In a pan, brown the ground beef with chopped onion and minced garlic until cooked through. Drain any excess fat.

3. In a bowl, combine the cooked rice, browned beef mixture, diced tomatoes, dried basil, dried oregano, salt, and black pepper.

4. Stuff each pepper with the rice and beef mixture.

5. Place the stuffed peppers in the crockpot.

6. Cover and cook on low heat for 3 hours or until the peppers are tender.

7. In the last 10 minutes of cooking, sprinkle the shredded mozzarella cheese over the top of each stuffed pepper and let it melt.

8. Serve the stuffed peppers hot from the crockpot. Enjoy your Crockpot Stuffed peppers!

Slow Cooker Cheese Straws

Serves: 4 Prep time: 10 minutes / Cook time: 2 hours

Ingredients:

- 200g puff pastry, rolled out
- 100g cheddar cheese, grated
- 1/2 tsp paprika
- 1/4 tsp garlic powder
- Salt and black pepper, to taste

Preparation instructions:

1. Preheat the slow cooker to low heat.

2. In a bowl, mix together grated cheddar cheese, paprika, garlic powder, salt, and black pepper.

3. Spread the cheese mixture evenly over the rolled-out puff pastry.

4. Cut the pastry into thin strips, about 1.5 cm wide.

5. Twist each strip and place it on a parchment-lined slow cooker insert.

6. Cover and cook on low heat for 2 hours or until the cheese straws are golden and crispy.

7. Let the cheese straws cool for a few minutes before serving. Enjoy your Slow Cooker Cheese Straws!

Crockpot Mini Quiches

Serves: 4 Prep time: 15 minutes / Cook time: 2 hours

Ingredients:
- 200g shortcrust pastry, rolled out
- 100g cooked ham, chopped
- 1/2 red pepper, finely diced
- 50g cheddar cheese, grated
- 3 large eggs
- 200ml double cream
- Salt and black pepper, to taste
- Fresh parsley, chopped (for garnish)

Preparation instructions:
1. Preheat the slow cooker to low heat.
2. Grease the cups of a muffin tin.
3. Cut circles from the rolled-out shortcrust pastry and line the muffin tin cups with the pastry circles.
4. Divide chopped cooked ham, diced red pepper, and grated cheddar cheese evenly among the pastry-lined cups.
5. In a bowl, whisk together eggs, double cream, salt, and black pepper.
6. Pour the egg mixture over the ham, pepper, and cheese in each cup, filling them almost to the top.
7. Cover the muffin tin with foil and place it in the slow cooker.
8. Cover the slow cooker and cook on low heat for 2 hours or until the quiches are set and golden.
9. Garnish with chopped fresh parsley before serving. Enjoy your Crockpot Mini Quiches!

Slow Cooker Herb Roasted Nuts

Serves: 4 Prep time: 10 minutes / Cook time: 2 hours

Ingredients:
- 200g mixed nuts (such as almonds, cashews, walnuts)
- 1 tbsp olive oil
- 1/2 tsp dried rosemary
- 1/2 tsp dried thyme
- 1/2 tsp dried oregano
- Salt and black pepper, to taste

Preparation instructions:
1. Preheat the slow cooker to low heat.
2. In a bowl, combine mixed nuts, olive oil, dried rosemary, dried thyme, dried oregano, salt, and black pepper. Toss to coat the nuts evenly with the seasoning.
3. Spread the seasoned nuts in an even layer in the slow cooker insert.
4. Cover and cook on low heat for 2 hours, stirring occasionally, until the nuts are roasted and fragrant.
5. Let the roasted nuts cool completely before serving. Enjoy your Slow Cooker Herb Roasted Nuts!

Crockpot Mediterranean Stuffed Mushrooms

Serves: 4 Prep time: 15 minutes / Cook time: 2 hours

Ingredients:
- 200g button mushrooms, stems removed and chopped
- 50g feta cheese, crumbled
- 30g black olives, finely chopped
- 1 small tomato, finely chopped
- 1 clove garlic, minced
- 1 tbsp fresh parsley, chopped
- Salt and black pepper, to taste
- Olive oil, for drizzling

Preparation instructions:
1. In a bowl, combine chopped mushroom stems, crumbled feta cheese, black olives, tomato, minced garlic, and fresh parsley. Season with salt and black pepper.
2. Stuff each mushroom cap with the Mediterranean filling mixture.
3. Arrange the stuffed mushrooms in the crock pot.
4. Drizzle with a bit of olive oil.
5. Cover and cook on low heat for 2 hours or until the mushrooms are tender and the filling is heated through.
6. Serve the Crockpot Mediterranean Stuffed Mushrooms warm.

Slow Cooker Spiced Apple Rings

Serves: 4 Prep time: 10 minutes / Cook time: 2 hours

Ingredients:
- 2 large apples, cored and sliced into rings
- 200ml apple juice
- 1/2 tsp ground cinnamon
- 1/4 tsp ground nutmeg
- 1 tbsp honey
- 1 tbsp lemon juice

Preparation instructions:
1. In a bowl, mix together apple juice, ground cinnamon, ground nutmeg, honey, and lemon juice.
2. Place the apple rings in the slow cooker.
3. Pour the spiced apple juice mixture over the apple rings.
4. Cover and cook on low heat for 2 hours or until the apples are tender and infused with spices.
5. Serve the Slow Cooker Spiced Apple Rings warm as a delightful dessert or snack.

Crockpot Mini Croque Monsieur

Serves: 4 Prep time: 15 minutes / Cook time: 2 hours

Ingredients:
- 8 slices white bread
- 50g butter, softened
- 100g ham, thinly sliced
- 100g Gruyère cheese, grated
- 300ml milk
- 2 large eggs
- 1/4 tsp ground nutmeg
- Salt and black pepper, to taste

Preparation instructions:
1. Butter each slice of bread on one side.
2. Place a layer of ham on the non-buttered side of 4 bread slices.
3. Sprinkle grated Gruyère cheese over the ham and top with

the remaining 4 bread slices, buttered side up, to form sandwiches.

4. Cut each sandwich into halves or quarters, creating mini Croque Monsieur sandwiches.

5. Arrange the mini sandwiches in the crock pot.

6. In a bowl, whisk together milk, eggs, ground nutmeg, salt, and black pepper.

7. Pour the egg mixture evenly over the mini sandwiches in the crock pot.

8. Cover and cook on low heat for 2 hours or until the sandwiches are set and golden brown on top.

9. Serve the Crockpot Mini Croque Monsieur warm for a delightful French-inspired treat.

Slow Cooker Chocolate Covered Strawberries

Serves: 4 Prep time: 15 minutes / Cook time: 1 hour

Ingredients:
- 200g fresh strawberries, washed and dried
- 150g dark chocolate, chopped
- 60ml double cream
- 1/2 tsp vanilla extract
- 1 tbsp unsalted butter
- White chocolate, melted, for drizzling (optional)

Preparation instructions:
1. In a small saucepan, heat the double cream over low heat until it starts to simmer.
2. Remove from heat and add the chopped dark chocolate. Let it sit for a minute to melt, then stir until smooth.
3. Stir in the vanilla extract and unsalted butter until well incorporated.
4. Dip each strawberry into the chocolate mixture, coating it evenly. Place the coated strawberries on a parchment-lined tray.
5. Transfer the strawberries to the slow cooker.
6. Cover and cook on low heat for 1 hour or until the chocolate is set.
7. Drizzle with melted white chocolate if desired.
8. Serve the Slow Cooker Chocolate Covered Strawberries as a delightful dessert.

Crockpot Mini Lemon Tarts

Serves: 4 Prep time: 15 minutes / Cook time: 2 hours

Ingredients:
- 200g digestive biscuits, crushed into fine crumbs
- 80g unsalted butter, melted
- Zest and juice of 2 lemons
- 200ml double cream
- 50g icing sugar
- Fresh mint leaves, for garnish

Preparation instructions:
1. In a bowl, combine the crushed digestive biscuits with melted unsalted butter until the mixture resembles wet sand.
2. Press the biscuit mixture firmly into the base of 4 silicone muffin cups to create the tart crust.

3. In another bowl, whisk together the lemon zest, lemon juice, double cream, and icing sugar until thick and creamy.
4. Pour the lemon cream mixture into each tart crust.
5. Place the muffin cups in the crock pot.
6. Cover and cook on low heat for 2 hours or until the lemon tarts are set.
7. Remove from the crock pot and let cool for a few minutes before serving.
8. Garnish with fresh mint leaves and serve the Crockpot Mini Lemon Tarts as a zesty dessert.

Slow Cooker Nutella Fondue

Serves: 4 Prep time: 10 minutes / Cook time: 1 hour

Ingredients:
- 200g Nutella hazelnut spread
- 120ml double cream
- 1/2 tsp vanilla extract
- Assorted fruits, marshmallows, and biscuits for dipping

Preparation instructions:
1. In a small saucepan, heat the double cream over low heat until it starts to simmer.
2. Remove from heat and add the Nutella hazelnut spread. Stir until smooth and well combined.
3. Stir in the vanilla extract until incorporated.
4. Transfer the Nutella fondue mixture to the slow cooker.
5. Cover and cook on low heat for 1 hour or until the fondue is smooth and creamy, stirring occasionally.
6. Serve the Slow Cooker Nutella Fondue with assorted fruits, marshmallows, and biscuits for dipping, creating a delightful dessert experience.

Crockpot Caprese Skewers

Serves: 4 Prep time: 15 minutes / Cook time: 1 hour

Ingredients:
- 200g cherry tomatoes
- 200g fresh mozzarella cheese, cut into small cubes
- 20 fresh basil leaves
- 60ml balsamic glaze
- Salt and black pepper, to taste

Preparation instructions:
1. Thread cherry tomatoes, fresh mozzarella cubes, and basil leaves alternately onto small skewers.
2. Place the skewers in the crock pot.
3. Drizzle the balsamic glaze over the skewers and season with salt and black pepper.
4. Cover and cook on low heat for 1 hour or until the tomatoes are softened and the cheese is slightly melted.
5. Serve the Crockpot Caprese Skewers as a delightful appetiser.

Slow Cooker Glazed Cinnamon Rolls

Serves: 4 Prep time: 15 minutes / Cook time: 2 hours

Ingredients:
- 400g refrigerated cinnamon roll dough

- 60g unsalted butter, melted
- 100g icing sugar
- 15 ml whole milk
- 1/2 tsp vanilla extract

Preparation instructions:

1. Roll each cinnamon roll into a small ball.
2. Dip each ball into the melted butter and place them in the bottom of the crock pot.
3. Cover and cook on low heat for 2 hours or until the cinnamon rolls are cooked through and golden brown.
4. In a bowl, whisk together the icing sugar, whole milk, and vanilla extract until smooth.
5. Drizzle the glaze over the cooked cinnamon rolls.
6. Serve the Slow Cooker Glazed Cinnamon Rolls as a sweet treat.

Crockpot Mini Chicken and Leek Pies

Serves: 4 Prep time: 20 minutes / Cook time: 4 hours

Ingredients:

- 400g boneless, skinless chicken thighs, diced
- 2 leeks, washed and sliced
- 200ml chicken stock
- 200ml double cream
- 30g plain flour
- 30g unsalted butter
- Salt and black pepper, to taste
- 400g puff pastry, thawed if frozen

Preparation instructions:

1. In a pan, melt the butter over medium heat. Add the diced chicken and cook until browned on all sides. Remove the chicken from the pan and set aside.
2. In the same pan, add the leeks and cook until softened.
3. Sprinkle the flour over the leeks and stir to create a roux. Gradually pour in the chicken stock and double cream, stirring constantly until the mixture thickens.
4. Add the cooked chicken back to the pan and season with salt and black pepper. Remove from heat and let the filling cool.
5. Roll out the puff pastry and cut out 8 circles to fit the tops of the muffin cups.
6. Grease the muffin cups and line them with the pastry circles, leaving some overhang.
7. Fill each pastry-lined cup with the chicken and leek filling.
8. Cover the pies with the overhanging pastry and seal the edges.
9. Place the muffin cups in the crock pot.
10. Cover and cook on low heat for 4 hours or until the pastry is golden and the filling is piping hot.
11. Serve the Crockpot Mini Chicken and Leek Pies with your favourite side dishes.

Slow Cooker Cheese and Spinach Stuffed Mushrooms

Serves: 4 Prep time: 15 minutes / Cook time: 2 hours

Ingredients:

- 200g button mushrooms, stems removed and finely chopped

- 100g fresh spinach, chopped
- 100g cream cheese
- 50g shredded cheddar cheese
- 1 garlic clove, minced
- Salt and black pepper, to taste
- 15ml olive oil

Preparation instructions:

1. In a bowl, combine the chopped mushroom stems, chopped spinach, cream cheese, shredded cheddar cheese, minced garlic, salt, and black pepper.
2. Stuff the mushroom caps with the cheese and spinach mixture.
3. Grease the bottom of the crock pot with olive oil and arrange the stuffed mushrooms in it.
4. Cover and cook on low heat for 2 hours or until the mushrooms are tender and the filling is melted and bubbly.
5. Serve the Slow Cooker Cheese and Spinach Stuffed Mushrooms as a delightful appetiser.

Crockpot Mini Raspberry Eclairs

Serves: 4 Prep time: 20 minutes / Cook time: 2 hours

Ingredients:

- 200ml water
- 100g unsalted butter
- 150g plain flour
- 4 large eggs
- 250ml whipping cream
- 50g icing sugar
- 150g fresh raspberries
- 50g dark chocolate, melted

Preparation instructions:

1. In a saucepan, combine water and butter and bring to a boil. Remove from heat and quickly stir in the flour until a dough forms.
2. Let the dough cool slightly, then beat in the eggs one at a time until smooth.
3. Transfer the dough into a piping bag fitted with a round tip.
4. Pipe small éclair shapes onto a greased baking sheet. Place the sheet in the freezer for 15 minutes.
5. Grease the bottom of the crock pot and arrange the frozen éclair shapes in it.
6. Cover and cook on low heat for 2 hours or until the éclairs are puffed up and golden.
7. In a separate bowl, whip the whipping cream and icing sugar until stiff peaks form.
8. Cut the cooled éclairs in half horizontally and fill them with whipped cream and fresh raspberries.
9. Drizzle the filled éclairs with melted chocolate.
10. Serve the Crockpot Mini Raspberry Eclairs as a delightful dessert.

Slow Cooker Sticky Date Pudding Bites

Serves: 4 Prep time: 15 minutes / Cook time: 2 hours

Ingredients:

- 200g pitted dates, chopped

- 250ml boiling water
- 1 tsp baking soda
- 100g unsalted butter, softened
- 150g brown sugar
- 2 large eggs
- 200g self-raising flour
- 1 tsp vanilla extract
- 250ml double cream, whipped
- For the sticky toffee sauce:
- 100g brown sugar
- 100g unsalted butter
- 150ml double cream

Preparation instructions:

1. In a bowl, combine the chopped dates, boiling water, and baking soda. Let it sit for 10 minutes.
2. In another bowl, cream together the softened butter and brown sugar. Beat in the eggs one at a time, then stir in the self-raising flour and vanilla extract.
3. Fold in the soaked dates into the batter.
4. Grease the bottom of the crock pot and pour the batter into it.
5. Cover and cook on low heat for 2 hours or until a toothpick inserted into the centre comes out clean.
6. In a saucepan, combine the brown sugar, butter, and double cream for the sticky toffee sauce. Cook over low heat until the sugar is dissolved and the sauce is smooth.
7. Serve the warm Sticky Date Pudding Bites drizzled with the sticky toffee sauce and topped with whipped cream.

Crockpot Mini Custard Tarts

Serves: 4 Prep time: 15 minutes / Cook time: 2 hours

Ingredients:

- 200g shortcrust pastry, rolled and cut into circles to fit the muffin cups
- 300ml whole milk
- 3 large eggs
- 50g caster sugar
- 1 tsp vanilla extract
- Freshly grated nutmeg, for garnish

Preparation instructions:

1. Grease the bottom and sides of 4 silicone muffin cups.
2. Line each muffin cup with a circle of shortcrust pastry, pressing gently to fit the cups.
3. In a saucepan, heat the milk until hot but not boiling.

4. In a bowl, whisk together the eggs, caster sugar, and vanilla extract.
5. Slowly pour the hot milk into the egg mixture, whisking constantly to avoid curdling.
6. Pour the custard mixture into the pastry-lined muffin cups, filling each cup up to 3/4 full.
7. Sprinkle freshly grated nutmeg over the top of each custard.
8. Place the muffin cups in the crockpot and cover. Cook on low heat for 2 hours or until the custards are set and a knife inserted into the centre comes out clean.
9. Carefully remove the custard tarts from the crockpot and let them cool for a few minutes before serving.

Slow Cooker Chocolate Dipped Shortbread Cookies

Makes: 4 servings Prep time: 15 minutes / Cook time: 2 hours

Ingredients:

- 200g plain flour
- 100g unsalted butter, softened
- 50g caster sugar
- 1 tsp vanilla extract
- 100g dark chocolate, melted
- Sprinkles, for decoration

Preparation instructions:

1. In a bowl, cream together the softened butter and caster sugar until light and fluffy. Stir in the vanilla extract.
2. Gradually add the flour and mix until a smooth dough forms.
3. Roll the dough into small balls and press each ball into a cookie shape.
4. Place the cookies on a parchment-lined tray and refrigerate for 15 minutes to firm up.
5. Grease the bottom of the crockpot and place the chilled cookies inside.
6. Cover and cook on low heat for 2 hours or until the cookies are firm and lightly golden.
7. Carefully dip half of each cookie into melted dark chocolate, allowing excess chocolate to drip off.
8. Place the chocolate-dipped cookies on a parchment-lined tray and decorate with sprinkles.
9. Allow the chocolate to set before serving the Slow Cooker Chocolate Dipped Shortbread Cookies.

Chapter 3: Lunch Recipes

Slow Cooker Beef and Guinness Stew

Serves: 4 Prep time: 15 minutes / Cook time: 6 hours

Ingredients:
- 500g stewing beef, cubed
- 2 tbsp plain flour
- Salt and black pepper, to taste
- 2 tbsp vegetable oil
- 2 onions, chopped
- 2 carrots, peeled and sliced
- 2 potatoes, peeled and cubed
- 2 cloves garlic, minced
- 500ml Guinness beer
- 250ml beef stock
- 2 tbsp tomato paste
- 1 tbsp Worcestershire sauce
- 1 tsp dried thyme
- 2 bay leaves
- Fresh parsley, chopped (for garnish)

Preparation instructions:
1. In a bowl, toss the stewing beef with plain flour, salt, and black pepper until coated.
2. Heat the vegetable oil in a frying pan over medium-high heat. Brown the beef cubes on all sides. Transfer the beef to the slow cooker.
3. In the same pan, add the chopped onions, carrots, and potatoes. Cook until the vegetables start to soften, about 5 minutes. Add minced garlic and cook for an additional minute.
4. Transfer the cooked vegetables to the slow cooker with the beef.
5. Pour Guinness beer and beef stock into the slow cooker. Add tomato paste, Worcestershire sauce, dried thyme, and bay leaves. Stir well to combine.
6. Cover and cook on low heat for 6 hours or until the beef is tender and the flavours are well blended.
7. Remove the bay leaves before serving. Garnish with fresh chopped parsley.

Crockpot Chicken Tikka Masala

Serves: 4 Prep time: 15 minutes / Cook time: 4 hours

Ingredients:
- 500g boneless, skinless chicken thighs, cubed
- 1 onion, finely chopped
- 3 cloves garlic, minced
- 1 tbsp fresh ginger, grated
- 400g canned chopped tomatoes
- 200ml double cream
- 2 tbsp tomato paste
- 2 tsp ground cumin
- 2 tsp ground coriander
- 1 tsp paprika
- 1/2 tsp turmeric powder
- Salt and black pepper, to taste
- Fresh coriander, chopped (for garnish)
- Cooked basmati rice, for serving

Preparation instructions:
1. In the crockpot, combine chicken cubes, chopped onion, minced garlic, grated ginger, canned chopped tomatoes, double cream, and tomato paste.
2. Add ground cumin, ground coriander, paprika, turmeric powder, salt, and black pepper. Stir well to combine all the Ingredients.
3. Cover and cook on low heat for 4 hours, allowing the flavours to meld together and the chicken to become tender.
4. Taste and adjust seasoning if necessary.
5. Serve the Chicken Tikka Masala over cooked basmati rice, garnished with fresh chopped coriander.

Slow Cooker Mushroom Risotto

Serves: 4 Prep time: 15 minutes / Cook time: 3 hours

Ingredients:
- 300g Arborio rice
- 500g mixed mushrooms (such as button mushrooms, cremini, and shiitake), sliced
- 1 onion, finely chopped
- 2 cloves garlic, minced
- 1 litre vegetable stock
- 60ml dry white wine
- 60g Parmesan cheese, grated
- 2 tbsp butter
- Salt and black pepper, to taste
- Fresh parsley, chopped (for garnish)

Preparation instructions:
1. In the slow cooker, combine Arborio rice, sliced mushrooms, chopped onion, minced garlic, vegetable stock, and dry white wine. Stir well to combine.
2. Cover and cook on low heat for 3 hours, stirring occasionally. The risotto should be creamy and the rice tender.
3. Stir in grated Parmesan cheese and butter. Season with salt and black pepper to taste.
4. Garnish with fresh chopped parsley before serving. Enjoy your creamy Mushroom Risotto straight from the slow cooker.

Crockpot Lamb Curry

Serves: 4 Prep time: 15 minutes / Cook time: 6 hours

Ingredients:
- 500g lamb shoulder, diced
- 2 onions, finely chopped
- 3 cloves garlic, minced

- 2 tbsp curry powder
- 1 tsp ground cumin
- 1 tsp ground coriander
- 1/2 tsp turmeric powder
- 400ml coconut milk
- 400g canned chopped tomatoes
- 200ml lamb or vegetable stock
- 2 potatoes, peeled and cubed
- Salt and black pepper, to taste
- Fresh coriander, chopped (for garnish)
- Cooked basmati rice, for serving

Preparation instructions:

1. In a pan, heat a little oil over medium heat. Add diced lamb and brown on all sides. Transfer the lamb to the crockpot.
2. In the same pan, add chopped onions and cook until softened. Add minced garlic and continue cooking for another minute.
3. Add curry powder, ground cumin, ground coriander, and turmeric powder to the onions and garlic. Stir well to combine the spices. Transfer the mixture to the crockpot.
4. Pour in coconut milk, canned chopped tomatoes, and lamb or vegetable stock. Add cubed potatoes. Season with salt and black pepper. Stir gently to combine all the Ingredients.
5. Cover and cook on low heat for 6 hours, allowing the flavours to meld together and the lamb to become tender.
6. Taste and adjust seasoning if necessary.
7. Serve the Lamb Curry over cooked basmati rice, garnished with fresh chopped coriander.

Slow Cooker Vegetable Soup

Serves: 4 Prep time: 15 minutes / Cook time: 6 hours

Ingredients:
- 500g mixed vegetables (carrots, potatoes, leeks, celery), peeled and chopped
- 1 onion, finely chopped
- 2 cloves garlic, minced
- 1 litre vegetable stock
- 400g canned chopped tomatoes
- 1 tsp dried mixed herbs
- Salt and black pepper, to taste
- Fresh parsley, chopped (for garnish)
- Crusty bread, for serving

Preparation instructions:

1. In the slow cooker, combine chopped mixed vegetables, chopped onion, minced garlic, vegetable stock, canned chopped tomatoes, and dried mixed herbs.
2. Season with salt and black pepper. Stir well to combine all the Ingredients.
3. Cover and cook on low heat for 6 hours, allowing the vegetables to soften and the flavours to meld together.
4. Taste and adjust seasoning if necessary.
5. Garnish with fresh chopped parsley before serving. Serve the Vegetable Soup hot with crusty bread.

Crockpot Pork and Apple Casserole

Serves: 4 Prep time: 15 minutes / Cook time: 6 hours

Ingredients:
- 500g pork shoulder, diced
- 2 apples, peeled, cored, and sliced
- 2 onions, finely chopped
- 2 cloves garlic, minced
- 300ml apple juice
- 1 tbsp Dijon mustard
- 1 tbsp honey
- 1 tsp dried sage
- Salt and black pepper, to taste
- Fresh parsley, chopped (for garnish)
- Mashed potatoes, for serving

Preparation instructions:

1. In the crockpot, combine diced pork shoulder, sliced apples, chopped onions, and minced garlic.
2. In a bowl, mix together apple juice, Dijon mustard, honey, dried sage, salt, and black pepper.
3. Pour the apple juice mixture over the pork and apples in the crockpot. Stir gently to combine.
4. Cover and cook on low heat for 6 hours, allowing the flavours to meld together and the pork to become tender.
5. Taste and adjust seasoning if necessary.
6. Garnish with fresh chopped parsley before serving. Serve the Pork and Apple Casserole hot with mashed potatoes.

Slow Cooker Spinach and Ricotta Lasagna

Serves: 4 Prep time: 15 minutes / Cook time: 4 hours

Ingredients:
- 250g lasagna noodles, uncooked
- 400g fresh spinach, chopped
- 250g ricotta cheese
- 500ml passata
- 1 onion, finely chopped
- 2 cloves garlic, minced
- 1 tsp dried oregano
- 1 tsp dried basil
- Salt and black pepper, to taste
- 200g shredded mozzarella cheese
- Fresh basil, chopped (for garnish)

Preparation instructions:

1. In a bowl, combine chopped fresh spinach and ricotta cheese. Season with salt and black pepper. Mix well.
2. In another bowl, mix passata with dried oregano, dried basil, salt, and black pepper.
3. In the slow cooker, layer uncooked lasagna noodles, followed by a layer of the spinach and ricotta mixture, a layer of chopped onions and minced garlic, and a layer of passata mixture. Repeat the layers until all Ingredients are used, finishing with a layer of passata mixture on top.
4. Cover and cook on low heat for 4 hours, allowing the lasagna to cook through and the flavours to meld together.

5. In the last 30 minutes of cooking, sprinkle shredded mozzarella cheese on top of the lasagna. Cover and let the cheese melt.
6. Garnish with fresh chopped basil before serving. Serve the Spinach and Ricotta Lasagna hot.

Crockpot Chicken and Leek Pie

Serves: 4 Prep time: 15 minutes / Cook time: 4 hours

Ingredients:
- 500g chicken breasts, diced
- 2 leeks, sliced
- 200ml chicken stock
- 200ml double cream
- 1 tbsp Dijon mustard
- 1 tbsp plain flour
- 1 tbsp butter
- Salt and black pepper, to taste
- Fresh parsley, chopped (for garnish)
- Puff pastry sheets, baked (for serving)

Preparation instructions:
1. In a pan, melt butter over medium heat. Add diced chicken and cook until browned on all sides. Transfer the chicken to the crockpot.
2. In the same pan, add sliced leeks and cook until softened. Transfer the leeks to the crockpot.
3. Sprinkle plain flour over the chicken and leeks in the crockpot. Stir to coat the Ingredients.
4. Pour in chicken stock, double cream, and Dijon mustard. Season with salt and black pepper. Stir well to combine all the Ingredients.
5. Cover and cook on low heat for 4 hours, allowing the flavours to meld together and the chicken to become tender.
6. Taste and adjust seasoning if necessary.
7. Garnish with fresh chopped parsley before serving. Serve the Chicken and Leek Pie hot, with baked puff pastry sheets on the side.

Slow Cooker Lentil Soup

Serves: 4 Prep time: 15 minutes / Cook time: 6 hours

Ingredients:
- 200g red lentils, rinsed and drained
- 1 onion, chopped
- 2 carrots, peeled and diced
- 2 celery sticks, chopped
- 2 cloves garlic, minced
- 1 tsp ground cumin
- 1 tsp ground turmeric
- 1/2 tsp ground coriander
- 2 litres vegetable stock
- Salt and black pepper, to taste
- Fresh coriander, chopped (for garnish)
- Crusty bread, for serving

Preparation instructions:
1. In the slow cooker, combine red lentils, chopped onion, diced carrots, chopped celery sticks, minced garlic, ground cumin, ground turmeric, ground coriander, vegetable stock, salt, and black pepper.
2. Stir well to combine all the Ingredients.
3. Cover and cook on low heat for 6 hours, allowing the lentils and vegetables to soften and the flavours to meld together.
4. Taste and adjust seasoning if necessary.
5. Garnish with fresh chopped coriander before serving. Serve the Lentil Soup hot with crusty bread.

Crockpot Beef and Ale Stew

Serves: 4 Prep time: 15 minutes / Cook time: 6 hours

Ingredients:
- 500g beef stewing meat, diced
- 2 onions, chopped
- 2 carrots, peeled and diced
- 2 potatoes, peeled and diced
- 2 cloves garlic, minced
- 500ml ale
- 500ml beef stock
- 2 tbsp plain flour
- 2 tbsp vegetable oil
- Salt and black pepper, to taste
- Fresh parsley, chopped (for garnish)

Preparation instructions:
1. In a bowl, coat the diced beef with plain flour, salt, and black pepper.
2. Heat vegetable oil in a pan over medium heat. Add the coated beef and cook until browned on all sides. Transfer the beef to the crockpot.
3. In the same pan, add chopped onions and minced garlic. Cook until softened. Transfer the onions and garlic to the crockpot.
4. Add diced carrots and potatoes to the crockpot.
5. Pour in ale and beef stock. Stir well to combine all the Ingredients.
6. Cover and cook on low heat for 6 hours, allowing the flavours to meld together and the beef to become tender.
7. Taste and adjust seasoning if necessary.
8. Garnish with fresh chopped parsley before serving. Serve the Beef and Ale Stew hot.

Slow Cooker Chicken Korma

Serves: 4 Prep time: 15 minutes / Cook time: 4 hours

Ingredients:
- 500g chicken breasts, diced
- 2 onions, finely chopped
- 4 cloves garlic, minced
- 1 tsp ground ginger
- 1 tsp ground turmeric
- 1 tsp ground cumin
- 1 tsp ground coriander
- 1/2 tsp chilli powder
- 200ml coconut milk
- 200ml natural yoghurt

- 2 tbsp vegetable oil
- Salt and black pepper, to taste
- Fresh coriander, chopped (for garnish)
- Basmati rice, cooked (for serving)

Preparation instructions:

1. In a pan, heat vegetable oil over medium heat. Add finely chopped onions and cook until golden brown.
2. Add minced garlic, ground ginger, ground turmeric, ground cumin, ground coriander, and chilli powder. Cook for a few minutes until fragrant. Transfer the mixture to the slow cooker.
3. Add diced chicken to the slow cooker.
4. Pour in coconut milk and natural yoghurt. Stir well to combine all the Ingredients.
5. Cover and cook on low heat for 4 hours, allowing the chicken to cook through and absorb the flavours.
6. Taste and adjust seasoning if necessary.
7. Garnish with fresh chopped coriander before serving. Serve the Chicken Korma hot with cooked basmati rice.

Crockpot Vegetarian Chilli

Serves: 4 Prep time: 15 minutes / Cook time: 6 hours

Ingredients:

- 2 cans (400g each) of mixed beans, drained and rinsed
- 1 can (400g) of chopped tomatoes
- 1 onion, chopped
- 2 cloves garlic, minced
- 2 carrots, peeled and diced
- 1 red pepper, diced
- 1 green pepper, diced
- 2 tbsp tomato paste
- 1 tsp ground cumin
- 1 tsp chilli powder
- 1/2 tsp paprika
- Salt and black pepper, to taste
- Fresh oregano, chopped (for garnish)
- Cooked rice, for serving

Preparation instructions:

1. In the crockpot, combine mixed beans, chopped tomatoes, chopped onion, minced garlic, diced carrots, diced red pepper, and diced green pepper.
2. Add tomato paste, ground cumin, chilli powder, paprika, salt, and black pepper. Stir well to combine all the Ingredients.
3. Cover and cook on low heat for 6 hours, allowing the flavours to meld together and the vegetables to soften.
4. Taste and adjust seasoning if necessary.
5. Garnish with fresh chopped oregano before serving. Serve the Vegetarian Chilli hot with cooked rice.

Slow Cooker Sausage and Bean Casserole

Serves: 4 Prep time: 15 minutes / Cook time: 6 hours

Ingredients:

- 400g sausages, sliced
- 1 onion, chopped

- 2 cloves garlic, minced
- 2 carrots, peeled and diced
- 2 celery sticks, diced
- 2 cans (400g each) of mixed beans, drained and rinsed
- 500ml vegetable stock
- 400g canned chopped tomatoes
- 1 tsp dried thyme
- 1 tsp dried rosemary
- Salt and black pepper, to taste
- Fresh parsley, chopped (for garnish)

Preparation instructions:

1. In a pan, brown the sausage slices over medium heat until cooked through. Transfer the sausages to the crockpot.
2. In the same pan, add chopped onions and minced garlic. Cook until softened. Transfer the onions and garlic to the crockpot.
3. Add diced carrots, diced celery, mixed beans, vegetable stock, chopped tomatoes, dried thyme, dried rosemary, salt, and black pepper to the crockpot. Stir well to combine all the Ingredients.
4. Cover and cook on low heat for 6 hours, allowing the flavours to meld together and the vegetables to become tender.
5. Taste and adjust seasoning if necessary.
6. Garnish with fresh chopped parsley before serving. Serve the Sausage and Bean Casserole hot.

Crockpot Tomato Basil Soup

Serves: 4 Prep time: 15 minutes / Cook time: 4 hours

Ingredients:

- 1 kg tomatoes, chopped
- 1 onion, chopped
- 2 cloves garlic, minced
- 500ml vegetable stock
- 2 tbsp tomato paste
- 1 tsp dried basil
- Salt and black pepper, to taste
- 60ml double cream
- Fresh basil leaves, for garnish
- Croutons, for serving

Preparation instructions:

1. In the crockpot, combine chopped tomatoes, chopped onions, minced garlic, vegetable stock, tomato paste, dried basil, salt, and black pepper. Stir well to combine all the Ingredients.
2. Cover and cook on low heat for 4 hours, allowing the tomatoes to soften and the flavours to meld together.
3. Use an immersion blender to blend the soup until smooth.
4. Stir in the double cream and adjust seasoning if necessary.
5. Garnish with fresh basil leaves before serving. Serve the Tomato Basil Soup hot with croutons.

Slow Cooker Chicken and Mushroom Pie

Serves: 4 Prep time: 20 minutes / Cook time: 6 hours

Ingredients:

- 500g chicken breasts, diced

- 250g mushrooms, sliced
- 1 onion, chopped
- 2 cloves garlic, minced
- 250ml chicken stock
- 250ml double cream
- 2 tbsp plain flour
- 2 tbsp butter
- Salt and black pepper, to taste
- Fresh parsley, chopped (for garnish)
- Puff pastry sheets, baked (for topping)

Preparation instructions:

1. In a pan, melt butter over medium heat. Add chopped onions and minced garlic. Cook until softened.
2. Add sliced mushrooms and diced chicken. Cook until the chicken is browned on all sides. Sprinkle plain flour over the mixture and stir well.
3. Transfer the mixture to the crockpot. Pour in chicken stock and double cream. Stir well to combine all the Ingredients.
4. Cover and cook on low heat for 6 hours, allowing the chicken to cook through and the flavours to meld together.
5. Taste and adjust seasoning if necessary.
6. Garnish with fresh chopped parsley before serving. Serve the Chicken and Mushroom Pie hot, topped with baked puff pastry sheets.

Crockpot Minestrone Soup

Serves: 4 Prep time: 15 minutes / Cook time: 4 hours

Ingredients:

- 1 tbsp olive oil
- 1 onion, chopped
- 2 cloves garlic, minced
- 2 carrots, peeled and diced
- 2 celery sticks, diced
- 400g canned chopped tomatoes
- 1 can (400g) cannellini beans, drained and rinsed
- 1.5 litres vegetable stock
- 100g small pasta (such as ditalini or macaroni)
- 1 tsp dried basil
- 1 tsp dried oregano
- Salt and black pepper, to taste
- 50g grated Parmesan cheese (for serving)
- Fresh basil leaves, chopped (for garnish)

Preparation instructions:

1. Heat olive oil in a pan over medium heat. Add chopped onions and minced garlic. Cook until softened.
2. Transfer the onions and garlic to the crockpot. Add diced carrots, diced celery, chopped tomatoes, cannellini beans, vegetable stock, small pasta, dried basil, dried oregano, salt, and black pepper. Stir well to combine all the Ingredients.
3. Cover and cook on low heat for 4 hours, allowing the flavours to meld together and the vegetables to become tender.
4. Taste and adjust seasoning if necessary.
5. Serve the Minestrone Soup hot, garnished with grated Parmesan cheese and fresh chopped basil.

Slow Cooker Lamb Tagine

Serves: 4 Prep time: 20 minutes / Cook time: 6 hours

Ingredients:

- 500g lamb stew meat, diced
- 2 onions, finely chopped
- 2 cloves garlic, minced
- 2 carrots, peeled and diced
- 400g canned chickpeas, drained and rinsed
- 400g canned chopped tomatoes
- 500ml vegetable stock
- 1 tsp ground cumin
- 1 tsp ground coriander
- 1/2 tsp ground cinnamon
- Salt and black pepper, to taste
- Fresh oregano leaves, chopped (for garnish)
- Cooked couscous (for serving)

Preparation instructions:

1. In a pan, brown the lamb stew meat over medium heat until browned on all sides. Transfer the meat to the crockpot.
2. In the same pan, add finely chopped onions and minced garlic. Cook until softened.
3. Add diced carrots, drained chickpeas, chopped tomatoes, vegetable stock, ground cumin, ground coriander, ground cinnamon, salt, and black pepper to the crockpot. Stir well to combine all the Ingredients.
4. Cover and cook on low heat for 6 hours, allowing the lamb to become tender and the flavours to meld together.
5. Taste and adjust seasoning if necessary.
6. Serve the Lamb Tagine hot, garnished with fresh chopped oregano, over cooked couscous.

Crockpot Sweet Potato and Chickpea Curry

Serves: 4 Prep time: 15 minutes / Cook time: 4 hours

Ingredients:

- 2 sweet potatoes, peeled and diced
- 400g canned chickpeas, drained and rinsed
- 1 onion, finely chopped
- 2 cloves garlic, minced
- 400ml coconut milk
- 250ml vegetable stock
- 2 tbsp curry paste
- 1 tsp ground turmeric
- 1 tsp ground cumin
- Salt and black pepper, to taste
- Fresh coriander leaves, chopped (for garnish)
- Cooked basmati rice (for serving)

Preparation instructions:

1. In the crockpot, combine diced sweet potatoes, drained chickpeas, finely chopped onions, minced garlic, coconut milk, vegetable stock, curry paste, ground turmeric, ground cumin, salt, and black pepper. Stir well to combine all the Ingredients.
2. Cover and cook on low heat for 4 hours, allowing the sweet potatoes to become tender and the flavours to meld

together.

3. Taste and adjust seasoning if necessary.
4. Serve the Sweet Potato and Chickpea Curry hot, garnished with fresh chopped coriander, over cooked basmati rice.

Slow Cooker Chicken Noodle Soup

Serves: 4 Prep time: 15 minutes / Cook time: 6 hours

Ingredients:

- 500g boneless, skinless chicken breasts, diced
- 1 onion, finely chopped
- 2 carrots, peeled and sliced
- 2 celery sticks, sliced
  1.5 litres chicken stock
- 200g dried egg noodles
- 1 tsp dried thyme
- Salt and black pepper, to taste
- Fresh parsley, chopped (for garnish)

Preparation instructions:

1. In the crockpot, combine diced chicken breasts, finely chopped onion, sliced carrots, sliced celery, chicken stock, dried thyme, salt, and black pepper. Stir well to combine all the Ingredients.
2. Cover and cook on low heat for 6 hours, allowing the flavours to meld together and the chicken to become tender.
3. In the last 30 minutes of cooking, add dried egg noodles to the crockpot. Stir well and let them cook until tender.
4. Taste and adjust seasoning if necessary.
5. Serve the Chicken Noodle Soup hot, garnished with fresh chopped parsley.

Crockpot Ratatouille

Serves: 4 Prep time: 20 minutes / Cook time: 4 hours

Ingredients:

- 2 courgettes (courgettes), diced
- 1 aubergine (aubergine), diced
- 2 red peppers, diced
- 1 onion, finely chopped
- 2 cloves garlic, minced
- 500g tomatoes, diced
- 2 tbsp tomato paste
- 1 tsp dried basil
- 1 tsp dried oregano
- Salt and black pepper, to taste
- 2 tbsp olive oil
- Fresh basil leaves, torn (for garnish)

Preparation instructions:

1. In a large pan, heat olive oil over medium heat. Add finely chopped onion and minced garlic. Cook until softened.
2. Transfer the onions and garlic to the crockpot. Add diced courgettes, diced aubergine, diced red peppers, diced tomatoes, tomato paste, dried basil, dried oregano, salt, and black pepper. Stir well to combine all the Ingredients.
3. Cover and cook on low heat for 4 hours, allowing the vegetables to become tender and the flavours to meld

together.

4. Taste and adjust seasoning if necessary.
5. Serve the Ratatouille hot, garnished with torn fresh basil leaves.

Slow Cooker Pork and Cider Stew

Serves: 4 Prep time: 15 minutes / Cook time: 6 hours

Ingredients:

- 500g pork shoulder, diced
- 2 onions, finely chopped
- 2 cloves garlic, minced
- 2 carrots, peeled and sliced
- 2 parsnips, peeled and sliced
- 500ml dry cider
- 250ml chicken stock
- 2 tbsp plain flour
- 1 tsp dried thyme
- Salt and black pepper, to taste
- Fresh parsley, chopped (for garnish)

Preparation instructions:

1. In a bowl, toss diced pork shoulder with plain flour until coated.
2. In the crockpot, combine floured pork, finely chopped onions, minced garlic, sliced carrots, sliced parsnips, dry cider, chicken stock, dried thyme, salt, and black pepper. Stir well to combine all the Ingredients.
3. Cover and cook on low heat for 6 hours, allowing the pork to become tender and the flavours to meld together.
4. Taste and adjust seasoning if necessary.
5. Serve the Pork and Cider Stew hot, garnished with fresh chopped parsley.

Crockpot Creamy Tomato Pasta

Serves: 4 Prep time: 10 minutes / Cook time: 4 hours

Ingredients:

- 400g penne pasta
- 500g cherry tomatoes, halved
- 1 onion, finely chopped
- 2 cloves garlic, minced
- 500ml passata (strained tomatoes)
- 250ml double cream
- 1 tsp dried basil
- 1 tsp dried oregano
- Salt and black pepper, to taste
- Fresh basil leaves, torn (for garnish)
- Grated Parmesan cheese (for serving)

Preparation instructions:

1. In the crockpot, combine penne pasta, halved cherry tomatoes, finely chopped onion, minced garlic, passata, dried basil, dried oregano, salt, and black pepper. Stir well to mix all the Ingredients.
2. Cover and cook on low heat for 4 hours, allowing the pasta to cook through and absorb the flavours.
3. In the last 30 minutes of cooking, pour in the double cream and stir well to incorporate.

4. Taste and adjust seasoning if necessary.
5. Serve the Creamy Tomato Pasta hot, garnished with torn fresh basil leaves and grated Parmesan cheese.

Slow Cooker Vegetable Curry

Serves: 4 Prep time: 15 minutes / Cook time: 4 hours

Ingredients:

- 1 onion, finely chopped
- 2 cloves garlic, minced
- 2 carrots, peeled and sliced
- 2 potatoes, peeled and diced
- 1 red pepper, diced
- 1 yellow pepper, diced
- 400g canned chickpeas, drained and rinsed
- 500ml vegetable stock
- 400ml coconut milk
- 2 tbsp curry powder
- Salt and black pepper, to taste
- Fresh coriander leaves, chopped (for garnish)
- Cooked basmati rice (for serving)

Preparation instructions:

1. In the crockpot, combine finely chopped onion, minced garlic, sliced carrots, diced potatoes, diced red pepper, diced yellow pepper, chickpeas, vegetable stock, coconut milk, curry powder, salt, and black pepper. Stir well to mix all the Ingredients.
2. Cover and cook on low heat for 4 hours, allowing the vegetables to become tender and the flavours to meld together.
3. Taste and adjust seasoning if necessary.
4. Serve the Vegetable Curry hot, garnished with chopped fresh coriander leaves. Serve over cooked basmati rice.

Crockpot Chicken and Rice Casserole

Serves: 4 Prep time: 15 minutes / Cook time: 4 hours

Ingredients:

- 500g boneless, skinless chicken thighs, diced
- 1 onion, finely chopped
- 2 cloves garlic, minced
- 200g button mushrooms, sliced
- 250g long-grain white rice
- 500ml chicken stock
- 250ml double cream
- 1 tsp dried thyme
- Salt and black pepper, to taste
- Fresh parsley, chopped (for garnish)

Preparation instructions:

1. In the crockpot, combine diced chicken thighs, finely chopped onion, minced garlic, sliced button mushrooms, long-grain white rice, chicken stock, double cream, dried thyme, salt, and black pepper. Stir well to mix all the Ingredients.
2. Cover and cook on low heat for 4 hours, allowing the chicken to become tender, and the rice to absorb the flavours.

3. Taste and adjust seasoning if necessary.
4. Serve the Chicken and Rice Casserole hot, garnished with chopped fresh parsley.

Slow Cooker Butternut Squash Soup

Serves: 4 Prep time: 15 minutes / Cook time: 4 hours

Ingredients:

- 800g butternut squash, peeled, seeded, and diced
- 1 onion, chopped
- 2 cloves garlic, minced
- 1 carrot, peeled and sliced
- 1 potato, peeled and diced
- 1 litre vegetable stock
- 250ml double cream
- 1/2 tsp ground nutmeg
- Salt and black pepper, to taste
- Fresh chives, chopped (for garnish)

Preparation instructions:

1. In the crockpot, combine diced butternut squash, chopped onion, minced garlic, sliced carrot, diced potato, vegetable stock, ground nutmeg, salt, and black pepper. Stir well to mix all the Ingredients.
2. Cover and cook on low heat for 4 hours, allowing the vegetables to become tender and the flavours to meld together.
3. Use an immersion blender to blend the soup until smooth.
4. Stir in the double cream, mixing well.
5. Taste and adjust seasoning if necessary.
6. Serve the Butternut Squash Soup hot, garnished with chopped fresh chives.

Crockpot Beef and Broccoli

Serves: 4 Prep time: 15 minutes / Cook time: 4 hours

Ingredients:

- 500g beef sirloin, thinly sliced
- 1 onion, thinly sliced
- 2 cloves garlic, minced
- 250ml beef broth
- 80 ml soy sauce
- 60ml oyster sauce
- 2 tbsp brown sugar
- 1 tbsp cornstarch
- 250g broccoli florets
- Sesame seeds (for garnish)
- Spring onions, sliced (for garnish)
- Cooked jasmine rice (for serving)

Preparation instructions:

1. In the crockpot, combine thinly sliced beef sirloin, thinly sliced onion, minced garlic, beef broth, soy sauce, oyster sauce, brown sugar, and cornstarch. Stir well to coat the beef evenly.
2. Cover and cook on low heat for 4 hours, allowing the beef to become tender and absorb the flavours.
3. In the last hour of cooking, add broccoli florets to the crock pot and stir well.

4. Taste and adjust seasoning if necessary.
5. Serve the Beef and Broccoli hot over cooked jasmine rice, garnished with sesame seeds and sliced spring onions.

Slow Cooker Cauliflower Cheese

Serves: 4 Prep time: 15 minutes / Cook time: 3 hours

Ingredients:
- 1 large cauliflower, cut into florets
- 50g unsalted butter
- 50g plain flour
- 500ml whole milk
- 200g cheddar cheese, grated
- 1/2 tsp mustard powder
- Salt and black pepper, to taste
- Fresh parsley, chopped (for garnish)

Preparation instructions:
1. In the crockpot, steam cauliflower florets until tender (about 1 hour on high or 2 hours on low). Drain any excess liquid.
2. In a saucepan, melt unsalted butter over medium heat. Stir in plain flour and cook for 1-2 minutes until golden brown.
3. Gradually whisk in whole milk to create a smooth sauce. Cook, stirring constantly, until the sauce thickens.
4. Remove the saucepan from heat and stir in grated cheddar cheese and mustard powder until the cheese is melted and the sauce is smooth.
5. Season the cheese sauce with salt and black pepper.
6. Pour the cheese sauce over the steamed cauliflower in the crockpot. Stir gently to coat the cauliflower evenly.
7. Cover and cook on low heat for an additional 2 hours, allowing the flavours to meld together.
8. Taste and adjust seasoning if necessary.
9. Serve the Cauliflower Cheese hot, garnished with chopped fresh parsley.

Crockpot Mushroom and Barley Soup

Serves: 4 Prep time: 15 minutes / Cook time: 6 hours

Ingredients:
- 200g pearl barley
- 400g button mushrooms, sliced
- 1 onion, finely chopped
- 2 cloves garlic, minced
- 1 carrot, peeled and diced
- 1 celery stalk, diced
- 1 litre vegetable stock
- 250ml water
- 1 bay leaf
- Salt and black pepper, to taste
- Fresh parsley, chopped (for garnish)

Preparation instructions:
1. Rinse the pearl barley under cold water and drain.
2. In the crockpot, combine pearl barley, sliced mushrooms, finely chopped onion, minced garlic, diced carrot, diced celery, vegetable stock, water, bay leaf, salt, and black pepper. Stir well to mix all the Ingredients.

3. Cover and cook on low heat for 6 hours, allowing the barley to become tender and the flavours to meld together.
4. Taste and adjust seasoning if necessary.
5. Remove the bay leaf before serving.
6. Serve the Mushroom and Barley Soup hot, garnished with chopped fresh parsley.

Slow Cooker Chicken and Spinach Curry

Serves: 4 Prep time: 15 minutes / Cook time: 4 hours

Ingredients:
- 500g boneless, skinless chicken thighs, cut into chunks
- 1 onion, finely chopped
- 2 cloves garlic, minced
- 2 tbsp curry powder
- 1 tsp ground turmeric
- 1 tsp ground cumin
- 400ml coconut milk
- 200ml chicken stock
- 200g fresh spinach leaves
- Salt and black pepper, to taste
- Fresh coriander, chopped (for garnish)
- Cooked basmati rice (for serving)

Preparation instructions:
1. In the crockpot, combine chicken chunks, finely chopped onion, minced garlic, curry powder, ground turmeric, ground cumin, coconut milk, and chicken stock. Stir well to coat the chicken evenly with the spices.
2. Cover and cook on low heat for 4 hours, allowing the chicken to become tender and absorb the flavours.
3. In the last 30 minutes of cooking, add fresh spinach leaves to the crock pot and stir well. Cover and continue cooking until the spinach wilts and the curry thickens.
4. Taste and adjust seasoning if necessary.
5. Serve the Chicken and Spinach Curry hot over cooked basmati rice, garnished with chopped fresh coriander.

Crockpot Vegan Chili

Serves: 4 Prep time: 15 minutes / Cook time: 6 hours

Ingredients:
- 2 cans (800g) mixed beans, drained and rinsed
- 1 can (400g) chopped tomatoes
- 1 onion, finely chopped
- 2 cloves garlic, minced
- 1 red pepper, diced
- 1 green pepper, diced
- 1 tbsp chilli powder
- 1 tsp ground cumin
- 1/2 tsp paprika
- 500ml vegetable stock
- Salt and black pepper, to taste
- Fresh oregano, chopped (for garnish)
- Vegan sour cream (for serving)

Preparation instructions:
1. In the crockpot, combine mixed beans, chopped tomatoes, finely chopped onion, minced garlic, diced red pepper,

diced green pepper, chilli powder, ground cumin, paprika, vegetable stock, salt, and black pepper. Stir well to mix all the Ingredients.

2. Cover and cook on low heat for 6 hours, allowing the flavours to meld together.

3. Taste and adjust seasoning if necessary.

4. Serve the Vegan Chili hot, garnished with chopped fresh oregano and a dollop of vegan sour cream.

Slow Cooker Beef and Vegetable Stew

Serves: 4 Prep time: 15 minutes / Cook time: 6 hours

Ingredients:

- 500g beef stewing meat, cubed
- 2 carrots, peeled and diced
- 2 potatoes, peeled and diced
- 1 onion, finely chopped
- 2 cloves garlic, minced
- 500ml beef stock
- 250ml water
- 2 tbsp tomato paste
- 1 tsp Worcestershire sauce
- 1 tsp dried thyme
- Salt and black pepper, to taste
- Fresh parsley, chopped (for garnish)

Preparation instructions:

1. In the crockpot, combine beef stewing meat, diced carrots, diced potatoes, finely chopped onion, minced garlic, beef stock, water, tomato paste, Worcestershire sauce, dried thyme, salt, and black pepper. Stir well to mix all the Ingredients.

2. Cover and cook on low heat for 6 hours, allowing the beef to become tender and the flavours to meld together.

3. Taste and adjust seasoning if necessary.

4. Serve the Beef and Vegetable Stew hot, garnished with chopped fresh parsley.

Crockpot Pumpkin Soup

Serves: 4 Prep time: 15 minutes / Cook time: 4 hours

Ingredients:

- 800g pumpkin, peeled and diced
- 1 onion, finely chopped
- 2 cloves garlic, minced
- 500ml vegetable stock
- 250ml coconut milk
- 1 tsp ground cumin
- 1/2 tsp ground coriander
- 1/4 tsp ground nutmeg
- Salt and black pepper, to taste
- Fresh chives, chopped (for garnish)
- Pumpkin seeds (for garnish)

Preparation instructions:

1. In the crockpot, combine diced pumpkin, finely chopped onion, minced garlic, vegetable stock, coconut milk, ground cumin, ground coriander, ground nutmeg, salt, and black pepper. Stir well to mix all the Ingredients.

2. Cover and cook on low heat for 4 hours, allowing the pumpkin to become tender and the flavours to meld together.

3. Use an immersion blender to blend the soup until smooth and creamy.

4. Taste and adjust seasoning if necessary.

5. Serve the Pumpkin Soup hot, garnished with chopped fresh chives and pumpkin seeds.

Slow Cooker Chicken and Sweetcorn Soup

Serves: 4 Prep time: 15 minutes / Cook time: 4 hours

Ingredients:

- 500g boneless, skinless chicken thighs, shredded
- 2 cans (400g each) creamed corn
- 1 can (400g) sweetcorn kernels, drained
- 1 onion, finely chopped
- 2 cloves garlic, minced
- 1 litre chicken stock
- 250ml water
- 2 tbsp soy sauce
- 1 tsp ground ginger
- 2 eggs, beaten
- Salt and white pepper, to taste
- Spring onions, chopped (for garnish)

Preparation instructions:

1. In the crockpot, combine shredded chicken thighs, creamed corn, sweetcorn kernels, finely chopped onion, minced garlic, chicken stock, water, soy sauce, and ground ginger. Stir well to mix all the Ingredients.

2. Cover and cook on low heat for 4 hours, allowing the flavours to meld together.

3. Slowly pour the beaten eggs into the soup while stirring gently to create ribbons of cooked egg.

4. Taste and adjust seasoning with salt and white pepper.

5. Serve the Chicken and Sweetcorn Soup hot, garnished with chopped spring onions.

Crockpot Red Lentil Curry

Serves: 4 Prep time: 15 minutes / Cook time: 6 hours

Ingredients:

- 200g red lentils, rinsed and drained
- 1 onion, finely chopped
- 2 cloves garlic, minced
- 1 can (400g) chopped tomatoes
- 400ml coconut milk
- 500ml vegetable stock
- 1 tbsp curry powder
- 1 tsp ground cumin
- 1 tsp ground coriander
- 1/2 tsp turmeric powder
- 1/4 tsp cayenne pepper (optional, for heat)
- Salt and black pepper, to taste
- Fresh coriander leaves, chopped (for garnish)

Preparation instructions:

1. In the crockpot, combine red lentils, finely chopped onion,

minced garlic, chopped tomatoes, coconut milk, vegetable stock, curry powder, ground cumin, ground coriander, turmeric powder, cayenne pepper (if using), salt, and black pepper. Stir well to mix all the Ingredients.

2. Cover and cook on low heat for 6 hours, allowing the lentils to become tender and the flavours to meld together.

3. Taste and adjust seasoning if necessary.

4. Serve the Red Lentil Curry hot, garnished with chopped fresh coriander.

Slow Cooker Aubergine Parmesan

Serves: 4 Prep time: 20 minutes / Cook time: 4 hours

Ingredients:
- 2 large aubergines, sliced into 1 cm thick rounds
- 500ml marinara sauce
- 200g mozzarella cheese, grated
- 100g Parmesan cheese, grated
- 1 tsp dried oregano
- 1 tsp dried basil
- Salt and black pepper, to taste
- Fresh basil leaves, chopped (for garnish)

Preparation instructions:
1. In the crockpot, spread a layer of marinara sauce at the bottom.
2. Arrange a layer of aubergine slices on top of the sauce.
3. Sprinkle with grated mozzarella and Parmesan cheese, and add a pinch of dried oregano and dried basil. Season with salt and black pepper.
4. Repeat the layers until all Ingredients are used, finishing with a layer of cheese and herbs on top.
5. Cover and cook on low heat for 4 hours, allowing the aubergine to become tender and the flavours to meld together.
6. Serve the aubergine Parmesan hot, garnished with chopped fresh basil.

Crockpot Corn Chowder

Serves: 4 Prep time: 15 minutes / Cook time: 6 hours

Ingredients:
- 500g potatoes, peeled and diced
- 500g frozen corn kernels
- 1 onion, finely chopped
- 2 cloves garlic, minced
- 500ml vegetable stock
- 250ml whole milk
- 250ml double cream
- 4 slices bacon, cooked and crumbled
- Salt and black pepper, to taste
- Fresh chives, chopped (for garnish)

Preparation instructions:
1. In the crockpot, combine diced potatoes, frozen corn kernels, finely chopped onion, minced garlic, vegetable stock, whole milk, and double cream. Stir well to mix all the Ingredients.
2. Cover and cook on low heat for 6 hours, allowing the

potatoes to become tender and the flavours to meld together.

3. Just before serving, stir in the crumbled cooked bacon. Taste and adjust seasoning if necessary.

4. Serve the Corn Chowder hot, garnished with chopped fresh chives.

Slow Cooker Chickpea and Spinach Stew

Serves: 4 Prep time: 15 minutes / Cook time: 4 hours

Ingredients:
- 400g canned chickpeas, drained and rinsed
- 200g fresh spinach leaves, roughly chopped
- 1 onion, finely chopped
- 2 cloves garlic, minced
- 400g canned chopped tomatoes
- 500ml vegetable stock
- 1 tsp ground cumin
- 1 tsp ground coriander
- 1/2 tsp smoked paprika
- Salt and black pepper, to taste
- Fresh oregano leaves, chopped (for garnish)

Preparation instructions:
1. In the crockpot, combine chickpeas, chopped fresh spinach, finely chopped onion, minced garlic, canned chopped tomatoes, vegetable stock, ground cumin, ground coriander, smoked paprika, salt, and black pepper. Stir well to mix all the Ingredients.
2. Cover and cook on low heat for 4 hours, allowing the flavours to meld together and the stew to thicken.
3. Taste and adjust seasoning if necessary.
4. Serve the Chickpea and Spinach Stew hot, garnished with chopped fresh oregano.

Crockpot Creamy Potato Soup

Serves: 4 Prep time: 15 minutes / Cook time: 6 hours

Ingredients:
- 500g potatoes, peeled and diced
- 1 onion, finely chopped
- 2 cloves garlic, minced
- 750ml vegetable stock
- 250ml whole milk
- 250ml double cream
- 50g butter
- Salt and black pepper, to taste
- Fresh chives, chopped (for garnish)

Preparation instructions:
1. In the crockpot, combine diced potatoes, finely chopped onion, minced garlic, vegetable stock, whole milk, double cream, and butter. Stir well to mix all the Ingredients.
2. Cover and cook on low heat for 6 hours, allowing the potatoes to become tender and the soup to thicken.
3. Use an immersion blender to blend the soup until smooth and creamy.
4. Season with salt and black pepper. Taste and adjust seasoning if necessary.

5. Serve the Creamy Potato Soup hot, garnished with chopped fresh chives.

Slow Cooker Moroccan Vegetable Tagine

Serves: 4 Prep time: 20 minutes / Cook time: 4 hours

Ingredients:
- 2 carrots, peeled and sliced
- 2 courgettes, sliced
- 1 onion, finely chopped
- 2 cloves garlic, minced
- 1 can (400g) chickpeas, drained and rinsed
- 400g canned chopped tomatoes
- 250ml vegetable stock
- 1 tsp ground cumin
- 1 tsp ground coriander
- 1/2 tsp ground cinnamon
- 1/4 tsp ground turmeric
- Salt and black pepper, to taste
- Fresh parsley leaves, chopped (for garnish)

Preparation instructions:
1. In the crockpot, combine sliced carrots, sliced courgettes, finely chopped onion, minced garlic, drained chickpeas, canned chopped tomatoes, vegetable stock, ground cumin, ground coriander, ground cinnamon, ground turmeric, salt, and black pepper. Stir well to mix all the Ingredients.
2. Cover and cook on low heat for 4 hours, allowing the vegetables to become tender and absorb the Moroccan spices.
3. Taste and adjust seasoning if necessary.
4. Serve the Moroccan Vegetable Tagine hot, garnished with chopped fresh parsley.

Crockpot Chicken and Chorizo Stew

Serves: 4 Prep time: 15 minutes / Cook time: 4 hours

Ingredients:
- 400g boneless, skinless chicken thighs, diced
- 150g chorizo sausage, sliced
- 1 onion, finely chopped
- 2 cloves garlic, minced
- 2 carrots, peeled and sliced
- 1 can (400g) chopped tomatoes
- 250ml chicken stock
- 1 tsp smoked paprika
- 1/2 tsp dried thyme
- Salt and black pepper, to taste
- Fresh parsley leaves, chopped (for garnish)

Preparation instructions:
1. In the crockpot, combine diced chicken thighs, sliced chorizo sausage, finely chopped onion, minced garlic, sliced carrots, chopped tomatoes, chicken stock, smoked paprika, dried thyme, salt, and black pepper. Stir well to mix all the Ingredients.
2. Cover and cook on low heat for 4 hours, allowing the flavours to meld together and the stew to thicken.
3. Taste and adjust seasoning if necessary.

4. Serve the Chicken and Chorizo Stew hot, garnished with chopped fresh parsley.

Slow Cooker Leek and Potato Soup

Serves: 4 Prep time: 15 minutes / Cook time: 4 hours

Ingredients:
- 400g leeks, sliced
- 400g potatoes, peeled and diced
- 1 onion, finely chopped
- 2 cloves garlic, minced
- 750ml vegetable stock
- 250ml whole milk
- 50g butter
- Salt and white pepper, to taste
- Fresh chives, chopped (for garnish)

Preparation instructions:
1. In the crockpot, combine sliced leeks, diced potatoes, finely chopped onion, minced garlic, vegetable stock, whole milk, and butter. Stir well to mix all the Ingredients.
2. Cover and cook on low heat for 4 hours, allowing the leeks and potatoes to become tender.
3. Use an immersion blender to blend the soup until smooth and creamy.
4. Season with salt and white pepper. Taste and adjust seasoning if necessary.
5. Serve the Leek and Potato Soup hot, garnished with chopped fresh chives.

Crockpot Spinach and Feta Stuffed Peppers

Serves: 4 Prep time: 15 minutes / Cook time: 4 hours

Ingredients:
- 4 large peppers, any colour
- 200g fresh spinach leaves, chopped
- 150g feta cheese, crumbled
- 1 onion, finely chopped
- 2 cloves garlic, minced
- 1 can (400g) chopped tomatoes
- 1 tsp dried oregano
- 1/2 tsp dried basil
- Salt and black pepper, to taste
- Grated Parmesan cheese (for topping)
- Fresh basil leaves, chopped (for garnish)

Preparation instructions:
1. Cut the tops off the peppers and remove the seeds and membranes.
2. In a bowl, combine chopped fresh spinach, crumbled feta cheese, finely chopped onion, minced garlic, chopped tomatoes, dried oregano, dried basil, salt, and black pepper. Mix well.
3. Stuff each pepper with the spinach and feta mixture.
4. Place the stuffed peppers in the crockpot.
5. Cover and cook on low heat for 4 hours, allowing the peppers to become tender and the filling to meld together.
6. In the last 15 minutes of cooking, sprinkle grated Parmesan cheese on top of each pepper and cover the crock pot to

melt the cheese.

7.Serve the Spinach and Feta Stuffed Peppers hot, garnished with chopped fresh basil.

Slow Cooker Carrot and Coriander Soup

Serves: 4 Prep time: 15 minutes / Cook time: 4 hours

Ingredients:

* 500g carrots, peeled and chopped
* 1 onion, finely chopped
* 2 cloves garlic, minced
* 1 potato, peeled and diced
1.2 litres vegetable stock
* 1 tsp ground coriander
* Salt and black pepper, to taste
* Fresh coriander leaves, chopped (for garnish)
* Cream (optional, for serving)

Preparation instructions:

1.In the crockpot, combine chopped carrots, finely chopped onion, minced garlic, diced potato, vegetable stock, and ground coriander. Stir well to mix all the Ingredients.

2.Cover and cook on low heat for 4 hours, allowing the vegetables to become tender.

3.Use an immersion blender to blend the soup until smooth and creamy.

4.Season with salt and black pepper. Taste and adjust seasoning if necessary.

5.Serve the Carrot and Coriander Soup hot, garnished with chopped fresh coriander. Add a swirl of cream on top if desired.

Crockpot Lentil and Vegetable Curry

Serves: 4 Prep time: 15 minutes / Cook time: 6 hours

Ingredients:

* 250g dried lentils, rinsed and drained
* 1 onion, finely chopped
* 2 cloves garlic, minced
* 1 can (400g) chopped tomatoes
* 500ml vegetable stock
* 400g mixed vegetables (such as carrots, peas, and peppers), chopped
* 2 tbsp curry powder
* 1 tsp ground cumin
* Salt and black pepper, to taste
* Fresh oregano leaves, chopped (for garnish)
* Cooked rice (for serving)

Preparation instructions:

1.In the crockpot, combine rinsed lentils, finely chopped onion, minced garlic, chopped tomatoes, vegetable stock, mixed vegetables, curry powder, and ground cumin. Stir well to mix all the Ingredients.

2.Cover and cook on low heat for 6 hours, allowing the lentils and vegetables to cook through and absorb the flavours.

3.Season with salt and black pepper. Taste and adjust seasoning if necessary.

4.Serve the Lentil and Vegetable Curry hot, garnished with chopped fresh oregano. Serve over cooked rice.

Slow Cooker Mushroom and Brie Soup

Serves: 4 Prep time: 15 minutes / Cook time: 4 hours

Ingredients:

* 500g mushrooms, sliced
* 1 onion, finely chopped
* 2 cloves garlic, minced
* 1 potato, peeled and diced
1.2 litres vegetable stock
* 200g Brie cheese, rind removed and diced
* Salt and black pepper, to taste
* Fresh parsley leaves, chopped (for garnish)
* Crusty bread (for serving)

Preparation instructions:

1.In the crockpot, combine sliced mushrooms, finely chopped onion, minced garlic, diced potato, vegetable stock, and diced Brie cheese. Stir well to mix all the Ingredients.

2.Cover and cook on low heat for 4 hours, allowing the mushrooms and potatoes to become tender and the flavours to meld together.

3.Use an immersion blender to blend the soup until smooth and creamy.

4.Season with salt and black pepper. Taste and adjust seasoning if necessary.

5.Serve the Mushroom and Brie Soup hot, garnished with chopped fresh parsley. Serve with crusty bread on the side.

Crockpot Quinoa and Vegetable Stew

Serves: 4 Prep time: 15 minutes / Cook time: 6 hours

Ingredients:

* 200g quinoa, rinsed and drained
* 500g mixed vegetables (such as carrots, peppers, and courgette), chopped
* 1 onion, finely chopped
* 2 cloves garlic, minced
* 1 can (400g) diced tomatoes
1.2 litres vegetable stock
* 1 tsp ground cumin
* 1/2 tsp paprika
* Salt and black pepper, to taste
* Fresh parsley leaves, chopped (for garnish)

Preparation instructions:

1.In the crockpot, combine rinsed quinoa, mixed vegetables, finely chopped onion, minced garlic, diced tomatoes, vegetable stock, ground cumin, and paprika. Stir well to mix all the Ingredients.

2.Cover and cook on low heat for 6 hours, allowing the quinoa and vegetables to cook through and absorb the flavours.

3.Season with salt and black pepper. Taste and adjust seasoning if necessary.

4.Serve the Quinoa and Vegetable Stew hot, garnished with

chopped fresh parsley.

Slow Cooker Thai Green Curry

Serves: 4 Prep time: 15 minutes / Cook time: 4 hours

Ingredients:

- 400ml coconut milk
- 400g chicken breast, diced (or tofu for a vegetarian option)
- 1 onion, finely chopped
- 2 cloves garlic, minced
- 2 tbsp Thai green curry paste
- 1 red pepper, sliced
- 1 green pepper, sliced
- 200g bamboo shoots, drained
- 1 tbsp fish sauce (or soy sauce for a vegetarian option)
- 1 tbsp brown sugar
- Fresh basil leaves, torn (for garnish)
- Cooked jasmine rice (for serving)

Preparation instructions:

1. In the crockpot, combine coconut milk, diced chicken (or tofu), finely chopped onion, minced garlic, Thai green curry paste, sliced red and green peppers, and drained bamboo shoots. Stir well to mix all the Ingredients.
2. Cover and cook on low heat for 4 hours, allowing the curry to simmer and the flavours to meld together.
3. Stir in fish sauce and brown sugar. Taste and adjust seasoning if necessary.
4. Serve the Thai Green Curry hot, garnished with torn fresh basil leaves. Serve over cooked jasmine rice.

Crockpot Sweet Potato and Lentil Soup

Serves: 4 Prep time: 15 minutes / Cook time: 6 hours

Ingredients:

- 500g sweet potatoes, peeled and diced
- 200g red lentils, rinsed and drained
- 1 onion, finely chopped
- 2 cloves garlic, minced
- 1.2 litres vegetable stock
- 1 tsp ground turmeric
- 1/2 tsp ground cumin
- Salt and black pepper, to taste
- Fresh coriander leaves, chopped (for garnish)

Preparation instructions:

1. In the crockpot, combine diced sweet potatoes, rinsed red lentils, finely chopped onion, minced garlic, vegetable stock, ground turmeric, and ground cumin. Stir well to mix all the Ingredients.
2. Cover and cook on low heat for 6 hours, allowing the sweet potatoes and lentils to become tender and the flavours to meld together.
3. Use an immersion blender to blend the soup until smooth and creamy.
4. Season with salt and black pepper. Taste and adjust seasoning if necessary.

5. Serve the Sweet Potato and Lentil Soup hot, garnished with chopped fresh coriander.

Slow Cooker Asparagus Risotto

Serves: 4 Prep time: 15 minutes / Cook time: 2 hours

Ingredients:

- 300g Arborio rice
- 1 bunch asparagus, trimmed and cut into bite-sized pieces
- 1 onion, finely chopped
- 2 cloves garlic, minced
- 1 litre vegetable stock, heated
- 125ml dry white wine
- 50g Parmesan cheese, grated
- Salt and black pepper, to taste
- Fresh chives, chopped (for garnish)

Preparation instructions:

1. In the crockpot, combine Arborio rice, trimmed asparagus pieces, finely chopped onion, minced garlic, heated vegetable stock, and dry white wine. Stir well to mix all the Ingredients.
2. Cover and cook on low heat for 2 hours, allowing the rice to absorb the liquid and become creamy.
3. Stir in grated Parmesan cheese, and season with salt and black pepper. Taste and adjust seasoning if necessary.
4. Serve the Asparagus Risotto hot, garnished with chopped fresh chives.

Crockpot Vegan Goulash

Serves: 4 Prep time: 15 minutes / Cook time: 6 hours

Ingredients:

- 500g mixed peppers (red, green, and yellow), sliced
- 1 onion, finely chopped
- 2 cloves garlic, minced
- 400g canned chickpeas, rinsed and drained
- 400g canned diced tomatoes
- 2 tbsp tomato paste
- 1 tbsp smoked paprika
- 1 tsp ground caraway seeds
- Salt and black pepper, to taste
- Fresh parsley leaves, chopped (for garnish)
- Cooked pasta (for serving)

Preparation instructions:

1. In the crockpot, combine sliced mixed peppers, finely chopped onion, minced garlic, rinsed chickpeas, canned diced tomatoes, tomato paste, smoked paprika, and ground caraway seeds. Stir well to mix all the Ingredients.
2. Cover and cook on low heat for 6 hours, allowing the flavours to meld together.
3. Season with salt and black pepper. Taste and adjust seasoning if necessary.
4. Serve the Vegan Goulash hot, garnished with chopped fresh parsley. Serve over cooked pasta.

Chapter 4: Dinner Recipes

Slow Cooker Beef Wellington

Serves: 4 Prep time: 20 minutes / Cook time: 6 hours

Ingredients:
- 500g beef fillet
- Salt and black pepper, to taste
- 2 tbsp olive oil
- 1 onion, finely chopped
- 200g mushrooms, finely chopped
- 2 tbsp fresh parsley, chopped
- 4 slices Parma ham
- 500g puff pastry, rolled out
- 1 egg, beaten (for egg wash)

Preparation instructions:
1. Season the beef fillet with salt and black pepper. In a hot skillet, heat the olive oil and sear the beef fillet on all sides until browned. Remove from the skillet and let it cool.
2. In the same skillet, sauté the fincly chopped onion and mushrooms until soft and golden. Stir in the fresh parsley and cook for another minute. Remove from heat and let it cool.
3. Lay out the Parma ham slices on a sheet of cling film, slightly overlapping. Spread the mushroom mixture over the Parma ham.
4. Place the seared beef fillet in the centre of the mushroom mixture. Roll it up tightly using the cling film, shaping it into a log. Chill in the fridge for 20 minutes.
5. Preheat the crockpot to low heat.
6. Roll out the puff pastry and unwrap the beef-mushroom log from the cling film. Place it in the centre of the puff pastry and wrap it tightly, sealing the edges. Brush the pastry with beaten egg for a golden finish.
7. Carefully transfer the wrapped Beef Wellington into the crockpot. Cover and cook on low heat for 6 hours.
8. Once cooked, remove from the crockpot and let it rest for a few minutes before slicing. Serve hot with your favourite sides.

Crockpot Chicken Casserole

Serves: 4 Prep time: 15 minutes / Cook time: 4 hours

Ingredients:
- 4 boneless, skinless chicken breasts, diced
- Salt and black pepper, to taste
- 2 tbsp olive oil
- 1 onion, finely chopped
- 2 garlic cloves, minced
- 200g carrots, peeled and sliced
- 200g potatoes, peeled and diced
- 200g green beans, trimmed and halved
- 1 can (400g) diced tomatoes
- 250ml chicken stock
- 1 tbsp fresh thyme leaves
- 1 tbsp fresh parsley, chopped (for garnish)

Preparation instructions:
1. Season the diced chicken breasts with salt and black pepper. In a hot skillet, heat the olive oil and brown the chicken pieces on all sides. Transfer to the crockpot.
2. In the same skillet, sauté the finely chopped onion and minced garlic until translucent. Add the sliced carrots, diced potatoes, and halved green beans. Cook for a few minutes until slightly softened.
3. Transfer the sautéed vegetables to the crockpot. Pour in the diced tomatoes and chicken stock. Add fresh thyme leaves.
4. Cover and cook on low heat for 4 hours, allowing the flavours to meld together.
5. Season with additional salt and black pepper, if necessary. Garnish with chopped fresh parsley before serving. Serve hot over rice or with crusty bread.

Slow Cooker Lamb Shank Stew

Serves: 4 Prep time: 20 minutes / Cook time: 8 hours

Ingredients:
- 4 lamb shanks
- Salt and black pepper, to taste
- 2 tbsp olive oil
- 2 onions, finely chopped
- 3 garlic cloves, minced
- 200g carrots, peeled and sliced
- 200g celery, sliced
- 2 tbsp tomato paste
- 1 can (400g) diced tomatoes
- 500ml beef stock
- 2 sprigs fresh rosemary
- 2 sprigs fresh thyme
- 1 bay leaf
- Fresh parsley, chopped (for garnish)

Preparation instructions:
1. Season the lamb shanks with salt and black pepper. In a hot skillet, heat the olive oil and brown the lamb shanks on all sides. Transfer to the crockpot.
2. In the same skillet, sauté the finely chopped onions and minced garlic until translucent. Add the sliced carrots and celery, cooking for a few minutes until slightly softened.
3. Stir in the tomato paste and diced tomatoes. Pour in the beef stock. Add fresh rosemary, thyme, and a bay leaf for flavour.
4. Cover and cook on low heat for 8 hours, allowing the lamb to become tender and the flavours to meld together.
5. Remove the herb sprigs and bay leaf before serving. Garnish with chopped fresh parsley. Serve the lamb shank stew hot with mashed potatoes or crusty bread.

Crockpot Fisherman's Pie

Serves: 4 Prep time: 15 minutes / Cook time: 6 hours

Ingredients:

- 500g mixed white fish fillets, cut into chunks
- 300g potatoes, peeled and diced
- 200g carrots, peeled and sliced
- 200g peas
- 1 onion, finely chopped
- 2 cloves garlic, minced
- 250ml fish stock
- 250ml whole milk
- 2 tbsp butter
- 2 tbsp all-purpose flour
- Salt and black pepper, to taste
- Fresh parsley, chopped (for garnish)

Preparation instructions:

1. In a hot skillet, sauté the chopped onion and minced garlic until translucent. Transfer to the crockpot.
2. Layer the mixed white fish fillets, diced potatoes, sliced carrots, and peas on top of the onions and garlic.
3. In the same skillet, melt the butter over low heat. Stir in the flour to create a roux. Gradually whisk in the fish stock and whole milk, ensuring there are no lumps. Cook until the sauce thickens.
4. Pour the thickened sauce over the Ingredients in the crockpot. Season with salt and black pepper.
5. Cover and cook on low heat for 6 hours, allowing the flavours to meld together and the fish to become tender.
6. Garnish with chopped fresh parsley before serving. Serve the Fisherman's Pie hot, spooned onto plates.

Slow Cooker Vegetable Curry

Serves: 4 Prep time: 15 minutes / Cook time: 4 hours

Ingredients:

- 400g mixed vegetables (such as carrots, peas, potatoes, cauliflower), diced
- 1 onion, finely chopped
- 2 cloves garlic, minced
- 400ml coconut milk
- 250ml vegetable stock
- 2 tbsp curry powder
- 1 tbsp vegetable oil
- Salt and black pepper, to taste
- Fresh oregano, chopped (for garnish)

Preparation instructions:

1. In a hot skillet, heat the vegetable oil and sauté the chopped onion and minced garlic until translucent. Transfer to the crockpot.
2. Add the diced mixed vegetables to the crockpot.
3. In a separate bowl, mix the curry powder with coconut milk until well combined. Pour the mixture over the vegetables.
4. Pour in the vegetable stock. Season with salt and black pepper.
5. Cover and cook on low heat for 4 hours, allowing the vegetables to absorb the flavours and become tender.
6. Stir well before serving. Garnish with chopped fresh oregano. Serve the vegetable curry hot, accompanied by

rice or naan bread.

Crockpot Sausage and Bean Stew

Serves: 4 Prep time: 15 minutes / Cook time: 6 hours

Ingredients:

- 8 pork sausages, sliced
- 400g canned white beans, drained and rinsed
- 1 onion, finely chopped
- 2 cloves garlic, minced
- 400g canned diced tomatoes
- 250ml beef stock
- 1 tsp dried oregano
- 1 tsp paprika
- Salt and black pepper, to taste
- Fresh parsley, chopped (for garnish)

Preparation instructions:

1. In a hot skillet, brown the sliced pork sausages. Transfer to the crockpot.
2. Add the drained white beans, chopped onion, and minced garlic to the crockpot.
3. Pour in the canned diced tomatoes and beef stock. Sprinkle dried oregano and paprika over the Ingredients. Season with salt and black pepper.
4. Cover and cook on low heat for 6 hours, allowing the flavours to meld together and the sausages to become tender.
5. Stir well before serving. Garnish with chopped fresh parsley. Serve the sausage and bean stew hot, accompanied by crusty bread.

Slow Cooker Chicken Tikka Masala

Serves: 4 Prep time: 15 minutes / Cook time: 4 hours

Ingredients:

- 500g boneless, skinless chicken thighs, cut into bite-sized pieces
- 200g plain yoghurt
- 2 tbsp tikka masala paste
- 1 onion, finely chopped
- 2 cloves garlic, minced
- 1 tsp ground cumin
- 1 tsp ground coriander
- 1 tsp paprika
- 1/2 tsp turmeric powder
- 400g canned diced tomatoes
- 150ml double cream
- Salt and black pepper, to taste
- Fresh coriander, chopped (for garnish)
- Steamed rice or naan bread (for serving)

Preparation instructions:

1. In a bowl, mix the plain yoghurt with tikka masala paste. Add the chicken pieces, ensuring they are well-coated. Marinate for at least 30 minutes.
2. In the preheated crockpot, combine the marinated chicken, chopped onion, minced garlic, ground cumin, ground coriander, paprika, and turmeric powder.

3. Pour in the canned diced tomatoes. Stir well to combine all the Ingredients.
4. Cover and cook on low heat for 4 hours, allowing the flavours to meld together and the chicken to become tender.
5. Stir in the double cream and season with salt and black pepper. Cook for an additional 15-30 minutes until the sauce thickens.
6. Garnish with chopped fresh coriander. Serve the chicken tikka masala hot, accompanied by steamed rice or naan bread.

Crockpot Beef and Guinness Stew

Serves: 4 Prep time: 20 minutes / Cook time: 6 hours

Ingredients:

- 600g stewing beef, cut into bite-sized pieces
- 2 tbsp vegetable oil
- 1 onion, chopped
- 2 cloves garlic, minced
- 3 carrots, peeled and sliced
- 2 potatoes, peeled and diced
- 2 tbsp all-purpose flour
- 500ml Guinness stout
- 250ml beef stock
- 2 tbsp tomato paste
- 1 tsp dried thyme
- Salt and black pepper, to taste
- Fresh parsley, chopped (for garnish)
- Mashed potatoes (for serving)

Preparation instructions:

1. In a skillet, heat the vegetable oil over medium-high heat. Brown the stewing beef on all sides. Transfer to the crockpot.
2. In the same skillet, sauté the chopped onion and minced garlic until translucent. Add the sliced carrots and diced potatoes. Cook for a few minutes.
3. Sprinkle the vegetables with all-purpose flour. Stir well to coat the vegetables evenly.
4. Transfer the vegetable mixture to the crockpot with the beef.
5. Pour in the Guinness stout, beef stock, and add the tomato paste and dried thyme. Season with salt and black pepper. Stir well to combine all the Ingredients.
6. Cover and cook on low heat for 6 hours, allowing the flavours to meld together and the beef to become tender.
7. Stir well before serving. Garnish with chopped fresh parsley. Serve the beef and Guinness stew hot, accompanied by mashed potatoes.

Slow Cooker Pork Roast with Apples

Serves: 4 Prep time: 15 minutes / Cook time: 6 hours

Ingredients:

1.2kg pork shoulder roast
- 2 apples, peeled, cored, and sliced
- 1 onion, sliced
- 3 cloves garlic, minced
- 250ml apple cider
- 2 tbsp honey
- 1 tsp ground cinnamon
- Salt and black pepper, to taste
- Fresh thyme, for garnish
- Roasted vegetables (such as carrots and potatoes, for serving)

Preparation instructions:

1. Season the pork shoulder roast with salt and black pepper. Place it in the crockpot.
2. Arrange the sliced apples, sliced onion, and minced garlic around the pork roast.
3. In a bowl, mix the apple cider, honey, and ground cinnamon. Pour the mixture over the pork and apples.
4. Cover and cook on low heat for 6 hours, allowing the pork to become tender and infused with the flavours of the apples and spices.
5. Remove the pork roast from the crockpot and let it rest for a few minutes before slicing.
6. Serve the sliced pork roast and apples hot, garnished with fresh thyme. Accompany with roasted vegetables.

Crockpot Vegetarian Lasagna

Serves: 4 Prep time: 20 minutes / Cook time: 4 hours

Ingredients:

- 250g lasagna noodles
- 500g ricotta cheese
- 400g canned crushed tomatoes
- 200g fresh spinach, chopped
- 150g button mushrooms, sliced
- 1 onion, finely chopped
- 2 cloves garlic, minced
- 200g shredded mozzarella cheese
- 50g grated Parmesan cheese
- 1 tsp dried oregano
- Salt and black pepper, to taste
- Fresh basil leaves, for garnish

Preparation instructions:

1. Cook the lasagna noodles according to the package instructions. Drain and set aside.
2. In a bowl, combine the ricotta cheese with chopped fresh spinach, sliced mushrooms, finely chopped onion, minced garlic, and dried oregano. Season with salt and black pepper. Mix well.
3. In the preheated crockpot, layer the bottom with a portion of the crushed tomatoes.
4. Place a layer of cooked lasagna noodles over the sauce.
5. Spread a layer of the ricotta cheese and vegetable mixture over the noodles.
6. Repeat the layers until all the Ingredients are used, finishing with a layer of crushed tomatoes on top.
7. Sprinkle the shredded mozzarella cheese and grated Parmesan cheese over the lasagna.
8. Cover and cook on low heat for 4 hours, allowing the flavours to meld together and the lasagna to become heated through and bubbly.

9. Garnish with fresh basil leaves before serving. Serve the vegetarian lasagna hot.

Slow Cooker Mushroom Risotto

Serves: 4 Prep time: 15 minutes / Cook time: 2.5 hours

Ingredients:
- 300g Arborio rice
- 500g mixed mushrooms (such as button, cremini, and shiitake), sliced
- 1 onion, finely chopped
- 2 cloves garlic, minced
- 1.2 litres vegetable stock
- 125ml white wine
- 50g grated Parmesan cheese
- 60ml double cream
- 2 tbsp unsalted butter
- 2 tbsp olive oil
- Salt and black pepper, to taste
- Fresh parsley, chopped (for garnish)

Preparation instructions:
1. In a skillet, heat the olive oil over medium heat. Sauté the chopped onion until translucent, then add the minced garlic and sliced mushrooms. Cook until the mushrooms are browned and tender. Transfer to the crockpot.
2. Add the Arborio rice to the crock pot and stir to combine with the mushrooms and onions.
3. Pour in the white wine and stir until the liquid is absorbed by the rice.
4. Slowly add the vegetable stock, one ladle at a time, stirring frequently and allowing the liquid to be absorbed before adding more. Cook on low heat for 2.5 hours or until the rice is creamy and cooked to al dente texture.
5. Stir in the grated Parmesan cheese, double cream, and unsalted butter. Season with salt and black pepper. Cook for an additional 10 minutes.
6. Garnish with chopped fresh parsley before serving. Serve the mushroom risotto hot.

Crockpot Chicken and Bacon Pie

Serves: 4 Prep time: 20 minutes / Cook time: 4 hours

Ingredients:
- 4 boneless, skinless chicken breasts, cut into bite-sized pieces
- 200g bacon, chopped
- 1 onion, finely chopped
- 2 cloves garlic, minced
- 200g button mushrooms, sliced
- 300ml chicken stock
- 200ml double cream
- 2 tbsp all-purpose flour
- 2 tbsp olive oil
- Salt and black pepper, to taste
- Fresh thyme leaves, for garnish
- Shortcrust pastry sheets (for serving)

Preparation instructions:
1. In a skillet, heat the olive oil over medium-high heat. Brown the chicken pieces and chopped bacon. Transfer to the crockpot.
2. In the same skillet, sauté the finely chopped onion until translucent. Add the minced garlic and sliced mushrooms. Cook until the mushrooms are browned. Transfer to the crockpot.
3. Sprinkle the flour over the chicken, bacon, onions, and mushrooms. Stir well to coat the Ingredients evenly.
4. Pour in the chicken stock and double cream. Stir until the mixture thickens. Season with salt and black pepper. Cook on low heat for 4 hours, allowing the flavours to meld together and the chicken to become tender.
5. Stir well before serving. Garnish with fresh thyme leaves. Serve the chicken and bacon pie hot, accompanied by shortcrust pastry sheets.

Slow Cooker Beef Bourguignon

Serves: 4 Prep time: 15 minutes / Cook time: 8 hours

Ingredients:
- 600g beef stew meat, cubed
- 200g bacon, chopped
- 200g button mushrooms, sliced
- 2 onions, finely chopped
- 2 carrots, peeled and sliced
- 2 cloves garlic, minced
- 500ml red wine
- 500ml beef stock
- 3 tbsp tomato paste
- 2 tbsp all-purpose flour
- 2 tbsp olive oil
- 2 sprigs fresh thyme
- Salt and black pepper, to taste
- Fresh parsley, chopped (for garnish)

Preparation instructions:
1. In a skillet, heat the olive oil over medium-high heat. Brown the beef cubes on all sides. Transfer the beef to the crockpot.
2. In the same skillet, cook the chopped bacon until crispy. Add the sliced mushrooms, finely chopped onions, sliced carrots, and minced garlic. Cook until the vegetables are tender. Transfer the mixture to the crockpot.
3. Sprinkle the flour over the beef and vegetable mixture in the crockpot. Stir to coat the Ingredients evenly.
4. Pour in the red wine and beef stock. Add the tomato paste and fresh thyme sprigs. Season with salt and black pepper.
5. Cover and cook on low heat for 8 hours, allowing the flavours to meld together and the beef to become tender and flavorful.
6. Stir well before serving. Garnish with chopped fresh parsley. Serve the beef bourguignon hot, accompanied by crusty bread or mashed potatoes.

Crockpot Lentil Curry

Serves: 4 Prep time: 15 minutes / Cook time: 6 hours

Ingredients:
- 250g green lentils, rinsed and drained
- 400ml coconut milk
- 1 onion, finely chopped
- 2 cloves garlic, minced
- 2 tomatoes, diced
- 1 can (400g) chickpeas, drained and rinsed
- 2 tbsp curry powder
- 1 tsp ground turmeric
- 1 tsp ground cumin
- 500ml vegetable stock
- 2 tbsp olive oil
- Salt and black pepper, to taste
- Fresh coriander leaves, chopped (for garnish)

Preparation instructions:
1. In a skillet, heat the olive oil over medium heat. Sauté the finely chopped onion until translucent. Add the minced garlic and diced tomatoes. Cook until the tomatoes are softened.
2. Transfer the sautéed onion and tomato mixture to the crockpot. Add the rinsed green lentils, drained chickpeas, curry powder, ground turmeric, ground cumin, coconut milk, and vegetable stock. Stir to combine.
3. Cover and cook on low heat for 6 hours, allowing the lentils to become tender and the flavours to meld together.
4. Season with salt and black pepper. Stir well before serving. Garnish with chopped fresh coriander leaves. Serve the lentil curry hot, accompanied by rice or naan bread.

Slow Cooker Seafood Chowder

Serves: 4 Prep time: 20 minutes / Cook time: 4 hours

Ingredients:
- 300g white fish fillets, cut into bite-sized pieces
- 200g peeled and deveined prawns
- 200g scallops
- 1 onion, finely chopped
- 2 cloves garlic, minced
- 2 potatoes, peeled and diced
- 200ml fish stock
- 250ml whole milk
- 250ml double cream
- 2 tbsp butter
- 2 tbsp all-purpose flour
- 2 tbsp fresh parsley, chopped
- Salt and black pepper, to taste
- Crusty bread (for serving)

Preparation instructions:
1. In a skillet, melt the butter over medium heat. Add the finely chopped onion and minced garlic. Sauté until the onion is translucent.
2. Sprinkle the flour over the onion and garlic mixture. Stir well to create a roux. Cook for a minute or two to remove the raw flour taste.

3. Transfer the roux to the crockpot. Add the diced potatoes, white fish fillets, prawns, scallops, fish stock, whole milk, and double cream. Stir to combine.
4. Cover and cook on low heat for 4 hours, allowing the seafood to cook through and the chowder to thicken.
5. Season with salt and black pepper. Stir in the chopped fresh parsley before serving. Serve the seafood chowder hot, accompanied by crusty bread.

Crockpot Moroccan Lamb Tagine

Serves: 4 Prep time: 15 minutes / Cook time: 6 hours

Ingredients:
- 500g lamb shoulder, cubed
- 1 onion, finely chopped
- 2 cloves garlic, minced
- 2 carrots, peeled and sliced
- 1 can (400g) chickpeas, drained and rinsed
- 2 tomatoes, diced
- 250ml vegetable stock
- 60g dried apricots, chopped
- 1 tsp ground cumin
- 1 tsp ground coriander
- 1/2 tsp ground cinnamon
- 1/4 tsp ground turmeric
- Salt and black pepper, to taste
- Fresh coriander leaves, chopped (for garnish)
- Cooked couscous (for serving)

Preparation instructions:
1. In a skillet, brown the cubed lamb over medium-high heat. Transfer the lamb to the crockpot.
2. In the same skillet, sauté the finely chopped onion until translucent. Add the minced garlic, sliced carrots, diced tomatoes, and drained chickpeas. Cook for a few minutes until the vegetables are slightly tender.
3. Transfer the vegetable mixture to the crockpot. Add the chopped dried apricots, ground cumin, ground coriander, ground cinnamon, ground turmeric, vegetable stock, salt, and black pepper. Stir to combine all Ingredients.
4. Cover and cook on low heat for 6 hours, allowing the flavours to meld together and the lamb to become tender.
5. Stir well before serving. Garnish with chopped fresh coriander leaves. Serve the Moroccan lamb tagine hot, accompanied by cooked couscous.

Slow Cooker Chicken and Mushroom Casserole

Serves: 4 Prep time: 15 minutes / Cook time: 4 hours

Ingredients:
- 4 chicken thighs, bone-in and skin-on
- 200g button mushrooms, sliced
- 1 onion, finely chopped
- 2 cloves garlic, minced
- 250ml chicken stock
- 125ml double cream
- 2 tbsp all-purpose flour
- 2 tbsp olive oil
- 1 tsp dried thyme

- Salt and black pepper, to taste
- Fresh parsley, chopped (for garnish)
- Mashed potatoes (for serving)

Preparation instructions:

1. Season the chicken thighs with salt and black pepper. In a skillet, heat the olive oil over medium-high heat. Brown the chicken thighs on both sides. Transfer the chicken to the crockpot.
2. In the same skillet, sauté the finely chopped onion until translucent. Add the minced garlic and sliced mushrooms. Cook until the mushrooms are tender.
3. Sprinkle the flour over the mushroom mixture. Stir well to create a roux. Cook for a minute to remove the raw flour taste.
4. Transfer the mushroom mixture to the crockpot. Add the chicken stock, double cream, and dried thyme. Stir to combine.
5. Cover and cook on low heat for 4 hours, allowing the chicken to become tender and flavorful.
6. Stir well before serving. Garnish with chopped fresh parsley. Serve the chicken and mushroom casserole hot, accompanied by creamy mashed potatoes.

Crockpot Vegetable Biryani

Serves: 4 Prep time: 20 minutes / Cook time: 4 hours

Ingredients:

- 300g basmati rice, rinsed and drained
- 2 onions, thinly sliced
- 1 carrot, peeled and diced
- 1 pepper, diced
- 100g green beans, trimmed and chopped
- 1 can (400g) chickpeas, drained and rinsed
- 60g plain yoghurt
- 500ml vegetable stock
- 2 tbsp ghee or vegetable oil
- 1 tbsp biryani spice mix (or garam masala)
- 1 tsp ground turmeric
- 1/2 tsp ground cumin
- 1/2 tsp ground coriander
- 1/4 tsp ground cinnamon
- Salt, to taste
- Fresh oregano leaves, chopped (for garnish)
- Plain yoghurt (for serving)

Preparation instructions:

1. In a skillet, heat the ghee or vegetable oil over medium heat. Sauté the thinly sliced onions until golden brown and crispy. Remove half of the onions and set aside for garnish.
2. To the remaining onions in the skillet, add the diced carrots, diced pepper, chopped green beans, and biryani spice mix. Cook for a few minutes until the vegetables are slightly tender.
3. Transfer the vegetable mixture to the crockpot. Add the rinsed basmati rice, drained chickpeas, plain yoghurt, ground turmeric, ground cumin, ground coriander, ground cinnamon, and vegetable stock. Stir to combine.

4. Cover and cook on low heat for 4 hours, allowing the rice to cook through and absorb the flavours.
5. Before serving, fluff the biryani with a fork. Garnish with the reserved crispy onions and chopped fresh oregano leaves. Serve the vegetable biryani hot, accompanied by a dollop of plain yoghurt.

Slow Cooker Pulled Pork Sandwiches

Serves: 4 Prep time: 15 minutes / Cook time: 6 hours

Ingredients:

- 800g pork shoulder, trimmed of excess fat and cut into chunks
- 1 onion, finely chopped
- 2 cloves garlic, minced
- 250ml barbecue sauce
- 60ml apple cider vinegar
- 1 tbsp brown sugar
- 1 tsp smoked paprika
- 1/2 tsp ground cumin
- Salt and black pepper, to taste
- 4 burger buns
- Coleslaw, for serving

Preparation instructions:

1. In a pan, heat a little oil over medium-high heat. Brown the pork chunks on all sides. Transfer the pork to the crockpot.
2. In the same pan, sauté the finely chopped onion until translucent. Add the minced garlic and cook for a minute more. Transfer the onion and garlic to the crockpot.
3. In a bowl, mix together the barbecue sauce, apple cider vinegar, brown sugar, smoked paprika, ground cumin, salt, and black pepper. Pour this mixture over the pork in the crockpot.
4. Cover and cook on low heat for 6 hours or until the pork is tender and easily shredded.
5. Use two forks to shred the pork directly in the crockpot. Stir well to coat the shredded pork in the sauce.
6. Toast the burger buns lightly. Spoon the pulled pork onto the bottom half of each bun. Top with coleslaw and cover with the other half of the bun. Serve hot, accompanied by your favourite side dishes.

Crockpot Ratatouille

Serves: 4 Prep time: 20 minutes / Cook time: 4 hours

Ingredients:

- 2 courgettes, diced
- 1 aubergine, diced
- 2 peppers (any colour), diced
- 1 onion, finely chopped
- 3 cloves garlic, minced
- 4 tomatoes, diced
- 2 tbsp tomato paste
- 1 tsp dried thyme
- 1 tsp dried oregano
- Salt and black pepper, to taste
- 2 tbsp olive oil
- Fresh basil leaves, chopped (for garnish)

- Cooked rice or crusty bread, for serving

Preparation instructions:

1. In a pan, heat the olive oil over medium heat. Sauté the finely chopped onion until translucent. Add the minced garlic and cook for a minute more. Transfer the onion and garlic to the crockpot.
2. Add the diced courgettes, aubergine, peppers, tomatoes, tomato paste, dried thyme, dried oregano, salt, and black pepper to the crockpot. Stir well to combine all Ingredients.
3. Cover and cook on low heat for 4 hours or until the vegetables are tender and flavorful.
4. Stir well before serving. Garnish with chopped fresh basil leaves. Serve the ratatouille hot, accompanied by cooked rice or crusty bread.

Slow Cooker Chicken and Spinach Curry

Serves: 4 Prep time: 15 minutes / Cook time: 4 hours

Ingredients:

- 500g boneless, skinless chicken thighs, cut into chunks
- 1 onion, finely chopped
- 3 cloves garlic, minced
- 1 thumb-sized piece of ginger, grated
- 200g fresh spinach leaves
- 250ml coconut milk
- 250ml chicken stock
- 2 tbsp curry powder
- 1 tsp ground turmeric
- 1/2 tsp ground cumin
- 1/2 tsp ground coriander
- Salt and black pepper, to taste
- Fresh coriander leaves, chopped (for garnish)
- Cooked rice, for serving

Preparation instructions:

1. In a pan, sauté the finely chopped onion until translucent. Add the minced garlic and grated ginger. Cook for a minute more. Transfer the mixture to the crockpot.
2. Add the chicken chunks, fresh spinach leaves, coconut milk, chicken stock, curry powder, ground turmeric, ground cumin, ground coriander, salt, and black pepper to the crockpot. Stir well to combine all Ingredients.
3. Cover and cook on low heat for 4 hours or until the chicken is cooked through and tender.
4. Stir well before serving. Garnish with chopped fresh coriander leaves. Serve the chicken and spinach curry hot, accompanied by cooked rice.

Crockpot Vegetarian Chilli

Serves: 4 Prep time: 15 minutes / Cook time: 6 hours

Ingredients:

- 400g canned kidney beans, drained and rinsed
- 400g canned black beans, drained and rinsed
- 400g canned chopped tomatoes
- 1 onion, finely chopped
- 2 cloves garlic, minced

- 1 pepper (any colour), diced
- 1 carrot, diced
- 1 celery stalk, diced
- 250ml vegetable stock
- 2 tbsp tomato paste
- 1 tbsp chilli powder
- 1 tsp ground cumin
- 1/2 tsp paprika
- Salt and black pepper, to taste
- Fresh oregano leaves, chopped (for garnish)
- Grated cheddar cheese, for serving
- Sour cream, for serving

Preparation instructions:

1. In the crockpot, combine the kidney beans, black beans, chopped tomatoes, finely chopped onion, minced garlic, diced pepper, diced carrot, and diced celery.
2. In a bowl, mix together the vegetable stock, tomato paste, chilli powder, ground cumin, paprika, salt, and black pepper. Pour this mixture over the vegetables and beans in the crockpot. Stir well to combine all Ingredients.
3. Cover and cook on low heat for 6 hours, allowing the flavours to meld together.
4. Stir well before serving. Garnish with chopped fresh oregano leaves. Serve the vegetarian chilli hot, topped with grated cheddar cheese and a dollop of sour cream.

Slow Cooker Beef and Ale Stew

Serves: 4 Prep time: 20 minutes / Cook time: 6 hours

Ingredients:

- 600g stewing beef, cut into chunks
- 1 onion, finely chopped
- 2 cloves garlic, minced
- 2 carrots, peeled and sliced
- 2 parsnips, peeled and sliced
- 500ml ale or stout
- 250ml beef stock
- 2 tbsp tomato paste
- 1 tbsp Worcestershire sauce
- 1 tsp dried thyme
- 1 bay leaf
- Salt and black pepper, to taste
- Fresh parsley, chopped (for garnish)
- Mashed potatoes, for serving

Preparation instructions:

1. In a pan, heat a little oil over medium-high heat. Brown the beef chunks on all sides. Transfer the beef to the crockpot.
2. In the same pan, sauté the finely chopped onion until translucent. Add the minced garlic and cook for a minute more. Transfer the onion and garlic to the crockpot.
3. Add the sliced carrots, sliced parsnips, ale or stout, beef stock, tomato paste, Worcestershire sauce, dried thyme, bay leaf, salt, and black pepper to the crockpot. Stir well to combine all Ingredients.
4. Cover and cook on low heat for 6 hours or until the beef is tender and flavorful.
5. Stir well before serving. Remove the bay leaf. Garnish

with chopped fresh parsley. Serve the beef and ale stew hot, accompanied by creamy mashed potatoes.

Crockpot Chicken and Rice Casserole

Serves: 4 Prep time: 15 minutes / Cook time: 4 hours

Ingredients:
- 500g boneless, skinless chicken thighs, cut into chunks
- 1 onion, finely chopped
- 2 cloves garlic, minced
- 250g mushrooms, sliced
- 200g long-grain rice
- 500ml chicken stock
- 250ml heavy cream
- 1 tsp dried thyme
- Salt and black pepper, to taste
- Fresh chives, chopped (for garnish)
- Steamed vegetables, for serving

Preparation instructions:
1. In a pan, sauté the finely chopped onion until translucent. Add the minced garlic and sliced mushrooms. Cook until the mushrooms are tender. Transfer the mixture to the crockpot.
2. Add the chicken chunks, long-grain rice, chicken stock, heavy cream, dried thyme, salt, and black pepper to the crockpot. Stir well to combine all Ingredients.
3. Cover and cook on low heat for 4 hours or until the chicken is cooked through, and the rice is tender.
4. Stir well before serving. Garnish with chopped fresh chives. Serve the chicken and rice casserole hot, accompanied by steamed vegetables.

Slow Cooker Mushroom and Barley Risotto

Serves: 4 Prep time: 10 minutes / Cook time: 4 hours

Ingredients:
- 200g pearl barley
- 500g mixed mushrooms, sliced (such as button mushrooms, cremini, and shiitake)
- 1 onion, finely chopped
- 2 cloves garlic, minced
- 1 litre vegetable stock
- 60ml white wine (optional)
- 60ml heavy cream
- 50g grated Parmesan cheese
- 2 tbsp butter
- 1 tbsp olive oil
- Salt and black pepper, to taste
- Fresh parsley, chopped (for garnish)

Preparation instructions:
1. In a pan, heat the olive oil over medium heat. Sauté the finely chopped onion until translucent. Add the minced garlic and cook for a minute more. Transfer the mixture to the slow cooker.
2. Add the pearl barley, sliced mushrooms, vegetable stock, and white wine (if using) to the slow cooker. Stir well to combine all Ingredients.

3. Cover and cook on low heat for 4 hours or until the barley is tender and creamy.
4. Stir in the heavy cream, grated Parmesan cheese, butter, salt, and black pepper. Let it cook for an additional 10 minutes.
5. Stir well before serving. Garnish with chopped fresh parsley. Serve the mushroom and barley risotto hot.

Crockpot Vegan Goulash

Serves: 4 Prep time: 15 minutes / Cook time: 6 hours

Ingredients:
- 400g potatoes, peeled and diced
- 400g carrots, peeled and sliced
- 1 onion, finely chopped
- 2 cloves garlic, minced
- 2 red peppers, chopped
- 2 tbsp tomato paste
- 1 tbsp sweet paprika
- 1 tsp smoked paprika
- 1 tsp caraway seeds
- 1 litre vegetable stock
- Salt and black pepper, to taste
- Fresh parsley, chopped (for garnish)
- Vegan sour cream, for serving

Preparation instructions:
1. In the crockpot, combine the diced potatoes, sliced carrots, finely chopped onion, minced garlic, and chopped red peppers.
2. In a bowl, mix together the tomato paste, sweet paprika, smoked paprika, caraway seeds, vegetable stock, salt, and black pepper. Pour this mixture over the vegetables in the crockpot. Stir well to combine all Ingredients.
3. Cover and cook on low heat for 6 hours, allowing the flavours to meld together.
4. Stir well before serving. Garnish with chopped fresh parsley. Serve the vegan goulash hot, with a dollop of vegan sour cream.

Slow Cooker Lamb Korma

Serves: 4 Prep time: 15 minutes / Cook time: 6 hours

Ingredients:
- 600g lamb shoulder, diced
- 1 onion, finely chopped
- 2 cloves garlic, minced
- 1-inch ginger, grated
- 200ml coconut milk
- 200g plain yoghurt
- 2 tbsp korma curry paste
- 1 tbsp vegetable oil
- 1 tsp ground coriander
- 1 tsp ground cumin
- 1/2 tsp turmeric powder
- Salt and black pepper, to taste
- Fresh coriander leaves, chopped (for garnish)
- Cooked basmati rice, for serving

Preparation instructions:

1. In a pan, heat the vegetable oil over medium-high heat. Brown the diced lamb on all sides. Transfer the lamb to the slow cooker.
2. In the same pan, sauté the finely chopped onion until translucent. Add the minced garlic and grated ginger. Cook for a few minutes until fragrant. Transfer this mixture to the slow cooker.
3. Add the korma curry paste, ground coriander, ground cumin, turmeric powder, coconut milk, and plain yoghurt to the slow cooker. Stir well to combine all Ingredients.
4. Cover and cook on low heat for 6 hours or until the lamb is tender and flavorful.
5. Stir well before serving. Garnish with chopped fresh coriander leaves. Serve the lamb korma hot, accompanied by cooked basmati rice.

Crockpot Sweet Potato and Chickpea Curry

Serves: 4 Prep time: 15 minutes / Cook time: 6 hours

Ingredients:

- 500g sweet potatoes, peeled and diced
- 400g canned chickpeas, drained and rinsed
- 1 onion, finely chopped
- 2 cloves garlic, minced
- 400ml coconut milk
- 200ml vegetable stock
- 2 tbsp curry powder
- 1 tsp ground turmeric
- 1 tsp ground cumin
- 1 tsp paprika
- Salt and black pepper, to taste
- Fresh coriander leaves, chopped (for garnish)
- Cooked basmati rice, for serving

Preparation instructions:

1. In the crockpot, combine the diced sweet potatoes, drained chickpeas, finely chopped onion, and minced garlic.
2. In a bowl, mix together the coconut milk, vegetable stock, curry powder, ground turmeric, ground cumin, paprika, salt, and black pepper. Pour this mixture over the Ingredients in the crockpot. Stir well to combine all Ingredients.
3. Cover and cook on low heat for 6 hours or until the sweet potatoes are tender and the flavours have melded together.
4. Stir well before serving. Garnish with chopped fresh coriander leaves. Serve the sweet potato and chickpea curry hot, with cooked basmati rice.

Slow Cooker Aubergine Parmesan

Serves: 4 Prep time: 20 minutes / Cook time: 4 hours

Ingredients:

- 2 large aubergines, sliced into 1/2-inch rounds
- 500ml tomato sauce
- 200g shredded mozzarella cheese
- 100g grated Parmesan cheese
- 2 eggs, beaten
- 120g breadcrumbs
- 1 tsp dried oregano
- 1 tsp dried basil
- Salt and black pepper, to taste
- Fresh basil leaves, for garnish

Preparation instructions:

1. In a shallow dish, combine the beaten eggs, dried oregano, dried basil, salt, and black pepper. Dip each aubergine slice into the egg mixture, allowing excess to drip off, then coat both sides with breadcrumbs.
2. In a pan, heat a little oil over medium-high heat. Cook the breaded aubergine slices until golden brown on both sides. Transfer to a paper towel-lined plate to drain excess oil.
3. In the slow cooker, spread a layer of tomato sauce at the bottom. Arrange a layer of fried aubergine slices over the sauce. Sprinkle it with shredded mozzarella and grated Parmesan cheese. Repeat the layers, ending with a layer of cheese on top.
4. Cover and cook on low heat for 4 hours or until the cheese is melted and bubbly.
5. Garnish with fresh basil leaves before serving. Serve the slow cooker aubergine Parmesan hot.

Crockpot Mediterranean Chicken

Serves: 4 Prep time: 15 minutes / Cook time: 4 hours

Ingredients:

- 4 boneless, skinless chicken breasts
- 200g cherry tomatoes, halved
- 1 red pepper, sliced
- 1 yellow pepper, sliced
- 1 red onion, thinly sliced
- 2 cloves garlic, minced
- 120ml chicken broth
- 60ml balsamic vinegar
- 2 tbsp olive oil
- 1 tsp dried oregano
- Salt and black pepper, to taste
- Fresh parsley, chopped (for garnish)
- Cooked couscous, for serving

Preparation instructions:

1. In the crockpot, place the chicken breasts at the bottom. Top with halved cherry tomatoes, sliced red and yellow peppers, thinly sliced red onion, and minced garlic.
2. In a bowl, whisk together the chicken broth, balsamic vinegar, olive oil, dried oregano, salt, and black pepper. Pour this mixture over the chicken and vegetables in the crockpot.
3. Cover and cook on low heat for 4 hours or until the chicken is cooked through and tender.
4. Stir well before serving. Garnish with chopped fresh parsley. Serve the Mediterranean chicken hot, with cooked couscous.

Slow Cooker Thai Green Curry

Serves: 4 Prep time: 15 minutes / Cook time: 4 hours

Ingredients:
- 500g boneless, skinless chicken thighs, cut into bite-sized pieces
- 400ml coconut milk
- 200g bamboo shoots, drained and sliced
- 1 red pepper, sliced
- 1 green pepper, sliced
- 1 onion, thinly sliced
- 2 tbsp green curry paste
- 2 tbsp fish sauce
- 1 tbsp brown sugar
- 1 lime, juiced
- Fresh basil leaves, for garnish
- Cooked jasmine rice, for serving

Preparation instructions:
1. In the slow cooker, combine the chicken pieces, coconut milk, sliced bamboo shoots, sliced red and green peppers, and thinly sliced onion.
2. In a bowl, mix together the green curry paste, fish sauce, brown sugar, and lime juice. Pour this mixture over the Ingredients in the slow cooker. Stir well to combine.
3. Cover and cook on low heat for 4 hours or until the chicken is cooked through and the vegetables are tender.
4. Stir well before serving. Garnish with fresh basil leaves. Serve the Thai green curry hot, with cooked jasmine rice.

Crockpot Beef Stroganoff

Serves: 4 Prep time: 15 minutes / Cook time: 6 hours

Ingredients:
- 500g beef sirloin, thinly sliced
- 1 onion, finely chopped
- 200g button mushrooms, sliced
- 2 cloves garlic, minced
- 250ml beef broth
- 200ml sour cream
- 2 tbsp Worcestershire sauce
- Salt and black pepper, to taste
- Fresh parsley, chopped (for garnish)
- Cooked egg noodles, for serving

Preparation instructions:
1. In the crockpot, combine the thinly sliced beef sirloin, finely chopped onion, sliced mushrooms, and minced garlic.
2. Pour in the beef broth and Worcestershire sauce. Season with salt and black pepper. Stir well to combine all Ingredients.
3. Cover and cook on low heat for 6 hours or until the beef is tender.
4. Stir in the sour cream before serving. Garnish with chopped fresh parsley. Serve the beef stroganoff hot, over cooked egg noodles.

Slow Cooker Cauliflower Cheese

Serves: 4 Prep time: 15 minutes / Cook time: 3 hours

Ingredients:
- 1 large cauliflower, cut into florets

- 500ml whole milk
- 200g shredded cheddar cheese
- 2 tbsp all-purpose flour
- 2 tbsp unsalted butter
- 1/4 tsp ground mustard
- 1/4 tsp garlic powder
- Salt and black pepper, to taste
- Fresh chives, chopped (for garnish)

Preparation instructions:
1. In a saucepan, melt the butter over medium heat. Stir in the flour to create a roux. Gradually whisk in the milk until the mixture thickens.
2. Stir in the shredded cheddar cheese, ground mustard, garlic powder, salt, and black pepper. Continue to stir until the cheese is melted and the sauce is smooth. Remove from heat.
3. In the slow cooker, layer the cauliflower florets. Pour the cheese sauce over the cauliflower.
4. Cover and cook on low heat for 3 hours or until the cauliflower is tender and the sauce is bubbling.
5. Stir well before serving. Garnish with chopped fresh chives. Serve the cauliflower cheese hot.

Crockpot Chicken Fajitas

Serves: 4 Prep time: 15 minutes / Cook time: 4 hours

Ingredients:
- 500g boneless, skinless chicken breasts, thinly sliced
- 1 onion, sliced
- 1 red pepper, sliced
- 1 yellow pepper, sliced
- 1 green pepper, sliced
- 2 cloves garlic, minced
- 1 tsp ground cumin
- 1 tsp paprika
- 1/2 tsp chilli powder
- Salt and black pepper, to taste
- 60ml olive oil
- 60ml fresh lime juice
- Fresh oregano leaves, for garnish
- Warm flour tortillas, for serving

Preparation instructions:
1. In the crockpot, combine the sliced chicken breasts, sliced onion, sliced red, yellow, and green peppers, and minced garlic.
2. In a small bowl, mix together the ground cumin, paprika, chilli powder, salt, black pepper, olive oil, and fresh lime juice. Pour this mixture over the Ingredients in the crockpot. Stir well to coat everything evenly.
3. Cover and cook on low heat for 4 hours or until the chicken is cooked through and the vegetables are tender.
4. Stir well before serving. Garnish with fresh oregano leaves. Serve the chicken fajitas hot, wrapped in warm flour tortillas.

Slow Cooker Butternut Squash Risotto

Serves: 4 Prep time: 15 minutes / Cook time: 3 hours

Ingredients:

- 400g butternut squash, peeled and diced
- 200g Arborio rice
- 1 onion, finely chopped
- 2 cloves garlic, minced
- 1 litre vegetable stock
- 60g Parmesan cheese, grated
- 60ml dry white wine
- 2 tbsp unsalted butter
- Salt and black pepper, to taste
- Fresh sage leaves, for garnish

Preparation instructions:

1. In the slow cooker, combine the diced butternut squash, Arborio rice, finely chopped onion, minced garlic, vegetable stock, grated Parmesan cheese, dry white wine, and unsalted butter.
2. Season with salt and black pepper. Stir well to combine all Ingredients.
3. Cover and cook on low heat for 3 hours or until the rice is creamy and the butternut squash is tender.
4. Stir well before serving. Garnish with fresh sage leaves. Serve the butternut squash risotto hot.

Crockpot Chicken and Chorizo Stew

Serves: 4 Prep time: 15 minutes / Cook time: 6 hours

Ingredients:

- 500g boneless, skinless chicken thighs, cut into bite-sized pieces
- 200g chorizo sausage, sliced
- 2 onions, chopped
- 2 cloves garlic, minced
- 400g canned chopped tomatoes
- 400g canned chickpeas, drained and rinsed
- 250ml chicken broth
- 1 tsp smoked paprika
- 1/2 tsp dried oregano
- Salt and black pepper, to taste
- Fresh parsley, chopped (for garnish)
- Crusty bread, for serving

Preparation instructions:

1. In the crockpot, combine the chicken pieces, sliced chorizo sausage, chopped onions, minced garlic, canned chopped tomatoes, chickpeas, chicken broth, smoked paprika, dried oregano, salt, and black pepper.
2. Stir well to combine all Ingredients.
3. Cover and cook on low heat for 6 hours or until the chicken is cooked through and tender.
4. Stir well before serving. Garnish with chopped fresh parsley. Serve the chicken and chorizo stew hot, with crusty bread.

Slow Cooker Quinoa and Vegetable Pilaf

Serves: 4 Prep time: 15 minutes / Cook time: 4 hours

Ingredients:

- 200g quinoa, rinsed and drained

- 400g mixed vegetables (such as carrots, peas, corn, and peppers), diced
- 1 onion, finely chopped
- 2 cloves garlic, minced
- 750ml vegetable broth
- 1 tsp ground cumin
- 1/2 tsp turmeric powder
- Salt and black pepper, to taste
- Fresh parsley, chopped (for garnish)

Preparation instructions:

1. In the slow cooker, combine the quinoa, mixed vegetables, finely chopped onion, minced garlic, vegetable broth, ground cumin, turmeric powder, salt, and black pepper.
2. Stir well to combine all Ingredients.
3. Cover and cook on low heat for 4 hours or until the quinoa is cooked through and the vegetables are tender.
4. Stir well before serving. Garnish with chopped fresh parsley. Serve the quinoa and vegetable pilaf hot.

Crockpot Mushroom and Brie Soup (served over pasta)

Serves: 4 Prep time: 15 minutes / Cook time: 4 hours

Ingredients:

- 400g mushrooms, sliced
- 1 onion, chopped
- 2 cloves garlic, minced
- 750ml vegetable broth
- 200ml heavy cream
- 150g Brie cheese, rind removed and chopped
- Salt and black pepper, to taste
- 300g pasta, cooked (for serving)
- Fresh chives, chopped (for garnish)

Preparation instructions:

1. In the crockpot, combine the sliced mushrooms, chopped onion, minced garlic, vegetable broth, and heavy cream.
2. Cover and cook on low heat for 4 hours or until the mushrooms are tender.
3. Using an immersion blender, blend the soup until smooth.
4. Add the chopped Brie cheese to the soup, stirring until melted and well incorporated.
5. Season with salt and black pepper to taste.
6. Serve the mushroom and Brie soup hot, ladled over cooked pasta. Garnish with chopped fresh chives.

Slow Cooker Veggie Enchiladas

Serves: 4 Prep time: 20 minutes / Cook time: 4 hours

Ingredients:

- 8 small corn tortillas
- 400g mixed vegetables (such as peppers, courgette, and corn), diced
- 1 onion, chopped
- 2 cloves garlic, minced
- 400g canned black beans, drained and rinsed
- 250ml enchilada sauce
- 200g shredded cheddar cheese

- Fresh oregano, chopped (for garnish)
- Sour cream, for serving

Preparation instructions:

1. In a pan, sauté the mixed vegetables, chopped onion, and minced garlic until tender.
2. Preheat the slow cooker on low heat.
3. Warm the corn tortillas in the microwave for a few seconds until pliable.
4. On each tortilla, place a spoonful of sautéed vegetables, a spoonful of black beans, and a sprinkle of shredded cheddar cheese. Roll the tortilla to form an enchilada.
5. Place the enchiladas seam side down in the slow cooker.
6. Pour the enchilada sauce over the top of the enchiladas, ensuring they are well covered.
7. Sprinkle the remaining shredded cheddar cheese on top.
8. Cover and cook on low heat for 4 hours or until the enchiladas are heated through and the cheese is melted and bubbly.
9. Garnish with chopped fresh oregano. Serve the veggie enchiladas hot, with a dollop of sour cream on the side.

Crockpot Lamb Rogan Josh

Serves: 4 Prep time: 15 minutes / Cook time: 6 hours

Ingredients:

- 600g boneless lamb, cut into cubes
- 1 onion, finely chopped
- 4 cloves garlic, minced
- 2 tsp ginger, grated
- 200g canned tomatoes, crushed
- 150ml natural yoghurt
- 2 tbsp Rogan Josh spice mix
- 250ml beef or vegetable broth
- Salt and black pepper, to taste
- Fresh coriander, chopped (for garnish)
- Cooked basmati rice, for serving

Preparation instructions:

1. In the crockpot, combine the lamb cubes, finely chopped onion, minced garlic, grated ginger, crushed tomatoes, natural yoghurt, Rogan Josh spice mix, and beef or vegetable broth.
2. Stir well to combine all Ingredients.
3. Cover and cook on low heat for 6 hours or until the lamb is tender and flavorful.
4. Season with salt and black pepper to taste.
5. Serve the Lamb Rogan Josh hot, garnished with chopped fresh coriander. Serve over cooked basmati rice.

Slow Cooker Chickpea and Spinach Stew

Serves: 4 Prep time: 15 minutes / Cook time: 4 hours

Ingredients:

- 400g canned chickpeas, drained and rinsed
- 200g fresh spinach leaves
- 1 onion, finely chopped
- 3 cloves garlic, minced
- 400g canned tomatoes, crushed

- 250ml vegetable broth
- 1 tsp ground cumin
- 1 tsp ground coriander
- 1/2 tsp smoked paprika
- Salt and black pepper, to taste
- Fresh parsley, chopped (for garnish)
- Crusty bread, for serving

Preparation instructions:

1. In the slow cooker, combine the chickpeas, fresh spinach leaves, finely chopped onion, minced garlic, crushed tomatoes, vegetable broth, ground cumin, ground coriander, and smoked paprika.
2. Stir well to combine all Ingredients.
3. Cover and cook on low heat for 4 hours or until the stew is bubbling and the flavours are well combined.
4. Season with salt and black pepper to taste.
5. Serve the Chickpea and Spinach Stew hot, garnished with chopped fresh parsley. Serve with crusty bread.

Crockpot Creamy Tomato Pasta

Serves: 4 Prep time: 10 minutes / Cook time: 3 hours

Ingredients:

- 400g pasta (such as penne or rigatoni)
- 400g canned tomatoes, crushed
- 200ml heavy cream
- 1 onion, finely chopped
- 3 cloves garlic, minced
- 1 tsp dried basil
- 1/2 tsp dried oregano
- Salt and black pepper, to taste
- Fresh basil leaves, chopped (for garnish)
- Grated Parmesan cheese, for serving

Preparation instructions:

1. Cook the pasta according to the package instructions until al dente. Drain and set aside.
2. In the crockpot, combine the crushed tomatoes, heavy cream, finely chopped onion, minced garlic, dried basil, and dried oregano.
3. Stir well to combine all Ingredients.
4. Cover and cook on low heat for 3 hours, stirring occasionally.
5. Season with salt and black pepper to taste.
6. Serve the Creamy Tomato Pasta over cooked pasta, garnished with chopped fresh basil leaves and grated Parmesan cheese.

Slow Cooker Seafood Paella

Serves: 4 Prep time: 15 minutes / Cook time: 3 hours

Ingredients:

- 300g mixed seafood (such as prawns, mussels, and squid), cleaned and deveined
- 300g Arborio rice
- 1 onion, finely chopped
- 2 cloves garlic, minced
- 1 red pepper, diced

- 1 yellow pepper, diced
- 400g canned chopped tomatoes
- 750ml vegetable broth
- 1/2 tsp smoked paprika
- 1/2 tsp saffron threads, soaked in 1 tbsp hot water
- Salt and black pepper, to taste
- Fresh parsley, chopped (for garnish)
- Lemon wedges, for serving

Preparation instructions:

1. In the crockpot, combine the mixed seafood, Arborio rice, finely chopped onion, minced garlic, diced red and yellow peppers, chopped tomatoes, vegetable broth, smoked paprika, and soaked saffron threads with water.
2. Stir well to combine all Ingredients.
3. Cover and cook on low heat for 3 hours or until the rice is tender and the seafood is cooked through.
4. Season with salt and black pepper to taste.
5. Garnish with chopped fresh parsley and serve the Seafood Paella hot, accompanied by lemon wedges.

Crockpot Vegan Chili

Serves: 4 Prep time: 15 minutes / Cook time: 4 hours

Ingredients:
- 400g canned kidney beans, drained and rinsed
- 400g canned black beans, drained and rinsed
- 400g canned diced tomatoes
- 1 onion, finely chopped
- 2 cloves garlic, minced
- 1 red pepper, diced
- 1 yellow pepper, diced
- 1 tbsp chilli powder
- 1 tsp ground cumin
- 1/2 tsp paprika
- Salt and black pepper, to taste
- Fresh oregano, chopped (for garnish)
- Vegan sour cream, for serving

Preparation instructions:

1. In the crockpot, combine the kidney beans, black beans, diced tomatoes, finely chopped onion, minced garlic, diced red and yellow peppers, chilli powder, ground cumin, and paprika.
2. Stir well to combine all Ingredients.
3. Cover and cook on low heat for 4 hours, allowing the flavours to meld together.
4. Season with salt and black pepper to taste.
5. Garnish with chopped fresh oregano and serve the Vegan Chili hot, with a dollop of vegan sour cream on top.

Slow Cooker Chicken and Sweetcorn Soup (served over rice)

Serves: 4 Prep time: 15 minutes / Cook time: 4 hours

Ingredients:
- 400g boneless, skinless chicken thighs, diced
- 1 onion, finely chopped
- 2 cloves garlic, minced

- 1 carrot, peeled and diced
- 1 can (300g) creamed corn
- 750ml chicken broth
- 60ml soy sauce
- 1 tbsp cornstarch, dissolved in 2 tbsp water
- Salt and white pepper, to taste
- Green onions, chopped (for garnish)
- Cooked rice, for serving

Preparation instructions:

1. In the crockpot, combine the diced chicken thighs, finely chopped onion, minced garlic, diced carrot, creamed corn, chicken broth, and soy sauce.
2. Stir well to combine all Ingredients.
3. Cover and cook on low heat for 4 hours or until the chicken is cooked through and tender.
4. Stir in the dissolved cornstarch mixture and cook for an additional 15 minutes to thicken the soup.
5. Season with salt and white pepper to taste.
6. Serve the Chicken and Sweetcorn Soup hot, ladled over cooked rice and garnished with chopped green onions.

Crockpot Spinach and Feta Stuffed Peppers

Serves: 4 Prep time: 15 minutes / Cook time: 3 hours

Ingredients:
- 4 large peppers, any colour
- 200g fresh spinach, chopped
- 150g feta cheese, crumbled
- 1 onion, finely chopped
- 2 cloves garlic, minced
- 200g cooked quinoa
- 400g canned diced tomatoes
- 1 tsp dried oregano
- Salt and black pepper, to taste
- Olive oil, for drizzling
- Fresh parsley, chopped (for garnish)

Preparation instructions:

1. Cut the tops off the peppers and remove the seeds and membranes.
2. In a bowl, combine chopped spinach, crumbled feta cheese, finely chopped onion, minced garlic, cooked quinoa, diced tomatoes, dried oregano, salt, and black pepper.
3. Stuff each pepper with the spinach and feta mixture.
4. Place the stuffed peppers into the crockpot.
5. Drizzle a little olive oil over the stuffed peppers.
6. Cover and cook on low heat for 3 hours or until the peppers are tender.
7. Garnish with chopped fresh parsley before serving.

Slow Cooker Mediterranean Vegetable Stew

Serves: 4 Prep time: 15 minutes / Cook time: 4 hours

Ingredients:
- 2 courgettes (courgettes), diced
- 2 aubergines (aubergines), diced
- 2 red onions, sliced

- 2 cloves garlic, minced
- 400g canned chickpeas, drained and rinsed
- 400g canned diced tomatoes
- 250ml vegetable broth
- 1 tsp dried basil
- 1 tsp dried oregano
- Salt and black pepper, to taste
- Fresh basil leaves, torn (for garnish)

Preparation instructions:

1. In the crockpot, combine diced courgettes, diced aubergines, sliced red onions, minced garlic, drained chickpeas, diced tomatoes, vegetable broth, dried basil, dried oregano, salt, and black pepper.
2. Stir well to combine all Ingredients.
3. Cover and cook on low heat for 4 hours or until the vegetables are tender.
4. Taste and adjust seasoning, if necessary.
5. Garnish with torn fresh basil leaves before serving.

Crockpot Chicken Korma

Serves: 4 Prep time: 15 minutes / Cook time: 4 hours

Ingredients:

- 600g boneless, skinless chicken thighs, diced
- 1 onion, finely chopped
- 2 cloves garlic, minced
- 1 red chilli, seeds removed and finely chopped
- 200ml coconut milk
- 150g natural yoghurt
- 2 tbsp korma curry paste
- 1 tsp ground turmeric
- 1 tsp ground cumin
- Salt and black pepper, to taste
- Fresh coriander leaves, chopped (for garnish)

Preparation instructions:

1. In the crockpot, combine diced chicken thighs, finely chopped onion, minced garlic, chopped red chilli, coconut milk, natural yoghurt, korma curry paste, ground turmeric, ground cumin, salt, and black pepper.
2. Stir well to coat the chicken with the sauce.
3. Cover and cook on low heat for 4 hours or until the chicken is cooked through and tender.
4. Taste and adjust seasoning, if necessary.
5. Garnish with chopped fresh coriander leaves before serving.

Slow Cooker Vegetable Tagine

Serves: 4 Prep time: 15 minutes / Cook time: 4 hours

Ingredients:

- 2 sweet potatoes, peeled and diced

- 2 carrots, peeled and sliced
- 2 red onions, sliced
- 2 cloves garlic, minced
- 1 can (400g) chickpeas, drained and rinsed
- 400g canned diced tomatoes
- 250ml vegetable broth
- 1 tsp ground cumin
- 1 tsp ground coriander
- 1/2 tsp ground cinnamon
- Salt and black pepper, to taste
- Fresh mint leaves, chopped (for garnish)

Preparation instructions:

1. In the crockpot, combine diced sweet potatoes, sliced carrots, sliced red onions, minced garlic, drained chickpeas, diced tomatoes, vegetable broth, ground cumin, ground coriander, ground cinnamon, salt, and black pepper.
2. Stir well to combine all Ingredients.
3. Cover and cook on low heat for 4 hours or until the vegetables are tender.
4. Taste and adjust seasoning, if necessary.
5. Garnish with chopped fresh mint leaves before serving.

Crockpot Sweet Potato and Lentil Curry

Serves: 4 Prep time: 15 minutes / Cook time: 4 hours

Ingredients:

- 2 sweet potatoes, peeled and diced
- 200g red lentils, rinsed
- 1 onion, finely chopped
- 2 cloves garlic, minced
- 400ml canned coconut milk
- 250ml vegetable broth
- 2 tbsp curry paste
- 1 tsp ground turmeric
- 1 tsp ground cumin
- Salt and black pepper, to taste
- Fresh oregano leaves, chopped (for garnish)

Preparation instructions:

1. In the crockpot, combine diced sweet potatoes, rinsed red lentils, finely chopped onion, minced garlic, coconut milk, vegetable broth, curry paste, ground turmeric, ground cumin, salt, and black pepper.
2. Stir well to combine all Ingredients.
3. Cover and cook on low heat for 4 hours or until the sweet potatoes are tender and the lentils are cooked through.
4. Taste and adjust seasoning, if necessary.
5. Garnish with chopped fresh oregano leaves before serving.

Chapter 5: Vegetable and Vegetarian Recipes

Slow Cooker Vegetable Curry

Serves: 4 Prep time: 15 minutes / Cook time: 4 hours

Ingredients:
- 400g mixed vegetables (such as carrots, peas, potatoes, and cauliflower), diced
- 1 onion, finely chopped • 2 cloves garlic, minced
- 1 can (400ml) coconut milk
- 250ml vegetable broth • 2 tbsp curry powder
- 1 tsp ground turmeric • 1 tsp ground cumin
- Salt and black pepper, to taste
- Fresh coriander leaves, chopped (for garnish)

Preparation instructions:
1. In the crockpot, combine diced mixed vegetables, finely chopped onion, minced garlic, coconut milk, vegetable broth, curry powder, ground turmeric, ground cumin, salt, and black pepper.
2. Stir well to combine all Ingredients.
3. Cover and cook on low heat for 4 hours or until the vegetables are tender and the curry is flavorful.
4. Taste and adjust seasoning, if necessary.
5. Garnish with chopped fresh coriander leaves before serving.

Crockpot Lentil Stew

Serves: 4 Prep time: 15 minutes / Cook time: 6 hours

Ingredients:
- 200g green or brown lentils, rinsed
- 1 onion, finely chopped • 2 cloves garlic, minced
- 2 carrots, peeled and sliced
- 2 celery stalks, sliced • 1 can (400g) diced tomatoes
- 1.2 litres vegetable broth • 1 tsp ground cumin
- 1 tsp paprika
- Salt and black pepper, to taste
- Fresh parsley leaves, chopped (for garnish)

Preparation instructions:
1. In the crockpot, combine rinsed lentils, finely chopped onion, minced garlic, sliced carrots, sliced celery, diced tomatoes, vegetable broth, ground cumin, paprika, salt, and black pepper.
2. Stir well to combine all Ingredients.
3. Cover and cook on low heat for 6 hours or until the lentils are tender and the stew is thickened.
4. Taste and adjust seasoning, if necessary.
5. Garnish with chopped fresh parsley leaves before serving.

Slow Cooker Spinach and Ricotta Lasagna

Serves: 4 Prep time: 20 minutes / Cook time: 4 hours

Ingredients:
- 9 lasagna noodles, cooked according to package instructions
- 400g fresh spinach leaves • 250g ricotta cheese
- 1 egg, beaten • 1 can (400g) crushed tomatoes
- 250ml vegetable broth
- 100g shredded mozzarella cheese
- 50g grated Parmesan cheese
- 1 tsp dried basil • Salt and black pepper, to taste
- Fresh basil leaves, torn (for garnish)

Preparation instructions:
1. In a bowl, combine fresh spinach leaves, ricotta cheese, beaten egg, salt, and black pepper.
2. In the crockpot, layer a small amount of crushed tomatoes, followed by a layer of cooked lasagna noodles.
3. Spread a portion of the spinach and ricotta mixture over the noodles.
4. Repeat the layers until all Ingredients are used, finishing with a layer of crushed tomatoes on top.
5. Pour vegetable broth around the edges of the lasagna.
6. Cover and cook on low heat for 4 hours or until the lasagna is cooked through and the flavours meld together.
7. During the last 10 minutes of cooking, sprinkle shredded mozzarella and grated Parmesan cheese on top.
8. Garnish with torn fresh basil leaves before serving.

Crockpot Ratatouille

Serves: 4 Prep time: 15 minutes / Cook time: 4 hours

Ingredients:
- 1 large aubergine (about 400g), diced
- 2 medium courgettes (about 300g), sliced
- 1 large red pepper (about 200g), diced
- 1 large yellow pepper (about 200g), diced
- 1 large onion (about 150g), chopped
- 2 cloves garlic, minced • 500g ripe tomatoes, diced
- 2 tbsp tomato paste • 2 tbsp olive oil
- 1 tsp dried thyme • 1 tsp dried basil
- Salt and black pepper, to taste
- Fresh basil leaves, chopped (for garnish)

Preparation instructions:
1. In the crockpot, combine diced aubergine, sliced courgettes, diced red pepper, diced yellow pepper, chopped onion, minced garlic, diced tomatoes, and tomato paste.
2. Drizzle olive oil over the vegetables and add dried thyme, dried basil, salt, and black pepper.
3. Stir well to combine all Ingredients.
4. Cover and cook on low heat for 4 hours or until the vegetables are tender and the flavours meld together.
5. Taste and adjust seasoning, if necessary.
6. Garnish with chopped fresh basil leaves before serving.

Slow Cooker Mushroom Risotto

Serves: 4 Prep time: 10 minutes / Cook time: 2 hours

Ingredients:
- 300g Arborio rice
- 500g mixed mushrooms (such as button, cremini, and

shiitake), sliced
- 1 onion, finely chopped • 2 cloves garlic, minced
- 1 litre vegetable broth • 60ml white wine
- 60g grated Parmesan cheese
- 2 tbsp butter
- Salt and black pepper, to taste
- Fresh parsley, chopped (for garnish)

Preparation instructions:

1. In the crockpot, combine Arborio rice, sliced mixed mushrooms, finely chopped onion, minced garlic, vegetable broth, and white wine.
2. Stir well to combine all Ingredients.
3. Cover and cook on low heat for 2 hours or until the rice is creamy and cooked through.
4. Stir in grated Parmesan cheese and butter until melted and creamy.
5. Season with salt and black pepper to taste.
6. Garnish with chopped fresh parsley before serving.

Crockpot Butternut Squash Soup

Serves: 4 Prep time: 15 minutes / Cook time: 4 hours

Ingredients:

- 600g butternut squash, peeled, seeded, and diced
- 1 large onion, chopped
- 2 cloves garlic, minced
- 1 carrot, peeled and chopped
- 1 apple, peeled, cored, and chopped
- 1 litre vegetable broth
- 1 tsp ground cumin
- 1/2 tsp ground coriander
- Salt and black pepper, to taste
- 120ml coconut milk
- Fresh chives, chopped (for garnish)

Preparation instructions:

1. In the crockpot, combine diced butternut squash, chopped onion, minced garlic, chopped carrot, chopped apple, vegetable broth, ground cumin, ground coriander, salt, and black pepper.
2. Stir well to combine all Ingredients.
3. Cover and cook on low heat for 4 hours or until the vegetables are tender.
4. Use an immersion blender to puree the soup until smooth.
5. Stir in coconut milk and adjust seasoning if necessary.
6. Garnish with chopped fresh chives before serving.

Slow Cooker Vegetarian Chilli

Serves: 4 Prep time: 15 minutes / Cook time: 4 hours

Ingredients:

- 400g canned black beans, drained and rinsed
- 400g canned kidney beans, drained and rinsed
- 1 large onion, chopped • 2 cloves garlic, minced
- 1 red pepper, chopped • 1 yellow pepper, chopped
- 400g canned chopped tomatoes
- 200ml vegetable broth • 2 tsp chilli powder
- 1 tsp ground cumin • 1/2 tsp paprika
- Salt and black pepper, to taste

- Fresh coriander, chopped (for garnish)
- Sour cream and grated cheddar cheese (optional, for serving)

Preparation instructions:

1. In the crockpot, combine black beans, kidney beans, chopped onion, minced garlic, chopped red pepper, chopped yellow pepper, chopped tomatoes, vegetable broth, chilli powder, ground cumin, paprika, salt, and black pepper.
2. Stir well to combine all Ingredients.
3. Cover and cook on low heat for 4 hours to allow the flavours to meld together.
4. Taste and adjust seasoning, if necessary.
5. Garnish with chopped fresh coriander before serving. Serve hot, and optionally, top with a dollop of sour cream and a sprinkle of grated cheddar cheese.

Crockpot Aubergine Parmesan

Serves: 4 Prep time: 20 minutes / Cook time: 3 hours

Ingredients:

- 1 large aubergine (about 600g), thinly sliced
- 500ml marinara sauce
- 200g shredded mozzarella cheese
- 100g grated Parmesan cheese
- 1 tsp dried basil
- 1 tsp dried oregano
- Salt and black pepper, to taste
- Fresh basil leaves (for garnish)

Preparation instructions:

1. In the crockpot, layer half of the aubergine slices, overlapping them slightly.
2. Spread half of the marinara sauce over the aubergine.
3. Sprinkle half of the shredded mozzarella and grated Parmesan over the sauce.
4. Sprinkle half of the dried basil and dried oregano over the cheese.
5. Repeat the layers with the remaining aubergine, marinara sauce, mozzarella, Parmesan, dried basil, and dried oregano.
6. Cover and cook on low heat for 3 hours or until the aubergine is tender and the cheese is melted and bubbly.
7. Season with salt and black pepper to taste.
8. Garnish with fresh basil leaves before serving.

Slow Cooker Chickpea Curry

Serves: 4 Prep time: 15 minutes / Cook time: 4 hours

Ingredients:

- 2 cans (400g each) chickpeas, drained and rinsed
- 1 large onion, chopped
- 2 cloves garlic, minced
- 1 can (400g) coconut milk
- 400g canned chopped tomatoes
- 200ml vegetable broth
- 2 tbsp curry powder
- 1 tsp ground turmeric
- 1/2 tsp cayenne pepper (optional, for heat)
- Salt and black pepper, to taste

- Fresh coriander, chopped (for garnish)
- Cooked basmati rice (for serving)

Preparation instructions:

1. In the crockpot, combine chickpeas, chopped onion, minced garlic, coconut milk, chopped tomatoes, vegetable broth, curry powder, ground turmeric, cayenne pepper (if using), salt, and black pepper.
2. Stir well to combine all Ingredients.
3. Cover and cook on low heat for 4 hours to allow the flavours to meld together.
4. Taste and adjust seasoning, if necessary.
5. Garnish with chopped fresh coriander before serving. Serve hot over cooked basmati rice.

Crockpot Vegetable Biryani

Serves: 4 Prep time: 15 minutes / Cook time: 4 hours

Ingredients:

- 300g basmati rice, rinsed and drained
- 500ml vegetable broth
- 1 large onion, thinly sliced
- 2 cloves garlic, minced
- 1 green pepper, chopped
- 1 red pepper, chopped
- 200g mixed vegetables (such as carrots, peas, and beans), chopped
- 2 tbsp biryani masala powder
- 1/2 tsp ground turmeric
- 1/2 tsp ground cumin
- Salt and black pepper, to taste
- Fresh coriander, chopped (for garnish)
- 60ml vegetable oil

Preparation instructions:

1. In the crockpot, layer half of the rice, followed by half of the sliced onion, minced garlic, chopped green pepper, chopped red pepper, and mixed vegetables.
2. Sprinkle half of the biryani masala powder, ground turmeric, ground cumin, salt, and black pepper over the vegetables.
3. Repeat the layers with the remaining rice, onion, garlic, peppers, mixed vegetables, biryani masala powder, ground turmeric, ground cumin, salt, and black pepper.
4. Pour vegetable broth evenly over the layers.
5. Drizzle vegetable oil on top.
6. Cover and cook on low heat for 4 hours or until the rice is cooked and the vegetables are tender.
7. Gently fluff the biryani with a fork before serving. Garnish with chopped fresh coriander.

Slow Cooker Spinach and Feta Stuffed Peppers

Serves: 4 Prep time: 20 minutes / Cook time: 3 hours

Ingredients:

- 4 large peppers (any colour), halved and seeds removed
- 200g fresh spinach, chopped
- 150g feta cheese, crumbled
- 1 small onion, finely chopped
- 2 cloves garlic, minced
- 200g canned chopped tomatoes

- 1 tsp dried oregano
- Salt and black pepper, to taste
- Fresh parsley, chopped (for garnish)

Preparation instructions:

1. In a bowl, combine chopped spinach, crumbled feta cheese, finely chopped onion, minced garlic, chopped tomatoes, dried oregano, salt, and black pepper.
2. Stuff each pepper half with the spinach and feta mixture.
3. Place the stuffed peppers in the crockpot.
4. Cover and cook on low heat for 3 hours or until the peppers are tender.
5. Garnish with chopped fresh parsley before serving.

Crockpot Cauliflower Cheese

Serves: 4 Prep time: 15 minutes / Cook time: 3 hours

Ingredients:

- 1 large cauliflower, cut into florets
- 300ml whole milk   • 200g shredded cheddar cheese
- 50g grated Parmesan cheese
- 2 tbsp plain flour   • 2 tbsp butter
- 1/2 tsp mustard powder
- Salt and black pepper, to taste
- Fresh chives, chopped (for garnish)

Preparation instructions:

1. In a saucepan, melt butter over medium heat. Stir in plain flour and mustard powder to create a roux.
2. Gradually whisk in the milk, stirring constantly until the sauce thickens.
3. Remove the saucepan from the heat and stir in shredded cheddar cheese and grated Parmesan cheese until smooth. Season with salt and black pepper to taste.
4. In the crockpot, layer cauliflower florets and cheese sauce, repeating the layers until all Ingredients are used.
5. Cover and cook on low heat for 3 hours or until the cauliflower is tender and the cheese is bubbly.
6. Garnish with chopped fresh chives before serving.

Slow Cooker Tomato Basil Soup

Serves: 4 Prep time: 10 minutes / Cook time: 4 hours

Ingredients:

- 800g ripe tomatoes, chopped
- 1 onion, finely chopped   • 2 cloves garlic, minced
- 500ml vegetable stock
- 400g canned chopped tomatoes
- 1 tbsp tomato paste   • 1 tsp dried basil
- Salt and black pepper, to taste
- 60ml double cream
- Fresh basil leaves, for garnish

Preparation instructions:

1. In the crockpot, combine fresh chopped tomatoes, finely chopped onion, minced garlic, vegetable stock, canned chopped tomatoes, tomato paste, dried basil, salt, and black pepper.
2. Cover and cook on low heat for 4 hours, allowing the flavours to meld together.

3. Use an immersion blender to blend the soup until smooth.
4. Stir in double cream, adjusting the seasoning if necessary.
5. Ladle the soup into bowls and garnish with fresh basil leaves before serving.

Crockpot Sweet Potato and Chickpea Curry

Serves: 4 Prep time: 15 minutes / Cook time: 6 hours

Ingredients:
- 500g sweet potatoes, peeled and diced
- 400g canned chickpeas, drained and rinsed
- 1 onion, finely chopped • 2 cloves garlic, minced
- 400ml coconut milk • 400ml vegetable stock
- 2 tbsp curry powder • 1 tsp ground turmeric
- Salt and black pepper, to taste
- Fresh coriander, chopped (for garnish)

Preparation instructions:
1. In the crockpot, combine diced sweet potatoes, drained chickpeas, finely chopped onion, minced garlic, coconut milk, vegetable stock, curry powder, ground turmeric, salt, and black pepper.
2. Stir well to combine all the Ingredients.
3. Cover and cook on low heat for 6 hours, allowing the flavours to meld together and the sweet potatoes to become tender.
4. Adjust the seasoning if necessary before serving.
5. Garnish with chopped fresh coriander.

Slow Cooker Vegetable Lasagna

Serves: 4 Prep time: 20 minutes / Cook time: 4 hours

Ingredients:
- 250g lasagna noodles, uncooked
- 400g ricotta cheese
- 200g shredded mozzarella cheese
- 500ml vegetable sauce (store-bought or homemade)
- 1 courgette, thinly sliced
- 1 red pepper, thinly sliced
- 1 yellow pepper, thinly sliced
- 1 onion, thinly sliced
- 1 tsp dried oregano
- Salt and black pepper, to taste
- Fresh parsley, chopped (for garnish)

Preparation instructions:
1. In a bowl, combine ricotta cheese, half of the shredded mozzarella cheese, dried oregano, salt, and black pepper.
2. In the crockpot, layer uncooked lasagna noodles, followed by a layer of vegetable sauce, a layer of courgette slices, red pepper slices, yellow pepper slices, and onion slices.
3. Spread a portion of the ricotta mixture over the vegetables.
4. Repeat the layers until all Ingredients are used, finishing with a layer of vegetable sauce on top.
5. Cover and cook on low heat for 4 hours or until the lasagna noodles are cooked through and the vegetables are tender.
6. Sprinkle the remaining mozzarella cheese over the top and cover until melted.
7. Garnish with chopped fresh parsley before serving.

Crockpot Lentil Curry

Serves: 4 Prep time: 10 minutes / Cook time: 6 hours

Ingredients:
- 250g dried red lentils, rinsed and drained
- 1 onion, finely chopped • 2 cloves garlic, minced
- 400ml canned coconut milk
- 400ml vegetable stock
- 400g canned chopped tomatoes
- 1 tbsp curry powder • 1 tsp ground turmeric
- 1 tsp ground cumin
- Salt and black pepper, to taste
- Fresh coriander, chopped (for garnish)

Preparation instructions:
1. In the crockpot, combine red lentils, finely chopped onion, minced garlic, canned coconut milk, vegetable stock, canned chopped tomatoes, curry powder, ground turmeric, ground cumin, salt, and black pepper.
2. Stir well to combine all the Ingredients.
3. Cover and cook on low heat for 6 hours, allowing the lentils to become tender and absorb the flavours.
4. Adjust the seasoning if necessary before serving.
5. Garnish with chopped fresh coriander.

Slow Cooker Mushroom and Barley Risotto

Serves: 4 Prep time: 10 minutes / Cook time: 4 hours

Ingredients:
- 200g pearl barley, rinsed and drained
- 500g mushrooms, sliced
- 1 onion, finely chopped
- 2 cloves garlic, minced
- 1 litre vegetable stock
- 60ml white wine (optional)
- 50g grated Parmesan cheese
- Salt and black pepper, to taste
- Fresh parsley, chopped (for garnish)

Preparation instructions:
1. In the crockpot, combine rinsed pearl barley, sliced mushrooms, finely chopped onion, minced garlic, vegetable stock, and white wine (if using).
2. Stir well to combine all the Ingredients.
3. Cover and cook on low heat for 4 hours, allowing the barley to become tender and absorb the flavours. Stir occasionally.
4. Stir in grated Parmesan cheese, salt, and black pepper. Adjust the seasoning if necessary.
5. Garnish with chopped fresh parsley before serving.

Crockpot Mediterranean Vegetable Stew

Serves: 4 Prep time: 15 minutes / Cook time: 6 hours

Ingredients:
- 2 aubergines, diced • 2 courgettes, diced
- 2 red peppers, diced • 1 onion, finely chopped
- 2 cloves garlic, minced • 400ml canned chopped tomatoes
- 60ml olive oil • 1 tsp dried oregano

- Salt and black pepper, to taste
- Fresh basil leaves, torn (for garnish)

Preparation instructions:

1. In the crockpot, combine diced aubergines, courgettes, red peppers, finely chopped onion, minced garlic, canned chopped tomatoes, olive oil, dried oregano, salt, and black pepper.
2. Stir well to combine all the Ingredients.
3. Cover and cook on low heat for 6 hours, allowing the vegetables to become tender and infused with the Mediterranean flavours.
4. Adjust the seasoning if necessary before serving.
5. Garnish with torn fresh basil leaves.

Slow Cooker Stuffed Mushrooms

Serves: 4 Prep time: 15 minutes / Cook time: 2 hours

Ingredients:

- 12 large mushrooms, cleaned and stems removed
- 100g cream cheese, softened
- 50g grated Parmesan cheese
- 2 cloves garlic, minced
- 1 tbsp fresh parsley, chopped
- Salt and black pepper, to taste
- Olive oil, for drizzling
- Fresh basil leaves, for garnish

Preparation instructions:

1. In a bowl, mix together softened cream cheese, grated Parmesan cheese, minced garlic, chopped fresh parsley, salt, and black pepper.
2. Stuff each mushroom cap with the cream cheese mixture.
3. Place the stuffed mushrooms in the crockpot.
4. Drizzle olive oil over the stuffed mushrooms.
5. Cover and cook on low heat for 2 hours or until the mushrooms are tender and the filling is melted and golden.
6. Garnish with fresh basil leaves before serving.

Crockpot Vegetable Paella

Serves: 4 Prep time: 15 minutes / Cook time: 3 hours

Ingredients:

- 300g paella rice
- 600ml vegetable stock
- 1 onion, finely chopped
- 2 cloves garlic, minced
- 1 red pepper, diced
- 1 yellow pepper, diced
- 150g cherry tomatoes, halved
- 100g frozen peas
- 1 tsp smoked paprika
- 1/2 tsp saffron threads (optional)
- Salt and black pepper, to taste
- Fresh parsley, chopped (for garnish)
- Lemon wedges, for serving

Preparation instructions:

1. In the crockpot, combine paella rice, vegetable stock, finely chopped onion, minced garlic, diced red pepper, diced yellow pepper, halved cherry tomatoes, frozen peas, smoked paprika, saffron threads (if using), salt, and black pepper.
2. Stir well to combine all the Ingredients.
3. Cover and cook on low heat for 3 hours or until the rice is cooked and the vegetables are tender.

4. Adjust the seasoning if necessary before serving.
5. Garnish with chopped fresh parsley and serve with lemon wedges.

Slow Cooker Spicy Vegetarian Goulash

Serves: 4 Prep time: 15 minutes / Cook time: 4 hours

Ingredients:

- 2 tbsp olive oil
- 1 onion, finely chopped
- 2 cloves garlic, minced
- 2 red peppers, diced
- 2 yellow peppers, diced
- 2 tsp smoked paprika
- 1 tsp ground cumin
- 1/2 tsp chilli powder
- 400g canned chopped tomatoes
- 400g canned kidney beans, drained and rinsed
- Salt and black pepper, to taste
- Fresh oregano, chopped (for garnish)
- Sour cream, for serving

Preparation instructions:

1. In a pan, heat olive oil over medium heat. Add finely chopped onion and minced garlic. Sauté until onion becomes translucent.
2. Transfer the sautéed onion and garlic to the crockpot.
3. Add diced red peppers, diced yellow peppers, smoked paprika, ground cumin, chilli powder, canned chopped tomatoes, and canned kidney beans to the crockpot.
4. Stir well to combine all the Ingredients.
5. Cover and cook on low heat for 4 hours, allowing the flavours to meld.
6. Adjust the seasoning if necessary before serving.
7. Garnish with chopped fresh oregano and serve with a dollop of sour cream.

Crockpot Quinoa and Vegetable Pilaf

Serves: 4 Prep time: 15 minutes / Cook time: 2 hours

Ingredients:

- 200g quinoa, rinsed and drained
- 400ml vegetable stock
- 1 onion, finely chopped
- 2 cloves garlic, minced
- 1 red pepper, diced
- 1 yellow pepper, diced
- 150g button mushrooms, sliced
- 100g frozen peas
- 1 tsp ground cumin
- 1/2 tsp turmeric powder
- Salt and black pepper, to taste
- Fresh parsley, chopped (for garnish)
- Lemon wedges, for serving

Preparation instructions:

1. In the crockpot, combine rinsed quinoa, vegetable stock, finely chopped onion, minced garlic, diced red pepper, diced yellow pepper, sliced button mushrooms, frozen peas, ground cumin, turmeric powder, salt, and black pepper.
2. Stir well to combine all the Ingredients.
3. Cover and cook on low heat for 2 hours or until the quinoa is cooked and the vegetables are tender.
4. Adjust the seasoning if necessary before serving.
5. Garnish with chopped fresh parsley and serve with lemon wedges.

Slow Cooker Thai Green Curry

Serves: 4 Prep time: 15 minutes / Cook time: 3 hours

Ingredients:

- 400ml coconut milk • 2 tbsp green curry paste
- 400g mixed vegetables (such as broccoli, carrots, and peppers), sliced
- 200g firm tofu, cubed • 1 tbsp soy sauce
- 1 tbsp brown sugar • Juice of 1 lime
- Fresh basil leaves, torn (for garnish)
- Cooked jasmine rice, for serving

Preparation instructions:

1. In the slow cooker, combine coconut milk and green curry paste. Stir well to combine.
2. Add sliced mixed vegetables and cubed firm tofu to the coconut milk mixture.
3. Add soy sauce, brown sugar, and lime juice. Stir to combine all the Ingredients.
4. Cover and cook on low heat for 3 hours or until the vegetables are tender and the flavours are well incorporated.
5. Adjust the seasoning if necessary before serving.
6. Serve the Thai green curry over cooked jasmine rice.
7. Garnish with torn fresh basil leaves.

Crockpot Spinach and Artichoke Dip

Serves: 4 Prep time: 10 minutes / Cook time: 2 hours

Ingredients:

- 200g fresh spinach, chopped
- 200g canned artichoke hearts, drained and chopped
- 200g cream cheese, softened
- 100g sour cream • 100g mayonnaise
- 1 clove garlic, minced
- 100g shredded mozzarella cheese
- 50g grated Parmesan cheese
- Salt and black pepper, to taste
- Bread slices or crackers, for serving

Preparation instructions:

1. In a bowl, combine chopped fresh spinach, chopped artichoke hearts, softened cream cheese, sour cream, mayonnaise, minced garlic, shredded mozzarella cheese, and grated Parmesan cheese.
2. Season with salt and black pepper. Mix well to combine all the Ingredients.
3. Transfer the mixture to the crockpot.
4. Cover and cook on low heat for 2 hours or until the dip is hot and bubbly.
5. Stir well before serving.
6. Serve the spinach and artichoke dip with bread slices or crackers.

Slow Cooker Potato and Leek Soup

Serves: 4 Prep time: 15 minutes / Cook time: 4 hours

Ingredients:

- 500g potatoes, peeled and diced

- 2 leeks, white and light green parts, sliced
- 1 onion, finely chopped • 2 cloves garlic, minced
- 1 litre vegetable stock • 250ml whole milk
- 60ml double cream
- Salt and black pepper, to taste
- Fresh chives, chopped (for garnish)

Preparation instructions:

1. In the slow cooker, combine diced potatoes, sliced leeks, finely chopped onion, minced garlic, and vegetable stock.
2. Cover and cook on low heat for 4 hours or until the potatoes are tender.
3. Use an immersion blender to blend the soup until smooth.
4. Stir in whole milk and double cream. Season with salt and black pepper. Cook for an additional 30 minutes.
5. Adjust the seasoning if necessary before serving.
6. Garnish with chopped fresh chives before serving.

Crockpot Vegetarian Enchiladas

Serves: 4 Prep time: 20 minutes / Cook time: 3 hours

Ingredients:

- 8 corn tortillas
- 400g black beans, cooked and drained
- 200g sweetcorn kernels • 1 red pepper, diced
- 1 green pepper, diced • 1 onion, finely chopped
- 400g enchilada sauce
- 200g shredded cheddar cheese
- Fresh oregano, chopped (for garnish)
- Sour cream, for serving

Preparation instructions:

1. In a bowl, mix together black beans, sweetcorn kernels, diced red pepper, diced green pepper, and finely chopped onion.
2. Warm the corn tortillas slightly in a dry skillet to make them pliable.
3. Spoon a portion of the bean and vegetable mixture onto each tortilla, roll them up, and place them seam side down in the crockpot.
4. Pour enchilada sauce over the rolled tortillas in the crockpot.
5. Sprinkle shredded cheddar cheese over the top.
6. Cover and cook on low heat for 3 hours or until the enchiladas are hot and bubbly.
7. Garnish with chopped fresh oregano.
8. Serve with a dollop of sour cream.

Slow Cooker Vegetable Korma

Serves: 4 Prep time: 15 minutes / Cook time: 4 hours

Ingredients:

- 500g mixed vegetables (such as cauliflower, carrots, and peas), chopped
- 1 onion, finely chopped • 2 cloves garlic, minced
- 400ml coconut milk • 150g plain yoghurt
- 50g almond meal • 2 tbsp korma paste
- 1 tsp ground turmeric • 1 tsp ground cumin
- Salt and black pepper, to taste
- Fresh coriander, chopped (for garnish)
- Cooked basmati rice, for serving

Preparation instructions:

1. In the slow cooker, combine chopped mixed vegetables, finely chopped onion, minced garlic, coconut milk, plain yoghurt, almond meal, korma paste, ground turmeric, ground cumin, salt, and black pepper.
2. Stir well to combine all the Ingredients.
3. Cover and cook on low heat for 4 hours or until the vegetables are tender and the flavours are well incorporated.
4. Adjust the seasoning if necessary before serving.
5. Garnish with chopped fresh coriander.
6. Serve the vegetable korma over cooked basmati rice.

Crockpot Lentil and Mushroom Casserole

Serves: 4 Prep time: 15 minutes / Cook time: 4 hours

Ingredients:

- 200g dried green lentils, rinsed and drained
- 250g mushrooms, sliced
- 1 onion, finely chopped
- 2 cloves garlic, minced
- 400ml vegetable broth
- 200ml coconut milk
- 2 tbsp tomato paste
- 1 tsp ground cumin
- 1 tsp ground coriander
- 1/2 tsp smoked paprika
- Salt and black pepper, to taste
- Fresh parsley, chopped (for garnish)
- Cooked rice or crusty bread, for serving

Preparation instructions:

1. In the crockpot, combine dried green lentils, sliced mushrooms, finely chopped onion, minced garlic, vegetable broth, coconut milk, tomato paste, ground cumin, ground coriander, smoked paprika, salt, and black pepper.
2. Stir well to combine all the Ingredients.
3. Cover and cook on low heat for 4 hours or until the lentils are tender and the flavours are well incorporated.
4. Adjust the seasoning if necessary before serving.
5. Garnish with chopped fresh parsley.
6. Serve the lentil and mushroom casserole over cooked rice or with crusty bread.

Slow Cooker Vegetable Tikka Masala

Serves: 4 Prep time: 20 minutes / Cook time: 4 hours

Ingredients:

- 500g mixed vegetables (such as cauliflower, carrots, and peas), chopped
- 1 onion, finely chopped
- 2 cloves garlic, minced
- 400ml coconut milk
- 200g tomato passata
- 2 tbsp tikka masala paste
- 1 tsp ground turmeric
- 1 tsp ground cumin
- 1/2 tsp ground ginger

- Salt and black pepper, to taste
- Fresh oregano, chopped (for garnish)
- Cooked basmati rice, for serving

Preparation instructions:

1. In the slow cooker, combine chopped mixed vegetables, finely chopped onion, minced garlic, coconut milk, tomato passata, tikka masala paste, ground turmeric, ground cumin, ground ginger, salt, and black pepper.
2. Stir well to combine all the Ingredients.
3. Cover and cook on low heat for 4 hours or until the vegetables are tender and the flavours are well incorporated.
4. Adjust the seasoning if necessary before serving.
5. Garnish with chopped fresh oregano.
6. Serve the vegetable tikka masala over cooked basmati rice.

Crockpot Ratatouille Pasta

Serves: 4 Prep time: 15 minutes / Cook time: 4 hours

Ingredients:

- 2 courgettes, diced
- 1 aubergine, diced
- 1 red pepper, diced
- 1 yellow pepper, diced
- 1 onion, finely chopped
- 2 cloves garlic, minced
- 400g tomato passata
- 2 tbsp tomato paste
- 1 tsp dried basil
- 1 tsp dried oregano
- Salt and black pepper, to taste
- 300g penne pasta, cooked according to package instructions
- Fresh basil, chopped (for garnish)
- Grated Parmesan cheese, for serving

Preparation instructions:

1. In the crockpot, combine diced courgettes, diced aubergine, diced red pepper, diced yellow pepper, finely chopped onion, minced garlic, tomato passata, tomato paste, dried basil, dried oregano, salt, and black pepper.
2. Stir well to combine all the Ingredients.
3. Cover and cook on low heat for 4 hours or until the vegetables are tender and the flavours are well incorporated.
4. Adjust the seasoning if necessary before serving.
5. Serve the ratatouille sauce over cooked penne pasta.
6. Garnish with chopped fresh basil and grated Parmesan cheese.

Slow Cooker Vegetable and Bean Soup

Serves: 4 Prep time: 15 minutes / Cook time: 4 hours

Ingredients:

- 300g mixed vegetables (carrots, peas, green beans), chopped
- 1 can (400g) mixed beans, drained and rinsed
- 1 onion, finely chopped

- 2 cloves garlic, minced
- 1 can (400g) chopped tomatoes
- 1 litre vegetable broth
- 1 tsp dried thyme
- 1 tsp dried rosemary
- Salt and black pepper, to taste
- Fresh parsley, chopped (for garnish)
- Crusty bread, for serving

Preparation instructions:

1. In the slow cooker, combine chopped mixed vegetables, mixed beans, finely chopped onion, minced garlic, chopped tomatoes, vegetable broth, dried thyme, dried rosemary, salt, and black pepper.
2. Stir well to combine all the Ingredients.
3. Cover and cook on low heat for 4 hours or until the vegetables are tender and the flavours are well incorporated.
4. Adjust the seasoning if necessary before serving.
5. Garnish with chopped fresh parsley.
6. Serve the vegetable and bean soup with crusty bread.

Crockpot Spinach and Cheese Stuffed Mushrooms

Serves: 4 Prep time: 15 minutes / Cook time: 3 hours

Ingredients:

- 12 large mushrooms, stems removed and chopped
- 200g fresh spinach, chopped
- 100g cream cheese
- 50g shredded cheddar cheese
- 1 clove garlic, minced
- Salt and black pepper, to taste
- Fresh parsley, chopped (for garnish)

Preparation instructions:

1. In a bowl, combine chopped mushroom stems, chopped fresh spinach, cream cheese, shredded cheddar cheese, minced garlic, salt, and black pepper.
2. Mix well to form the stuffing mixture.
3. Stuff each mushroom cap with the spinach and cheese mixture.
4. Place the stuffed mushrooms in the crockpot.
5. Cover and cook on low heat for 3 hours or until the mushrooms are tender and the filling is hot and melty.
6. Garnish with chopped fresh parsley before serving.

Slow Cooker Chickpea and Spinach Stew

Serves: 4 Prep time: 15 minutes / Cook time: 4 hours

Ingredients:

- 2 cans (800g) chickpeas, drained and rinsed
- 1 onion, finely chopped
- 2 cloves garlic, minced
- 400g chopped tomatoes
- 200ml vegetable broth
- 200g fresh spinach leaves
- 1 tsp ground cumin
- 1 tsp ground coriander
- 1/2 tsp smoked paprika

- Salt and black pepper, to taste
- Fresh oregano, chopped (for garnish)
- Cooked couscous, for serving

Preparation instructions:

1. In the slow cooker, combine chickpeas, finely chopped onion, minced garlic, chopped tomatoes, vegetable broth, fresh spinach leaves, ground cumin, ground coriander, smoked paprika, salt, and black pepper.
2. Stir well to combine all the Ingredients.
3. Cover and cook on low heat for 4 hours or until the stew is hot and the flavours are well incorporated.
4. Adjust the seasoning if necessary before serving.
5. Garnish with chopped fresh oregano.
6. Serve the chickpea and spinach stew over cooked couscous.

Crockpot Aubergine and Tomato Curry

Serves: 4 Prep time: 15 minutes / Cook time: 4 hours

Ingredients:

- 1 large aubergine, diced
- 400g chopped tomatoes
- 1 onion, finely chopped
- 2 cloves garlic, minced
- 200ml coconut milk
- 1 tbsp curry powder
- 1 tsp ground turmeric
- 1/2 tsp chilli powder
- Salt and black pepper, to taste
- Fresh coriander, chopped (for garnish)
- Cooked rice, for serving

Preparation instructions:

1. In the crockpot, combine diced aubergine, chopped tomatoes, finely chopped onion, minced garlic, coconut milk, curry powder, ground turmeric, chilli powder, salt, and black pepper.
2. Stir well to combine all the Ingredients.
3. Cover and cook on low heat for 4 hours or until the aubergine is tender and the flavours are well incorporated.
4. Adjust the seasoning if necessary before serving.
5. Garnish with chopped fresh coriander.
6. Serve the aubergine and tomato curry over cooked rice.

Slow Cooker Vegetable Stir-Fry

Serves: 4 Prep time: 15 minutes / Cook time: 3 hours

Ingredients:

- 300g mixed vegetables (peppers, broccoli, carrots), sliced
- 200g mushrooms, sliced
- 1 onion, thinly sliced
- 3 cloves garlic, minced
- 60ml soy sauce
- 30ml hoisin sauce
- 30ml vegetable broth
- 1 tbsp brown sugar
- 1 tsp grated ginger
- 1 tsp sesame oil
- Sesame seeds and sliced green onions, for garnish

- Cooked rice, for serving

Preparation instructions:

1. In the slow cooker, combine sliced mixed vegetables, sliced mushrooms, thinly sliced onion, minced garlic, soy sauce, hoisin sauce, vegetable broth, brown sugar, grated ginger, and sesame oil.
2. Stir well to combine all the Ingredients.
3. Cover and cook on low heat for 3 hours or until the vegetables are tender and the flavours are well incorporated.
4. Adjust the seasoning if necessary before serving.
5. Garnish with sesame seeds and sliced green onions.
6. Serve the vegetable stir-fry over cooked rice.

Crockpot Veggie Burritos

Serves: 4 Prep time: 15 minutes / Cook time: 4 hours

Ingredients:

- 400g canned black beans, drained and rinsed
- 200g corn kernels
- 1 red pepper, diced
- 1 green pepper, diced
- 1 onion, finely chopped
- 2 cloves garlic, minced
- 1 tsp ground cumin
- 1 tsp chilli powder
- 200g cooked quinoa
- 200g shredded cheddar cheese
- 4 large whole wheat tortillas
- Fresh oregano, chopped (for garnish)
- Sour cream and salsa, for serving

Preparation instructions:

1. In the crockpot, combine black beans, corn kernels, diced red pepper, diced green pepper, finely chopped onion, minced garlic, ground cumin, and chilli powder.
2. Stir well to combine all the Ingredients.
3. Cover and cook on low heat for 4 hours or until the vegetables are tender and the flavours are well incorporated.
4. Adjust the seasoning if necessary before serving.
5. Warm the tortillas according to the package instructions.
6. Spoon the veggie mixture onto each tortilla, top with cooked quinoa and shredded cheddar cheese.
7. Garnish with chopped fresh oregano.
8. Roll up the tortillas into burritos.
9. Serve the veggie burritos with sour cream and salsa on the side.

Slow Cooker Garlic Herb Mushrooms

Serves: 4 Prep time: 10 minutes / Cook time: 2 hours

Ingredients:

- 500g button mushrooms, cleaned and halved
- 3 cloves garlic, minced
- 2 tbsp fresh parsley, chopped
- 1 tbsp fresh thyme leaves
- 60ml olive oil
- Salt and black pepper, to taste
- Fresh parsley, chopped (for garnish)
- Crusty bread, for serving

Preparation instructions:

1. In the slow cooker, combine halved button mushrooms, minced garlic, chopped fresh parsley, fresh thyme leaves, olive oil, salt, and black pepper.
2. Stir well to combine all the Ingredients.
3. Cover and cook on low heat for 2 hours or until the mushrooms are tender and infused with the flavours.
4. Adjust the seasoning if necessary before serving.
5. Garnish with chopped fresh parsley.
6. Serve the garlic herb mushrooms with crusty bread.

Crockpot Vegetable Tagine

Serves: 4 Prep time: 20 minutes / Cook time: 4 hours

Ingredients:

- 2 large carrots, peeled and sliced
- 2 large potatoes, peeled and diced
- 1 onion, finely chopped
- 2 cloves garlic, minced
- 1 can (400g) chickpeas, drained and rinsed
- 400g chopped tomatoes
- 200ml vegetable broth
- 1 tsp ground cumin
- 1 tsp ground coriander
- 1/2 tsp ground cinnamon
- Salt and black pepper, to taste
- Fresh oregano, chopped (for garnish)
- Cooked couscous, for serving

Preparation instructions:

1. In the crockpot, combine sliced carrots, diced potatoes, finely chopped onion, minced garlic, chickpeas, chopped tomatoes, vegetable broth, ground cumin, ground coriander, ground cinnamon, salt, and black pepper.
2. Stir well to combine all the Ingredients.
3. Cover and cook on low heat for 4 hours or until the vegetables are tender and the flavours are well incorporated.
4. Adjust the seasoning if necessary before serving.
5. Garnish with chopped fresh oregano.
6. Serve the vegetable tagine over cooked couscous.

Slow Cooker Sweet Potato and Lentil Stew

Serves: 4 Prep time: 15 minutes / Cook time: 4 hours

Ingredients:

- 500g sweet potatoes, peeled and diced
- 200g red lentils, rinsed and drained
- 1 onion, finely chopped
- 2 cloves garlic, minced
- 1 can (400g) chopped tomatoes
- 1.2 litres vegetable broth
- 1 tsp ground cumin
- 1 tsp ground turmeric
- Salt and black pepper, to taste
- Fresh parsley, chopped (for garnish)

Preparation instructions:

1. In the slow cooker, combine diced sweet potatoes, rinsed red lentils, finely chopped onion, minced garlic, chopped

tomatoes, vegetable broth, ground cumin, and ground turmeric.
2. Stir well to combine all the Ingredients.
3. Cover and cook on low heat for 4 hours or until the sweet potatoes and lentils are tender and the stew has thickened.
4. Adjust the seasoning with salt and black pepper if necessary before serving.
5. Garnish with chopped fresh parsley.
6. Serve the sweet potato and lentil stew hot.

Crockpot Mushroom and Brie Soup

Serves: 4 Prep time: 15 minutes / Cook time: 4 hours

Ingredients:
- 500g mushrooms, cleaned and sliced
- 1 onion, finely chopped
- 2 cloves garlic, minced
- 1 litre vegetable broth
- 200ml heavy cream
- 200g Brie cheese, rind removed and chopped
- 2 tbsp olive oil
- Salt and black pepper, to taste
- Fresh chives, chopped (for garnish)

Preparation instructions:
1. In the crockpot, combine sliced mushrooms, finely chopped onion, minced garlic, vegetable broth, and heavy cream.
2. Stir well to combine all the Ingredients.
3. Cover and cook on low heat for 4 hours or until the mushrooms are tender.
4. In a pan, heat olive oil over medium heat. Add Brie cheese and stir until melted and smooth.
5. Add the melted Brie cheese to the mushroom mixture in the crockpot.
6. Blend the soup using an immersion blender until smooth and creamy.
7. Season with salt and black pepper to taste.
8. Garnish with chopped fresh chives.
9. Serve the mushroom and Brie soup hot.

Slow Cooker Ratatouille Pizza

Serves: 4 Prep time: 20 minutes / Cook time: 4 hours

Ingredients:
- 2 large aubergines, diced
- 2 courgettes, diced
- 2 red peppers, diced
- 2 yellow peppers, diced
- 1 onion, finely chopped
- 3 cloves garlic, minced
- 1 can (400g) crushed tomatoes
- 2 tbsp tomato paste
- 1 tsp dried basil
- 1 tsp dried oregano
- Salt and black pepper, to taste
- 200g mozzarella cheese, shredded
- Fresh basil leaves, for garnish
- Pizza dough, for serving

Preparation instructions:
1. In the slow cooker, combine diced aubergines, diced courgettes, diced red peppers, diced yellow peppers, finely chopped onion, minced garlic, crushed tomatoes, tomato paste, dried basil, dried oregano, salt, and black pepper.
2. Stir well to combine all the Ingredients.
3. Cover and cook on low heat for 4 hours or until the vegetables are tender and the flavours are well incorporated.
4. Preheat the oven to the temperature recommended on the pizza dough package.
5. Roll out the pizza dough on a baking sheet.
6. Spread the ratatouille mixture evenly over the pizza dough.
7. Sprinkle shredded mozzarella cheese on top.
8. Bake in the preheated oven according to the pizza dough instructions or until the cheese is melted and bubbly.
9. Garnish with fresh basil leaves.
10. Slice and serve the ratatouille pizza hot.

Crockpot Vegetable Bolognese

Serves: 4 Prep time: 15 minutes / Cook time: 4 hours

Ingredients:
- 2 large carrots, peeled and diced
- 2 celery stalks, diced
- 1 onion, finely chopped
- 2 cloves garlic, minced
- 2 cans (800g) crushed tomatoes
- 2 tbsp tomato paste
- 1 tsp dried basil
- 1 tsp dried oregano
- Salt and black pepper, to taste
- 200g cooked spaghetti, for serving
- Fresh parsley, chopped (for garnish)
- Grated Parmesan cheese, for serving

Preparation instructions:
1. In the crockpot, combine diced carrots, diced celery, finely chopped onion, minced garlic, crushed tomatoes, tomato paste, dried basil, dried oregano, salt, and black pepper.
2. Stir well to combine all the Ingredients.
3. Cover and cook on low heat for 4 hours or until the vegetables are tender and the sauce is flavorful.
4. Adjust the seasoning with salt and black pepper if necessary before serving.
5. Serve the vegetable Bolognese sauce over cooked spaghetti.
6. Garnish with chopped fresh parsley and grated Parmesan cheese.
7. Enjoy your hearty vegetable Bolognese!

Slow Cooker Spinach and Ricotta Cannelloni

Serves: 4 Prep time: 20 minutes / Cook time: 4 hours

Ingredients:
- 250g fresh spinach, chopped
- 250g ricotta cheese
- 200g cannelloni tubes
- 500ml tomato passata
- 1 onion, finely chopped

- 2 cloves garlic, minced
- 1 tsp dried basil
- 1 tsp dried oregano
- Salt and black pepper, to taste
- 100g grated Parmesan cheese
- Fresh basil leaves, for garnish

Preparation instructions:

1. In a bowl, combine chopped fresh spinach and ricotta cheese. Season with salt and black pepper.
2. Carefully stuff the cannelloni tubes with the spinach and ricotta mixture.
3. In the slow cooker, mix together tomato passata, finely chopped onion, minced garlic, dried basil, and dried oregano. Season with salt and black pepper.
4. Arrange the stuffed cannelloni tubes in the tomato sauce in the slow cooker.
5. Cover and cook on low heat for 4 hours or until the cannelloni is tender and the flavours are well incorporated.
6. Sprinkle grated Parmesan cheese over the top.
7. Garnish with fresh basil leaves.
8. Serve the spinach and ricotta cannelloni hot.

Crockpot Vegetarian Shepherd's Pie

Serves: 4 Prep time: 20 minutes / Cook time: 4 hours

Ingredients:

- 500g potatoes, peeled and diced
- 50g butter
- 60ml milk
- 2 tbsp olive oil
- 1 onion, finely chopped
- 2 carrots, diced
- 2 celery stalks, diced
- 200g mushrooms, sliced
- 2 cloves garlic, minced
- 2 tbsp tomato paste
- 1 can (400g) lentils, drained and rinsed
- 250ml vegetable broth
- 1 tsp dried thyme
- Salt and black pepper, to taste
- Fresh parsley, chopped (for garnish)

Preparation instructions:

1. Boil the diced potatoes until tender. Drain and mash with butter and milk until smooth. Set aside.
2. In a pan, heat olive oil over medium heat. Add finely chopped onion, diced carrots, diced celery, sliced mushrooms, and minced garlic. Cook until the vegetables are tender.
3. Stir in tomato paste, lentils, vegetable broth, and dried thyme. Cook for a few minutes until the mixture thickens. Season with salt and black pepper.
4. Transfer the lentil and vegetable mixture to the crockpot.
5. Spread the mashed potatoes over the lentil mixture in the crockpot.
6. Cover and cook on low heat for 4 hours or until the shepherd's pie is heated through and bubbly.
7. Garnish with chopped fresh parsley.
8. Serve the vegetarian shepherd's pie hot.

Slow Cooker Vegetarian Fajitas

Serves: 4 Prep time: 15 minutes / Cook time: 3 hours

Ingredients:

- 2 peppers, sliced
- 1 onion, sliced
- 200g button mushrooms, sliced
- 2 cloves garlic, minced
- 1 can (400g) black beans, drained and rinsed
- 1 tsp ground cumin
- 1 tsp chilli powder
- Salt and black pepper, to taste
- 8 small flour tortillas
- Sour cream, guacamole, and salsa, for serving

Preparation instructions:

1. In the slow cooker, combine sliced peppers, sliced onion, sliced mushrooms, and minced garlic.
2. Add black beans, ground cumin, chilli powder, salt, and black pepper. Toss to combine all the Ingredients.
3. Cover and cook on low heat for 3 hours or until the vegetables are tender and flavorful.
4. Warm the flour tortillas according to the package instructions.
5. Spoon the vegetable and black bean mixture onto each tortilla.
6. Serve with sour cream, guacamole, and salsa.
7. Enjoy your vegetarian fajitas!

Crockpot Tomato and Basil Risotto

Serves: 4 Prep time: 15 minutes / Cook time: 2 hours

Ingredients:

- 300g Arborio rice
- 1 onion, finely chopped
- 2 cloves garlic, minced
- 1 can (400g) crushed tomatoes
- 1.2 litres vegetable broth
- 1 tsp dried basil
- Salt and black pepper, to taste
- 50g grated Parmesan cheese
- Fresh basil leaves, for garnish

Preparation instructions:

1. In the crockpot, combine Arborio rice, finely chopped onion, minced garlic, crushed tomatoes, vegetable broth, and dried basil.
2. Season with salt and black pepper. Stir well to combine all the Ingredients.
3. Cover and cook on low heat for 2 hours or until the risotto is creamy and the rice is tender. Stir occasionally.
4. Stir in grated Parmesan cheese until melted and well incorporated.
5. Garnish with fresh basil leaves.
6. Serve the tomato and basil risotto hot.

Slow Cooker Vegetable and Lentil Curry

Serves: 4 Prep time: 15 minutes / Cook time: 4 hours

Ingredients:

- 200g red lentils, rinsed and drained
- 1 onion, finely chopped

- 2 cloves garlic, minced
- 1 can (400g) chickpeas, drained and rinsed
- 400g mixed vegetables (such as carrots, potatoes, and peas), diced
- 1 can (400g) coconut milk
- 500ml vegetable broth
- 2 tbsp curry powder
- 1 tsp ground turmeric
- Salt and black pepper, to taste
- Fresh coriander leaves, for garnish
- Cooked basmati rice, for serving

Preparation instructions:

1. In the slow cooker, combine red lentils, finely chopped onion, minced garlic, chickpeas, mixed vegetables, coconut milk, vegetable broth, curry powder, and ground turmeric.
2. Season with salt and black pepper. Stir well to combine all the Ingredients.
3. Cover and cook on low heat for 4 hours or until the lentils and vegetables are tender and the flavours are well blended.
4. Serve the vegetable and lentil curry over cooked basmati rice.
5. Garnish with fresh coriander leaves.
6. Enjoy your delicious and hearty vegetable and lentil curry!

Crockpot Spinach and Cheese Pasta

Serves: 4 Prep time: 10 minutes / Cook time: 2 hours

Ingredients:

- 300g penne pasta
- 250g ricotta cheese
- 500ml tomato passata
- 2 cloves garlic, minced
- 1 tsp dried basil
- 1/2 tsp dried oregano
- Salt and black pepper, to taste
- Grated Parmesan cheese, for serving
- 200g fresh spinach leaves
- 100g shredded mozzarella cheese

Preparation instructions:

1. Cook the penne pasta according to the package instructions. Drain and set aside.
2. In the crockpot, combine fresh spinach leaves, ricotta cheese, shredded mozzarella cheese, tomato passata, minced garlic, dried basil, and dried oregano.
3. Season with salt and black pepper. Mix well to combine all the Ingredients.
4. Add the cooked penne pasta to the crockpot and toss to coat the pasta with the sauce and cheese mixture.
5. Cover and cook on low heat for 2 hours or until the pasta is heated through and the cheese is melted and bubbly.
6. Serve the spinach and cheese pasta hot, sprinkled with grated Parmesan cheese.
7. Enjoy your creamy and flavorful pasta dish!

Slow Cooker Vegetarian Pho

Serves: 4 Prep time: 15 minutes / Cook time: 4 hours

Ingredients:

- 200g rice noodles
- 2 cloves garlic, minced
- 1 thumb-sized piece of ginger, sliced
- 1 cinnamon stick
- 4 cups vegetable broth
- 1 tbsp hoisin sauce
- 200g tofu, cubed
- Fresh basil leaves, bean sprouts, lime wedges, and sliced chilli, for serving
- 1 onion, sliced
- 2 star anise
- 2 tbsp soy sauce
- 1 tbsp brown sugar

Preparation instructions:

1. Cook the rice noodles according to the package instructions. Drain and set aside.
2. In the slow cooker, combine sliced onion, minced garlic, sliced ginger, cinnamon stick, star anise, vegetable broth, soy sauce, hoisin sauce, and brown sugar.
3. Cover and cook on low heat for 4 hours to allow the flavours to meld together.
4. About 30 minutes before serving, add the cubed tofu to the slow cooker and continue cooking.
5. To serve, divide the cooked rice noodles among bowls and ladle the hot broth and tofu over the noodles.
6. Garnish with fresh basil leaves, bean sprouts, lime wedges, and sliced chilli.
7. Enjoy your comforting and aromatic vegetarian pho!

Crockpot Roasted Vegetable Soup

Serves: 4 Prep time: 15 minutes / Cook time: 4 hours

Ingredients:

- 2 large carrots, peeled and diced
- 2 parsnips, peeled and diced
- 1 large sweet potato, peeled and diced
- 1 red pepper, diced
- 1 yellow pepper, diced
- 1 onion, chopped
- 2 cloves garlic, minced
- 1 can (400g) chopped tomatoes
- 1.2 litres vegetable broth
- 1 tsp dried thyme
- Salt and black pepper, to taste
- Fresh parsley, chopped, for garnish

Preparation instructions:

1. In the crockpot, combine diced carrots, diced parsnips, diced sweet potato, diced red pepper, diced yellow pepper, chopped onion, minced garlic, chopped tomatoes, vegetable broth, dried thyme, salt, and black pepper.
2. Stir well to combine all the Ingredients.
3. Cover and cook on low heat for 4 hours or until the vegetables are tender and the flavours are well blended.
4. Use an immersion blender to blend the soup until smooth and creamy.
5. Adjust the seasoning if necessary.
6. Ladle the roasted vegetable soup into bowls.
7. Garnish with chopped fresh parsley.
8. Enjoy your flavorful and nutritious vegetable soup!

Chapter 6: Sides & Appetiser Recipes

Slow Cooker Garlic Bread

Serves: 4 Prep time: 5 minutes / Cook time: 2 hours

Ingredients:
- 4 slices of bread
- 60g unsalted butter, melted
- 2 cloves garlic, minced
- 1 tbsp fresh parsley, finely chopped
- Salt and black pepper, to taste

Preparation instructions:
1. In a small bowl, mix melted unsalted butter, minced garlic, fresh parsley, salt, and black pepper.
2. Spread the garlic butter mixture evenly over one side of each bread slice.
3. Stack the bread slices and wrap them in foil.
4. Place the wrapped bread in the slow cooker.
5. Cover and cook on low heat for 2 hours or until the bread is warm and infused with the garlic butter flavour.
6. Serve the slow cooker garlic bread hot with your favourite dishes.
7. Enjoy the deliciously aromatic and buttery garlic bread!

Crockpot Spinach and Artichoke Dip

Serves: 4 Prep time: 10 minutes / Cook time: 2 hours

Ingredients:
- 200g fresh spinach, chopped
- 1 can (400g) artichoke hearts, drained and chopped
- 150g cream cheese, softened
- 100g sour cream
- 100g shredded mozzarella cheese
- 50g grated Parmesan cheese
- 2 cloves garlic, minced
- 1/2 tsp onion powder
- Salt and black pepper, to taste
- Tortilla chips or bread slices, for serving

Preparation instructions:
1. In the crockpot, combine chopped fresh spinach, chopped artichoke hearts, softened cream cheese, sour cream, shredded mozzarella cheese, grated Parmesan cheese, minced garlic, onion powder, salt, and black pepper.
2. Stir well to combine all the Ingredients.
3. Cover and cook on low heat for 2 hours or until the dip is hot and bubbly, and the cheeses are melted and blended.
4. Stir the dip before serving to ensure a smooth texture.
5. Serve the spinach and artichoke dip hot with tortilla chips or bread slices.
6. Enjoy the creamy and cheesy goodness of this dip!

Slow Cooker Stuffed Mushrooms

Serves: 4 Prep time: 15 minutes / Cook time: 2 hours

Ingredients:
- 12 large mushrooms, stems removed and finely chopped
- 50g breadcrumbs
- 50g shredded mozzarella cheese
- 2 cloves garlic, minced
- 1 tbsp fresh parsley, finely chopped
- 2 tbsp olive oil
- Salt and black pepper, to taste

Preparation instructions:
1. In a bowl, combine finely chopped mushroom stems, breadcrumbs, shredded mozzarella cheese, minced garlic, fresh parsley, olive oil, salt, and black pepper.
2. Stuff each mushroom cap with the mixture, pressing gently to pack the filling.
3. Place the stuffed mushrooms in the slow cooker.
4. Cover and cook on low heat for 2 hours or until the mushrooms are tender and the filling is golden brown and crispy.
5. Serve the slow cooker stuffed mushrooms hot, garnished with additional fresh parsley if desired.
6. Enjoy these flavorful and savoury stuffed mushrooms!

Crockpot Mozzarella Sticks

Serves: 4 Prep time: 10 minutes / Cook time: 1.5 hours

Ingredients:
- 200g mozzarella cheese sticks, cut into halves
- 100g breadcrumbs
- 2 eggs, beaten
- 1/2 tsp dried oregano
- 1/2 tsp garlic powder
- 1/2 tsp paprika
- Cooking spray

Preparation instructions:
1. In a small bowl, combine breadcrumbs, dried oregano, garlic powder, and paprika.
2. Dip each mozzarella stick half into the beaten eggs and then coat with the breadcrumb mixture, pressing gently to adhere.
3. Place the coated mozzarella sticks in the slow cooker, making sure they are not touching each other.
4. Lightly spray the mozzarella sticks with cooking spray.
5. Cover and cook on low heat for 1.5 hours or until the mozzarella sticks are crispy and golden brown.
6. Carefully remove the mozzarella sticks from the slow cooker and let them cool for a few minutes before serving.
7. Serve the crockpot mozzarella sticks hot with your favourite dipping sauce.
8. Enjoy these delightful and cheesy snacks!

Slow Cooker Meatballs in Tomato Sauce

Serves: 4 Prep time: 15 minutes / Cook time: 4 hours

Ingredients:
- 400g lean ground beef
- 1/4 cup breadcrumbs
- 1/4 cup grated Parmesan cheese
- 1 egg, beaten
- 1/2 tsp garlic powder
- 1/2 tsp dried oregano
- Salt and black pepper, to taste

- 800g canned crushed tomatoes
- 1 tbsp tomato paste
- 1/2 tsp dried basil
- 1/2 tsp dried thyme
- 1/2 tsp sugar
- Fresh basil leaves, for garnish
- Cooked spaghetti or pasta, for serving

Preparation instructions:
1. In a bowl, combine ground beef, breadcrumbs, grated Parmesan cheese, beaten egg, garlic powder, dried oregano, salt, and black pepper. Mix until well combined.
2. Shape the mixture into small meatballs, about 1 inch in diameter.
3. In the crockpot, mix crushed tomatoes, tomato paste, dried basil, dried thyme, sugar, salt, and black pepper.
4. Gently place the meatballs into the sauce mixture in the slow cooker.
5. Cover and cook on low heat for 4 hours or until the meatballs are cooked through and the sauce is flavorful.
6. Stir the sauce occasionally to coat the meatballs evenly.
7. Serve the meatballs and tomato sauce over cooked spaghetti or pasta.
8. Garnish with fresh basil leaves before serving.
9. Enjoy this classic Italian dish prepared with ease in your slow cooker!

Crockpot Sweet and Spicy Nuts

Serves: 4 Prep time: 10 minutes / Cook time: 2 hours

Ingredients:
- 200g mixed nuts (such as almonds, cashews, and pecans)
- 2 tbsp honey
- 1/2 tsp chilli powder
- 1/2 tsp paprika
- 1/2 tsp salt
- 1/4 tsp cayenne pepper (adjust to taste)
- Cooking spray

Preparation instructions:
1. In a bowl, combine mixed nuts, honey, chilli powder, paprika, salt, and cayenne pepper. Toss to coat the nuts evenly.
2. Lightly spray the inside of the crockpot with cooking spray.
3. Place the coated nuts in the crockpot, spreading them out into an even layer.
4. Cover and cook on low heat for 2 hours, stirring occasionally, until the nuts are toasted and the coating is caramelised.
5. Spread the nuts on a parchment paper-lined tray to cool completely.
6. Once cooled, break apart any clusters.
7. Serve the sweet and spicy nuts as a snack or appetiser.
8. Enjoy the delightful combination of sweet and heat in this crunchy treat!

Slow Cooker Cheese Fondue

Serves: 4 Prep time: 10 minutes / Cook time: 1.5 hours

Ingredients:
- 200g Swiss cheese, grated
- 200g Gruyère cheese, grated
- 240ml dry white wine
- 1 garlic clove, halved
- 1 tbsp lemon juice
- 1/2 tsp Dijon mustard
- 1/4 tsp nutmeg
- Salt and black pepper, to taste
- Assorted dipping foods (such as bread cubes, vegetables, and sausages), for serving

Preparation instructions:
1. Rub the inside of the crockpot with the halved garlic clove.
2. Pour the white wine and lemon juice into the crockpot and heat on high until hot but not boiling.
3. Gradually add the grated Swiss cheese and Gruyère cheese, stirring constantly until melted and smooth.
4. Stir in Dijon mustard and nutmeg. Season with salt and black pepper to taste.
5. Reduce the heat to low and keep the fondue warm and smooth.
6. Serve the cheese fondue in the crockpot, accompanied by assorted dipping foods.
7. Enjoy a cosy and delicious fondue experience right at home!

Crockpot Bruschetta

Serves: 4 Prep time: 15 minutes / Cook time: 2 hours

Ingredients:
- 400g fresh tomatoes, diced
- 1/4 red onion, finely chopped
- 2 cloves garlic, minced
- 2 tbsp fresh basil, chopped
- 1 tbsp balsamic vinegar
- 2 tbsp extra virgin olive oil
- Salt and black pepper, to taste
- 1 baguette, sliced and toasted

Preparation instructions:
1. In a bowl, combine diced tomatoes, red onion, minced garlic, fresh basil, balsamic vinegar, extra virgin olive oil, salt, and black pepper. Mix well to combine.
2. Cover and refrigerate the mixture for at least 1 hour to let the flavours meld.
3. Just before serving, spoon the bruschetta mixture onto the toasted baguette slices.
4. Arrange the bruschetta-topped baguette slices in the crockpot.
5. Cover and cook on low heat for 2 hours or until the bruschetta is warm and the bread remains crispy.
6. Serve the crockpot bruschetta immediately as a delightful appetiser.

Slow Cooker Caprese Skewers

Serves: 4 Prep time: 15 minutes / Cook time: 1.5 hours

Ingredients:
- 200g cherry tomatoes
- 200g fresh mozzarella cheese, cut into cubes
- Fresh basil leaves
- Balsamic glaze, for drizzling
- Salt and black pepper, to taste

Preparation instructions:
1. Thread cherry tomatoes, fresh mozzarella cheese cubes,

and fresh basil leaves alternately onto skewers.
2. Arrange the skewers in the crockpot in a single layer.
3. Season the skewers with salt and black pepper.
4. Cover and cook on low heat for 1.5 hours or until the mozzarella cheese is slightly melted and the tomatoes are tender.
5. Drizzle with balsamic glaze just before serving.
6. Enjoy these delightful caprese skewers as a tasty and visually appealing appetiser.

Crockpot Buffalo Cauliflower Bites

Serves: 4 Prep time: 15 minutes / Cook time: 2 hours

Ingredients:
- 400g cauliflower florets
- 60g plain flour
- 60ml milk
- 1/4 tsp garlic powder
- 1/4 tsp onion powder
- 1/2 tsp paprika
- 1/2 cup buffalo sauce
- 30g unsalted butter, melted
- Fresh parsley, chopped, for garnish
- Ranch or blue cheese dressing, for dipping

Preparation instructions:
1. In a bowl, combine plain flour, milk, garlic powder, onion powder, and paprika to create a batter.
2. Dip each cauliflower floret into the batter, coating it evenly, and place it in the crockpot.
3. In a separate bowl, mix buffalo sauce and melted unsalted butter.
4. Pour the buffalo sauce mixture over the cauliflower in the crockpot, ensuring the florets are well-coated.
5. Cover and cook on low heat for 2 hours or until the cauliflower is tender.
6. Sprinkle with chopped fresh parsley before serving.
7. Serve the buffalo cauliflower bites with ranch or blue cheese dressing for dipping.

Slow Cooker Chilli Cheese Dip

Serves: 4 Prep time: 10 minutes / Cook time: 1.5 hours

Ingredients:
- 200g cheddar cheese, grated
- 120ml milk
- 1/2 tsp chilli powder
- 1/4 tsp cayenne pepper
- 1/4 tsp garlic powder
- 1/4 tsp onion powder
- 1 can (400g) canned chilli
- Fresh chives, chopped, for garnish
- Tortilla chips, for dipping

Preparation instructions:
1. In the crockpot, combine grated cheddar cheese, milk, chilli powder, cayenne pepper, garlic powder, and onion powder. Mix well.
2. Add canned chilli to the cheese mixture, stirring until combined.
3. Cover and cook on low heat for 1.5 hours or until the dip is

hot and bubbly, stirring occasionally.
4. Garnish with chopped fresh chives just before serving.
5. Serve the chilli cheese dip warm with tortilla chips for dipping.

Crockpot Teriyaki Meatballs

Serves: 4 Prep time: 10 minutes / Cook time: 2 hours

Ingredients:
- 400g beef or pork meatballs
- 120ml teriyaki sauce
- 60ml soy sauce
- 2 tbsp honey
- 1 clove garlic, minced
- 1/2 tsp ginger, grated
- 1 tbsp cornstarch, dissolved in 60ml water
- Sesame seeds and chopped spring onions, for garnish

Preparation instructions:
1. In the crockpot, combine meatballs, teriyaki sauce, soy sauce, honey, minced garlic, and grated ginger. Mix well to coat the meatballs evenly.
2. Cover and cook on low heat for 2 hours, allowing the meatballs to absorb the flavours.
3. Stir in the dissolved cornstarch mixture to thicken the sauce. Cook for an additional 15-20 minutes until the sauce is thickened.
4. Garnish with sesame seeds and chopped spring onions before serving.
5. Serve the teriyaki meatballs hot as a delicious appetiser.

Slow Cooker Spinach and Cheese Dip

Serves: 4 Prep time: 10 minutes / Cook time: 2 hours

Ingredients:
- 200g fresh spinach, chopped
- 200g cream cheese, softened
- 200g shredded mozzarella cheese
- 60ml sour cream
- 1 clove garlic, minced
- 1/4 tsp black pepper
- 1/4 tsp paprika
- Tortilla chips or bread, for dipping

Preparation instructions:
1. In the crockpot, combine chopped fresh spinach, softened cream cheese, shredded mozzarella cheese, sour cream, minced garlic, black pepper, and paprika. Mix well to blend the Ingredients.
2. Cover and cook on low heat for 2 hours, stirring occasionally until the dip is hot and creamy.
3. Serve the spinach and cheese dip warm with tortilla chips or bread for dipping.

Crockpot Crab and Artichoke Dip

Serves: 4 Prep time: 10 minutes / Cook time: 2 hours

Ingredients:
- 200g crab meat, drained and flaked
- 200g artichoke hearts, chopped
- 200g cream cheese, softened

- 60ml mayonnaise
- 60ml sour cream
- 1 clove garlic, minced
- 1/2 tsp lemon juice
- 1/4 tsp cayenne pepper
- Salt and black pepper, to taste
- Chopped fresh parsley, for garnish
- Tortilla chips or bread, for dipping

Preparation instructions:

1. In the crockpot, combine crab meat, chopped artichoke hearts, softened cream cheese, mayonnaise, sour cream, minced garlic, lemon juice, cayenne pepper, salt, and black pepper. Mix well to combine the Ingredients.
2. Cover and cook on low heat for 2 hours, stirring occasionally until the dip is creamy and heated through.
3. Garnish with chopped fresh parsley before serving.
4. Serve the crab and artichoke dip warm with tortilla chips or bread for dipping.

Slow Cooker Mini Quiches

Serves: 4 Prep time: 15 minutes / Cook time: 2 hours

Ingredients:

- 4 large eggs
- 120ml milk
- 100g shredded cheddar cheese
- 60g cooked bacon, chopped
- 60g mushrooms, sliced
- 1/4 tsp garlic powder
- 1/4 tsp black pepper
- Fresh chives, chopped, for garnish

Preparation instructions:

1. In a bowl, whisk together eggs, milk, shredded cheddar cheese, chopped cooked bacon, sliced mushrooms, garlic powder, and black pepper.
2. Grease the muffin cups of the crockpot.
3. Pour the egg mixture into each muffin cup until it's 3/4 full.
4. Cover and cook on low heat for 2 hours or until the quiches are set and cooked through.
5. Garnish with chopped fresh chives before serving.
6. Serve the mini quiches warm as a delightful appetiser.

Crockpot Garlic Herb Mushrooms

Serves: 4 Prep time: 10 minutes / Cook time: 2 hours

Ingredients:

- 400g button mushrooms, cleaned and halved
- 60g unsalted butter, melted
- 2 cloves garlic, minced
- 1/2 tsp dried thyme
- 1/2 tsp dried rosemary
- Salt and black pepper, to taste
- Fresh parsley, chopped, for garnish

Preparation instructions:

1. In the crockpot, combine halved button mushrooms, melted unsalted butter, minced garlic, dried thyme, dried rosemary, salt, and black pepper. Mix well to coat the mushrooms evenly.
2. Cover and cook on low heat for 2 hours, stirring occasionally, until the mushrooms are tender and infused with the flavours.
3. Garnish with chopped fresh parsley before serving.
4. Serve the garlic herb mushrooms hot as a delightful side dish.

Slow Cooker BBQ Meatballs

Serves: 4 Prep time: 10 minutes / Cook time: 2 hours

Ingredients:

- 400g beef or pork meatballs
- 120ml barbecue sauce
- 60ml ketchup
- 2 tbsp brown sugar
- 1 tbsp Worcestershire sauce
- 1/2 tsp smoked paprika
- 1/4 tsp black pepper
- Chopped fresh parsley, for garnish

Preparation instructions:

1. In the crockpot, combine meatballs, barbecue sauce, ketchup, brown sugar, Worcestershire sauce, smoked paprika, and black pepper. Mix well to coat the meatballs evenly.
2. Cover and cook on low heat for 2 hours, allowing the meatballs to absorb the barbecue flavours.
3. Stir occasionally to ensure the meatballs are well-coated in the sauce.
4. Garnish with chopped fresh parsley before serving.
5. Serve the BBQ meatballs hot as a tasty appetiser or main dish.

Crockpot Baked Camembert with Cranberries

Serves: 4 Prep time: 10 minutes / Cook time: 1.5 hours

Ingredients:

- 250g Camembert cheese wheel
- 60g fresh cranberries
- 2 tbsp honey
- 1 tbsp balsamic vinegar
- Fresh thyme sprigs, for garnish
- Sliced baguette or crackers, for dipping

Preparation instructions:

1. Remove the Camembert cheese from its packaging and place it in a small heatproof dish that fits inside the crockpot.
2. In a bowl, combine fresh cranberries, honey, and balsamic vinegar. Mix well.
3. Spoon the cranberry mixture over the Camembert cheese.
4. Place the dish with the cheese and cranberries inside the crockpot.
5. Cover and cook on low heat for 1.5 hours or until the cheese is gooey and the cranberries are softened.
6. Carefully remove the dish from the crockpot (it will be hot) and garnish with fresh thyme sprigs.
7. Serve the baked Camembert with cranberries hot with sliced baguette or crackers for dipping.

Slow Cooker Chicken Wings

Serves: 4 Prep time: 10 minutes / Cook time: 3 hours

Ingredients:

- 800g chicken wings, split at joints, tips discarded
- 120ml barbecue sauce
- 60ml soy sauce
- 2 tbsp honey
- 1/2 tsp garlic powder
- 1/4 tsp black pepper
- Sesame seeds and chopped green onions, for garnish

Preparation instructions:

1. In the crockpot, combine chicken wings, barbecue sauce, soy sauce, honey, garlic powder, and black pepper. Mix well to coat the wings evenly.
2. Cover and cook on low heat for 3 hours, stirring occasionally to ensure the wings are coated in the sauce.
3. Preheat the grill to medium-high heat.
4. Transfer the wings from the crockpot to the grill and cook for 5-7 minutes per side, basting with the remaining sauce, until the wings are crispy and caramelised.
5. Garnish with sesame seeds and chopped green onions before serving.
6. Serve the chicken wings hot as a flavourful appetiser or main dish.

Crockpot Veggie Stuffed Peppers

Serves: 4 Prep time: 15 minutes / Cook time: 4 hours

Ingredients:

- 4 large peppers, any colour
- 200g cooked quinoa
- 200g mixed vegetables (such as corn, peas, and carrots), cooked
- 100g shredded cheddar cheese
- 1 can (400g) crushed tomatoes
- 1/2 tsp dried basil
- 1/2 tsp dried oregano
- Salt and black pepper, to taste
- Fresh parsley, chopped, for garnish

Preparation instructions:

1. Cut the tops off the peppers and remove the seeds and membranes.
2. In a bowl, combine cooked quinoa, mixed vegetables, shredded cheddar cheese, crushed tomatoes, dried basil, dried oregano, salt, and black pepper. Mix well.
3. Stuff each pepper with the quinoa mixture.
4. Place the stuffed peppers in the crockpot.
5. Cover and cook on low heat for 4 hours or until the peppers are tender and the filling is hot and bubbly.
6. Garnish with chopped fresh parsley before serving.
7. Serve the veggie stuffed peppers hot as a nutritious and delicious main dish.

Slow Cooker Shrimp Scampi

Serves: 4 Prep time: 10 minutes / Cook time: 2 hours

Ingredients:

- 400g large shrimp, peeled and deveined
- 3 cloves garlic, minced
- 60ml white wine
- 60ml chicken broth
- 60g unsalted butter
- 1/4 tsp red pepper flakes
- Zest and juice of 1 lemon
- Salt and black pepper, to taste
- Fresh parsley, chopped, for garnish
- Cooked linguine or spaghetti, for serving

Preparation instructions:

1. In the crockpot, combine large shrimp, minced garlic, white wine, chicken broth, unsalted butter, red pepper flakes, lemon zest, lemon juice, salt, and black pepper. Mix well.
2. Cover and cook on low heat for 2 hours, stirring occasionally, until the shrimp are cooked through and the sauce is fragrant.
3. Cook linguine or spaghetti according to package instructions.
4. Serve the shrimp scampi over cooked linguine or spaghetti.
5. Garnish with chopped fresh parsley before serving.
6. Enjoy the slow cooker shrimp scampi as a delightful seafood pasta dish.

Crockpot Chicken Satay Skewers

Serves: 4 Prep time: 15 minutes / Cook time: 3 hours

Ingredients:

- 500g boneless, skinless chicken thighs, cut into bite-sized pieces
- 60ml coconut milk
- 2 tbsp peanut butter
- 2 tbsp soy sauce
- 1 tbsp honey
- 1 clove garlic, minced
- 1/2 tsp ground cumin
- 1/4 tsp turmeric powder
- 1/4 tsp red pepper flakes
- Fresh oregano, chopped, for garnish
- Cooked rice, for serving

Preparation instructions:

1. In a bowl, combine chicken pieces, coconut milk, peanut butter, soy sauce, honey, minced garlic, ground cumin, turmeric powder, and red pepper flakes. Mix well to coat the chicken evenly.
2. Thread the marinated chicken pieces onto skewers.
3. Place the chicken skewers in the crockpot.
4. Cover and cook on low heat for 3 hours, turning the skewers occasionally, until the chicken is cooked through and tender.
5. Serve the chicken satay skewers over cooked rice.
6. Garnish with chopped fresh oregano before serving.
7. Enjoy the chicken satay skewers as a flavourful and aromatic dish.

Slow Cooker Spinach and Feta Stuffed Mushrooms

Serves: 4 Prep time: 15 minutes / Cook time: 2 hours

Ingredients:

- 12 large mushrooms, cleaned and stems removed
- 200g fresh spinach, chopped
- 100g feta cheese, crumbled
- 1/4 tsp garlic powder
- 1/4 tsp onion powder
- Salt and black pepper, to taste
- Fresh parsley, chopped, for garnish

Preparation instructions:

1. In a bowl, combine chopped fresh spinach, crumbled feta cheese, garlic powder, onion powder, salt, and black pepper. Mix well.
2. Stuff each mushroom cap with the spinach and feta mixture.
3. Place the stuffed mushrooms in the crockpot.
4. Cover and cook on low heat for 2 hours or until the mushrooms are tender and the filling is hot.
5. Garnish with chopped fresh parsley before serving.
6. Serve the spinach and feta stuffed mushrooms hot as a delightful appetiser or side dish.

Crockpot Cheesy Jalapeño Dip

Serves: 4 Prep time: 10 minutes / Cook time: 2 hours

Ingredients:

- 200g cream cheese, cubed
- 100g shredded cheddar cheese
- 60ml sour cream
- 2 jalapeño peppers, seeds removed and finely chopped
- 1 clove garlic, minced
- 1/4 tsp onion powder
- Salt and black pepper, to taste
- Fresh parsley, chopped, for garnish
- Tortilla chips, for dipping

Preparation instructions:

1. In the crockpot, combine cubed cream cheese, shredded cheddar cheese, sour cream, finely chopped jalapeño peppers, minced garlic, onion powder, salt, and black pepper. Mix well.
2. Cover and cook on low heat for 2 hours, stirring occasionally, until the cheeses are melted and the dip is smooth and creamy.
3. Garnish with chopped fresh parsley before serving.
4. Serve the cheesy jalapeño dip hot with tortilla chips for dipping.

Slow Cooker Spanakopita Triangles

Serves: 4 Prep time: 15 minutes / Cook time: 2 hours

Ingredients:

- 200g frozen spinach, thawed and drained
- 100g feta cheese, crumbled
- 1/4 tsp garlic powder
- 1/4 tsp onion powder
- Salt and black pepper, to taste
- 8 sheets filo pastry
- 60g unsalted butter, melted
- Fresh dill, chopped, for garnish

Preparation instructions:

1. In a bowl, combine thawed and drained frozen spinach, crumbled feta cheese, garlic powder, onion powder, salt, and black pepper. Mix well.
2. Lay out one sheet of filo pastry and brush it lightly with melted butter. Place another sheet on top and repeat until you have four layers.
3. Cut the filo pastry stack into squares.
4. Place a spoonful of the spinach and feta mixture in the centre of each square.
5. Fold the squares into triangles, sealing the edges with a little melted butter.
6. Arrange the spanakopita triangles in the crockpot.
7. Cover and cook on low heat for 2 hours or until the pastry is golden brown and crispy.
8. Garnish with chopped fresh dill before serving.
9. Serve the spanakopita triangles hot as a delightful appetiser.

Crockpot Artichoke and Spinach Dip

Serves: 4 Prep time: 10 minutes / Cook time: 2 hours

Ingredients:

- 200g frozen chopped spinach, thawed and drained
- 200g canned artichoke hearts, drained and chopped
- 100g cream cheese, cubed
- 60ml sour cream
- 60g grated Parmesan cheese
- 1 clove garlic, minced
- 1/4 tsp onion powder
- Salt and black pepper, to taste
- Tortilla chips or bread slices, for dipping

Preparation instructions:

1. In the crockpot, combine thawed and drained chopped spinach, chopped artichoke hearts, cubed cream cheese, sour cream, grated Parmesan cheese, minced garlic, onion powder, salt, and black pepper. Mix well.
2. Cover and cook on low heat for 2 hours, stirring occasionally, until the dip is hot and creamy.
3. Serve the artichoke and spinach dip hot with tortilla chips or bread slices for dipping.

Slow Cooker Teriyaki Chicken Wings

Serves: 4 Prep time: 10 minutes / Cook time: 2.5 hours

Ingredients:

- 500g chicken wings, split at joints, tips discarded
- 120ml soy sauce
- 60ml honey
- 2 cloves garlic, minced
- 1/2 tsp ginger, grated
- 1 tbsp cornstarch
- Sesame seeds and chopped green onions, for garnish

Preparation instructions:

1. In the crockpot, combine chicken wings, soy sauce, honey, minced garlic, and grated ginger. Mix well to coat the wings evenly.
2. Cover and cook on low heat for 2.5 hours, stirring occasionally, until the chicken wings are cooked through and tender.
3. In a small bowl, mix cornstarch with a tablespoon of water to create a slurry. Stir the slurry into the crockpot to thicken the sauce. Cook for an additional 10 minutes.
4. Garnish with sesame seeds and chopped green onions before serving.
5. Serve the teriyaki chicken wings hot as a flavourful appetiser or main dish.

Crockpot Garlic Herb Breadsticks

Serves: 4 Prep time: 10 minutes / Cook time: 2 hours

Ingredients:

- 300g all-purpose flour
- 7g instant yeast
- 1/2 tsp salt
- 1/2 tsp garlic powder
- 1/4 tsp dried oregano
- 1/4 tsp dried basil
- 200ml warm water
- 30ml olive oil
- 2 cloves garlic, minced
- Fresh parsley, chopped, for garnish
- 30g grated Parmesan cheese, for topping

Preparation instructions:

1. In a bowl, combine all-purpose flour, instant yeast, salt, garlic powder, dried oregano, and dried basil. Mix well.
2. Add warm water and olive oil to the flour mixture. Knead the dough until smooth and elastic, about 5-7 minutes.
3. Cover the dough and let it rise in a warm place for 1 hour or until it doubles in size.
4. In a small bowl, mix minced garlic with a tablespoon of olive oil.
5. Preheat the crockpot to 150°C for 5 minutes.
6. Divide the dough into 12 equal portions and roll each portion into a thin rope.
7. Dip each rope into the garlic oil mixture and arrange them in the crockpot.
8. Cover and cook on low heat for 2 hours or until the breadsticks are cooked through and golden brown.
9. Sprinkle with chopped fresh parsley and grated Parmesan cheese before serving.
10. Serve the garlic herb breadsticks warm as a delightful accompaniment.

Slow Cooker Bruschetta Chicken

Serves: 4 Prep time: 10 minutes / Cook time: 4 hours

Ingredients:

- 4 boneless, skinless chicken breasts
- Salt and black pepper, to taste
- 400g cherry tomatoes, halved
- 2 cloves garlic, minced
- 30ml balsamic vinegar
- 60ml olive oil
- 1/4 tsp dried basil
- 1/4 tsp dried oregano
- 100g mozzarella cheese, sliced
- Fresh basil leaves, for garnish

Preparation instructions:

1. Season chicken breasts with salt and black pepper, then place them in the crockpot.
2. In a bowl, combine cherry tomatoes, minced garlic, balsamic vinegar, olive oil, dried basil, and dried oregano. Mix well.
3. Pour the tomato mixture over the chicken breasts.
4. Cover and cook on low heat for 4 hours or until the chicken is cooked through and tender.
5. During the last 10 minutes of cooking, place mozzarella cheese slices on top of each chicken breast to melt.
6. Garnish with fresh basil leaves before serving.
7. Serve the bruschetta chicken hot, accompanied by your favourite sides.

Crockpot Baked Brie with Cranberries

Serves: 4 Prep time: 5 minutes / Cook time: 1.5 hours

Ingredients:

- 250g wheel of Brie cheese
- 100g dried cranberries
- 60ml honey
- 30ml water
- 1/4 tsp dried rosemary
- Crackers or bread slices, for serving

Preparation instructions:

1. Place the Brie cheese in the crockpot.
2. In a small bowl, combine dried cranberries, honey, water, and dried rosemary. Mix well.
3. Pour the cranberry mixture over the Brie cheese.
4. Cover and cook on low heat for 1.5 hours or until the Brie cheese is soft and gooey.
5. Serve the baked Brie with cranberries warm, accompanied by crackers or bread slices.

Slow Cooker Pigs in Blankets

Serves: 4 Prep time: 10 minutes / Cook time: 2 hours

Ingredients:

- 8 pork sausages
- 8 rashers streaky bacon
- 60ml maple syrup
- 1/4 tsp black pepper
- Toothpicks, for securing

Preparation instructions:

1. Preheat the crockpot to 150°C for 5 minutes.
2. Wrap each pork sausage with a rasher of streaky bacon and secure with toothpicks.
3. Place the pigs in blankets in the crockpot.
4. Drizzle maple syrup over the top and sprinkle with black

pepper.

5. Cover and cook on low heat for 2 hours or until the sausages are cooked through and the bacon is crispy.
6. Remove toothpicks before serving.
7. Serve the pigs in blankets hot as a delightful appetiser or snack.

Crockpot Veggie Spring Rolls

Serves: 4 Prep time: 15 minutes / Cook time: 2 hours

Ingredients:
- 200g bean sprouts
- 150g carrots, julienned
- 150g cabbage, finely shredded
- 100g mushrooms, thinly sliced
- 1 red pepper, thinly sliced
- 2 spring onions, chopped
- 50g bamboo shoots, thinly sliced
- 2 cloves garlic, minced
- 30ml soy sauce
- 15ml hoisin sauce
- 10ml sesame oil
- 1/4 tsp black pepper
- 16 spring roll wrappers
- 30ml vegetable oil, for brushing

Preparation instructions:
1. In a crockpot, combine bean sprouts, carrots, cabbage, mushrooms, red pepper, spring onions, bamboo shoots, and minced garlic.
2. In a small bowl, mix soy sauce, hoisin sauce, sesame oil, and black pepper. Pour the sauce over the vegetable mixture and stir well.
3. Cover and cook on low heat for 2 hours or until the vegetables are tender and cooked through.
4. Preheat the crockpot to 180°C for 5 minutes.
5. Place a spoonful of the vegetable mixture onto a spring roll wrapper. Fold the sides and roll up tightly. Seal the edges with a bit of water.
6. Brush the spring rolls with vegetable oil and arrange them in the crockpot.
7. Cook for an additional 20-30 minutes or until the spring rolls are crispy and golden brown.
8. Serve the veggie spring rolls hot with your favourite dipping sauce.

Slow Cooker Stuffed Grape Leaves

Serves: 4 Prep time: 20 minutes / Cook time: 4 hours

Ingredients:
- 200g grape leaves, rinsed and drained
- 150g rice, washed and drained
- 1 onion, finely chopped
- 2 tomatoes, finely chopped
- 1/4 cup fresh parsley, chopped
- 1/4 cup fresh mint, chopped
- 2 cloves garlic, minced
- 30ml olive oil
- 15ml lemon juice

- 1/4 tsp black pepper
- 1/4 tsp ground cinnamon
- 300ml vegetable broth

Preparation instructions:
1. In a bowl, combine rice, onion, tomatoes, parsley, mint, garlic, olive oil, lemon juice, black pepper, and ground cinnamon. Mix well.
2. Place a grape leaf flat on a working surface. Put a spoonful of the rice mixture in the centre of the leaf. Fold the sides and roll up tightly.
3. Repeat with the remaining grape leaves and rice mixture.
4. Arrange the stuffed grape leaves in the crockpot.
5. Pour vegetable broth over the stuffed grape leaves.
6. Cover and cook on low heat for 4 hours or until the grape leaves are tender.
7. Serve the stuffed grape leaves warm, accompanied by yoghurt or tzatziki sauce.

Crockpot Mini Samosas

Serves: 4 Prep time: 25 minutes / Cook time: 3 hours

Ingredients:
- 200g potatoes, peeled and diced
- 100g peas
- 1 onion, finely chopped
- 2 cloves garlic, minced
- 1 tsp ground cumin
- 1/2 tsp ground coriander
- 1/2 tsp turmeric powder
- 1/4 tsp red chilli powder
- Salt, to taste
- 16 samosa wrappers (spring roll pastry sheets)
- 30ml vegetable oil, for brushing

Preparation instructions:
1. Boil diced potatoes and peas until tender. Drain and set aside.
2. In a pan, heat a bit of oil and sauté chopped onion until golden brown. Add minced garlic and cook until fragrant.
3. Add ground cumin, ground coriander, turmeric powder, red chilli powder, and salt. Stir well.
4. Add boiled potatoes and peas to the spice mixture. Mix thoroughly and cook for a few minutes. Remove from heat and let it cool.
5. Preheat the crockpot to 160°C for 5 minutes.
6. Cut samosa wrappers into halves to form triangles.
7. Place a spoonful of the potato mixture in the centre of each triangle. Fold into a samosa shape, sealing the edges with water.
8. Brush the samosas with vegetable oil and arrange them in the crockpot.
9. Cover and cook for 2-3 hours or until the samosas are crispy and golden brown.
10. Serve the mini samosas hot with your favourite chutney or sauce.

Slow Cooker Crispy Chickpeas

Serves: 4 Prep time: 10 minutes / Cook time: 2 hours

Ingredients:

- 400g canned chickpeas, drained and rinsed
- 30ml olive oil
- 1 tsp ground cumin
- 1/2 tsp smoked paprika
- 1/4 tsp cayenne pepper
- Salt and black pepper, to taste

Preparation instructions:

1. In a bowl, combine chickpeas, olive oil, ground cumin, smoked paprika, cayenne pepper, salt, and black pepper. Toss until the chickpeas are well coated.
2. Preheat the crockpot to 150°C for 5 minutes.
3. Place the chickpea mixture in the crockpot.
4. Cover and cook on low heat for 2 hours, stirring occasionally, until the chickpeas are crispy and golden brown.
5. Serve the crispy chickpeas hot as a tasty and healthy snack.

Crockpot Mushroom and Brie Soup (Served as a Dip)

Serves: 4 Prep time: 10 minutes / Cook time: 3 hours

Ingredients:

- 300g mushrooms, sliced
- 100g Brie cheese, rind removed and chopped
- 1 onion, finely chopped
- 2 cloves garlic, minced
- 500ml vegetable broth
- 250ml double cream
- 30ml olive oil
- Salt and black pepper, to taste
- Fresh parsley, chopped, for garnish
- Bread slices, for dipping

Preparation instructions:

1. Preheat the crockpot to 160°C for 5 minutes.
2. In a pan, heat olive oil and sauté chopped onion and minced garlic until translucent.
3. Add sliced mushrooms and cook until they release their moisture and become tender.
4. Transfer the mushroom mixture to the crockpot. Add chopped Brie cheese, vegetable broth, and double cream. Stir well.
5. Cover and cook on low heat for 3 hours, allowing the flavours to meld together.
6. Season with salt and black pepper to taste.
7. Garnish with fresh parsley and serve the creamy mushroom and Brie soup hot with bread slices for dipping.

Slow Cooker Buffalo Cauliflower Wings

Serves: 4 Prep time: 15 minutes / Cook time: 2 hours

Ingredients:

- 1 large cauliflower, cut into florets
- 100g plain flour
- 150ml unsweetened plant-based milk (such as almond or soy milk)
- 1 tsp garlic powder
- 1 tsp onion powder
- 1/2 tsp smoked paprika
- 1/2 tsp cayenne pepper
- Salt and black pepper, to taste
- 150ml buffalo sauce
- 30ml vegetable oil

Preparation instructions:

1. Preheat the crockpot to 160°C for 5 minutes.
2. In a bowl, whisk together flour, plant-based milk, garlic powder, onion powder, smoked paprika, cayenne pepper, salt, and black pepper to create a batter.
3. Dip each cauliflower floret into the batter, ensuring it's well coated, and place it in the crockpot.
4. Cover and cook on low heat for 2 hours or until the cauliflower is tender.
5. In a small saucepan, heat buffalo sauce and vegetable oil over medium heat until well combined.
6. Pour the buffalo sauce mixture over the cooked cauliflower in the crockpot. Gently stir to coat the cauliflower evenly.
7. Cover and cook for an additional 15-20 minutes until the buffalo sauce thickens and coats the cauliflower wings.
8. Serve the buffalo cauliflower wings hot, accompanied by your favourite dipping sauce.

Crockpot Spinach and Cheese Stuffed Mushrooms

Serves: 4 Prep time: 15 minutes / Cook time: 2 hours

Ingredients:

- 16 large button mushrooms, stems removed and finely chopped
- 100g fresh spinach, chopped
- 100g cream cheese
- 50g grated Parmesan cheese
- 1 clove garlic, minced
- 1/4 tsp black pepper
- 30ml olive oil
- Fresh parsley, chopped, for garnish

Preparation instructions:

1. Preheat the crockpot to 160°C for 5 minutes.
2. In a bowl, combine chopped mushroom stems, chopped spinach, cream cheese, grated Parmesan cheese, minced garlic, and black pepper. Mix well.
3. Stuff each mushroom cap with the spinach and cheese mixture.
4. Drizzle olive oil in the crockpot and place the stuffed mushrooms inside.
5. Cover and cook on low heat for 2 hours or until the mushrooms are tender and the filling is hot and bubbly.
6. Garnish with fresh parsley and serve the spinach and cheese stuffed mushrooms hot.

Slow Cooker Caramelized Onion Dip

Serves: 4 Prep time: 10 minutes / Cook time: 4 hours

Ingredients:

- 4 large onions, thinly sliced
- 30ml olive oil
- 1/2 tsp brown sugar

- 150ml sour cream
- 150ml mayonnaise
- Salt and black pepper, to taste
- Fresh chives, chopped, for garnish
- Vegetable sticks and crisps, for dipping

Preparation instructions:

1. In a pan, heat olive oil over medium heat. Add thinly sliced onions and cook until soft and golden brown, stirring occasionally.
2. Sprinkle brown sugar over the onions and continue cooking until they caramelise, about 20-25 minutes. Remove from heat and let them cool slightly.
3. In a bowl, combine caramelised onions, sour cream, mayonnaise, salt, and black pepper. Mix well.
4. Preheat the crockpot to 140°C for 5 minutes.
5. Transfer the onion mixture to the crockpot.
6. Cover and cook on low heat for 4 hours, allowing the flavours to meld together.
7. Garnish with fresh chives and serve the caramelised onion dip warm with vegetable sticks and crisps for dipping.

Crockpot Mini Caprese Skewers

Serves: 4 Prep time: 15 minutes / Cook time: 1 hour

Ingredients:

- 200g cherry tomatoes
- 200g mini mozzarella balls
- Fresh basil leaves
- 30ml balsamic glaze
- Salt and black pepper, to taste

Preparation instructions:

1. Preheat the crockpot to 160°C for 5 minutes.
2. Thread cherry tomatoes, mini mozzarella balls, and fresh basil leaves onto small skewers, creating mini Caprese skewers.
3. Place the skewers in the crockpot.
4. Drizzle balsamic glaze over the skewers and season with salt and black pepper to taste.
5. Cover and cook on low heat for 1 hour, allowing the flavours to meld together and the cheese to soften slightly.
6. Serve the warm mini Caprese skewers as a delightful appetiser.

Slow Cooker Onion Rings

Serves: 4 Prep time: 15 minutes / Cook time: 2 hours

Ingredients:

- 2 large onions, sliced into rings
- 150g plain flour
- 2 eggs, beaten
- 100ml milk
- 100g breadcrumbs
- 1/2 tsp paprika
- 1/2 tsp garlic powder
- 1/2 tsp onion powder
- Salt and black pepper, to taste
- Vegetable oil, for frying

Preparation instructions:

1. Preheat the crockpot to 160°C for 5 minutes.
2. In one bowl, combine plain flour, paprika, garlic powder, onion powder, salt, and black pepper.
3. In another bowl, mix beaten eggs with milk.
4. Dip each onion ring into the flour mixture, then into the egg mixture, and finally coat with breadcrumbs. Press gently to adhere the breadcrumbs to the rings.
5. Heat vegetable oil in a pan over medium heat. Fry the onion rings until golden brown and crispy. Drain excess oil on a paper towel.
6. Transfer the fried onion rings to the crockpot.
7. Cover and cook on low heat for 2 hours to keep the onion rings warm and maintain their crispiness.
8. Serve the slow-cooked onion rings hot, accompanied by your favourite dipping sauce.

Crockpot Garlic Parmesan Pretzels

Serves: 4 Prep time: 15 minutes / Cook time: 1 hour

Ingredients:

- 200g pretzel bites
- 60g unsalted butter, melted
- 2 cloves garlic, minced
- 30g grated Parmesan cheese
- 1/2 tsp dried parsley flakes
- Salt, to taste

Preparation instructions:

1. Preheat the crockpot to 160°C for 5 minutes.
2. In a bowl, combine melted butter and minced garlic.
3. Place pretzel bites in the crockpot and drizzle the garlic butter mixture over them, tossing gently to coat evenly.
4. Sprinkle grated Parmesan cheese, dried parsley flakes, and salt over the pretzel bites. Toss again to combine.
5. Cover and cook on low heat for 1 hour, allowing the flavours to meld together.
6. Serve the warm and flavorful garlic Parmesan pretzels as a tasty snack or appetiser.

Slow Cooker Stuffed Peppers

Serves: 4 Prep time: 15 minutes / Cook time: 4 hours

Ingredients:

- 4 large peppers, any colour
- 200g cooked rice
- 400g lean minced beef
- 1 can (400g) chopped tomatoes
- 1 onion, finely chopped
- 2 cloves garlic, minced
- 1 tsp dried oregano
- 1 tsp dried basil
- Salt and black pepper, to taste
- 100g shredded cheddar cheese

Preparation instructions:

1. Cut the tops off the peppers and remove the seeds and membranes.
2. In a bowl, combine cooked rice, minced beef, chopped

tomatoes, onion, garlic, dried oregano, dried basil, salt, and black pepper.

3. Stuff the peppers with the rice and beef mixture, packing it tightly.
4. Place the stuffed peppers in the crock pot.
5. Cover and cook on low heat for 4 hours or until the peppers are tender and the filling is cooked through.
6. In the last 30 minutes of cooking, sprinkle shredded cheddar cheese over the stuffed peppers and cover to melt the cheese.
7. Serve the hot and cheesy stuffed peppers with your favourite side dishes.

Crockpot Cheese Straws

Serves: 4 Prep time: 15 minutes / Cook time: 2 hours

Ingredients:

- 200g plain flour
- 100g cold unsalted butter, cubed
- 200g grated cheddar cheese
- 1/2 tsp salt
- 1/4 tsp cayenne pepper
- 1/4 tsp smoked paprika
- 60ml milk

Preparation instructions:

1. In a food processor, combine plain flour, cold cubed butter, grated cheddar cheese, salt, cayenne pepper, and smoked paprika. Pulse until the mixture resembles breadcrumbs.
2. Add milk and process until the dough comes together.
3. Roll out the dough on a floured surface to 1/4-inch thickness.
4. Cut the dough into thin strips or straws.
5. Place the cheese straws in the crockpot, arranging them in a single layer.
6. Cover and cook on low heat for 2 hours or until the cheese straws are crisp and golden.
7. Let the cheese straws cool slightly before serving as a delightful snack or appetiser.

Slow Cooker Potato Skins

Serves: 4 Prep time: 15 minutes / Cook time: 4 hours

Ingredients:

- 4 large baking potatoes
- 100g shredded cheddar cheese
- 4 slices cooked bacon, crumbled
- 2 green onions, chopped
- 60ml sour cream
- Salt and black pepper, to taste

Preparation instructions:

1. Scrub the potatoes and pierce them with a fork. Rub the skins with olive oil and sprinkle with salt.
2. Place the potatoes in the crockpot and cook on low heat for 4 hours or until the potatoes are tender.
3. Preheat the oven to 220°C. Cut the potatoes in half lengthwise and scoop out the flesh, leaving a thin layer attached to the skin.

4. Place the potato skins on a baking sheet. Fill each skin with shredded cheddar cheese and crumbled bacon.
5. Bake in the oven for about 10 minutes or until the cheese is melted and bubbly.
6. Remove from the oven and sprinkle with chopped green onions. Serve with a dollop of sour cream on top.

Crockpot Sweet Potato Fritters

Serves: 4 Prep time: 15 minutes / Cook time: 3 hours

Ingredients:

- 2 large sweet potatoes, peeled and grated
- 1 small onion, finely chopped
- 2 cloves garlic, minced
- 2 eggs, beaten
- 60g plain flour
- 1 tsp baking powder
- 1/2 tsp ground cumin
- 1/2 tsp ground coriander
- Salt and black pepper, to taste
- Vegetable oil, for frying

Preparation instructions:

1. In a large bowl, combine grated sweet potatoes, chopped onion, minced garlic, beaten eggs, plain flour, baking powder, ground cumin, ground coriander, salt, and black pepper. Mix well.
2. Heat a small amount of vegetable oil in a pan over medium heat.
3. Scoop spoonfuls of the sweet potato mixture and drop them into the hot oil, flattening slightly with the back of the spoon.
4. Fry the fritters in batches until golden brown and crispy, about 3-4 minutes per side.
5. Transfer the fried fritters to the crockpot to keep them warm and crisp.
6. Serve the hot and crispy sweet potato fritters as a tasty side dish or appetiser, accompanied by your favourite dipping sauce.

Slow Cooker Mini Vegetable Pies

Serves: 4 Prep time: 15 minutes / Cook time: 4 hours

Ingredients:

- 300g mixed vegetables (carrots, peas, corn), cooked and chopped
- 1 small onion, finely chopped
- 1 clove garlic, minced
- 200g potatoes, peeled, boiled, and mashed
- 60g cheddar cheese, grated
- 1 tbsp olive oil
- 1/2 tsp dried thyme
- Salt and black pepper, to taste
- 250g ready-made shortcrust pastry, rolled out and cut into circles

Preparation instructions:

1. In a pan, heat olive oil over medium heat. Add chopped onion and minced garlic, sauté until translucent.

2. Add the mixed vegetables to the pan, season with dried thyme, salt, and black pepper. Cook for a few minutes until heated through. Remove from heat and let it cool.
3. Preheat the slow cooker on low. Grease the muffin cups in the slow cooker.
4. Line the muffin cups with the rolled-out shortcrust pastry circles, ensuring they cover the bottom and sides.
5. Spoon the vegetable mixture into each pastry-lined cup.
6. Top each mini pie with a layer of mashed potatoes and sprinkle grated cheddar cheese on top.
7. Cover and cook on low for 4 hours or until the pastry is golden brown and the filling is hot and bubbling.
8. Carefully remove the mini vegetable pies from the slow cooker and let them cool for a few minutes before serving.

Crockpot Mushroom and Thyme Stuffed Mushrooms

Serves: 4 Prep time: 15 minutes / Cook time: 3 hours

Ingredients:
- 12 large mushrooms, stems removed and finely chopped
- 1 small onion, finely chopped
- 1 clove garlic, minced
- 50g breadcrumbs
- 50g cheddar cheese, grated
- 1 tbsp fresh thyme leaves
- Salt and black pepper, to taste
- 2 tbsp olive oil

Preparation instructions:
1. In a pan, heat olive oil over medium heat. Add chopped mushroom stems, onion, and minced garlic. Cook until the mushrooms release their moisture and the mixture becomes fragrant.
2. Remove the pan from heat and transfer the mushroom mixture to a bowl. Let it cool for a few minutes.
3. Add breadcrumbs, grated cheddar cheese, fresh thyme leaves, salt, and black pepper to the bowl. Mix until well combined.
4. Stuff each mushroom cap with the filling mixture, pressing gently to pack it in.
5. Arrange the stuffed mushrooms in the greased crockpot.
6. Cover and cook on low for 3 hours or until the mushrooms are tender and the filling is golden brown and crispy.
7. Carefully remove the stuffed mushrooms from the crockpot and serve them hot as a delightful appetiser or side dish.

Slow Cooker Polenta Bites

Serves: 4 Prep time: 15 minutes / Cook time: 2 hours

Ingredients:
- 200g polenta
- 800ml vegetable stock
- 50g cheddar cheese, grated
- 2 tbsp fresh parsley, chopped
- Salt and black pepper, to taste
- Olive oil, for brushing

Preparation instructions:
1. In a saucepan, bring the vegetable stock to a boil. Gradually whisk in the polenta, stirring constantly to avoid lumps. Cook according to the package instructions until thickened.
2. Remove the polenta from heat and stir in grated cheddar cheese, chopped parsley, salt, and black pepper. Let it cool slightly.
3. Grease a baking dish and spread the polenta evenly in it, smoothing the top.
4. Refrigerate the polenta for about 1 hour or until firm.
5. Preheat the slow cooker on low. Using a cookie cutter, cut out bite-sized shapes from the chilled polenta.
6. Brush the polenta bites with olive oil and arrange them in the slow cooker.
7. Cover and cook on low for 2 hours or until the polenta bites are heated through and have a slight crispness on the outside.
8. Carefully remove the polenta bites from the slow cooker and serve them hot as a tasty snack or appetiser.

Crockpot Ratatouille Stuffed Peppers

Serves: 4 Prep time: 20 minutes / Cook time: 4 hours

Ingredients:
- 4 large peppers, any colour
- 1 small aubergine, diced
- 1 courgette, diced
- 1 onion, finely chopped
- 2 cloves garlic, minced
- 400g canned chopped tomatoes
- 1 tsp dried basil
- 1 tsp dried oregano
- Salt and black pepper, to taste
- 2 tbsp olive oil
- Fresh basil leaves, for garnish

Preparation instructions:
1. Cut the tops off the peppers and remove the seeds and membranes.
2. In a pan, heat olive oil over medium heat. Add chopped onion and minced garlic, sauté until translucent.
3. Add diced aubergine and courgette to the pan, cook until slightly softened.
4. Stir in canned chopped tomatoes, dried basil, dried oregano, salt, and black pepper. Simmer for 10 minutes.
5. Preheat the slow cooker on low. Grease the peppers and place them in the crockpot.
6. Fill each pepper with the ratatouille mixture, pressing gently to pack it in.
7. Cover and cook on low for 4 hours or until the peppers are tender.
8. Carefully remove the stuffed peppers from the slow cooker and garnish with fresh basil leaves before serving.

Chapter 7: Soup & Stews

Slow Cooker Minestrone Soup

Serves: 4 Prep time: 15 minutes / Cook time: 4 hours

Ingredients:
- 400g canned cannellini beans, drained and rinsed
- 400g canned kidney beans, drained and rinsed
- 400g canned chopped tomatoes
- 200g carrots, peeled and diced
- 200g celery, diced   • 200g courgette, diced
- 1 onion, finely chopped • 2 cloves garlic, minced
- 1.5 litres vegetable broth
- 80g small pasta (such as ditalini or macaroni)
- 2 tsp dried basil   • 1 tsp dried oregano
- Salt and black pepper, to taste
- 60g grated Parmesan cheese, for serving
- Fresh basil leaves, for garnish

Preparation instructions:
1. In the slow cooker, combine cannellini beans, kidney beans, chopped tomatoes, carrots, celery, courgette, onion, and garlic.
2. Pour in the vegetable broth and add dried basil, dried oregano, salt, and black pepper. Stir well to combine.
3. Cover and cook on low for 4 hours or until the vegetables are tender.
4. In the last 30 minutes of cooking, stir in the small pasta and continue cooking until the pasta is al dente.
5. Ladle the minestrone soup into bowls. Garnish with grated Parmesan cheese and fresh basil leaves before serving.

Crockpot Chicken and Vegetable Stew

Serves: 4 Prep time: 15 minutes / Cook time: 4 hours

Ingredients:
- 600g boneless, skinless chicken thighs, diced
- 400g potatoes, peeled and diced
- 200g carrots, peeled and sliced
- 200g green beans, trimmed and cut into 2-inch pieces
- 1 onion, finely chopped • 2 cloves garlic, minced
- 1.5 litres chicken broth • 2 tbsp tomato paste
- 1 tsp dried thyme
- Salt and black pepper, to taste
- Fresh parsley, chopped, for garnish

Preparation instructions:
1. In the crockpot, combine diced chicken thighs, potatoes, carrots, green beans, onion, and garlic.
2. In a bowl, whisk together chicken broth, tomato paste, dried thyme, salt, and black pepper.
3. Pour the broth mixture over the chicken and vegetables in the slow cooker. Stir to combine.
4. Cover and cook on low for 4 hours or until the chicken is cooked through and the vegetables are tender.
5. Ladle the chicken and vegetable stew into bowls. Garnish with chopped fresh parsley before serving.

Slow Cooker Tomato Basil Soup

Serves: 4 Prep time: 10 minutes / Cook time: 4 hours

Ingredients:
- 800g canned whole tomatoes
- 1 onion, finely chopped • 2 cloves garlic, minced
- 600ml vegetable broth • 2 tbsp tomato paste
- 1 tsp dried basil   • 1/2 tsp dried oregano
- Salt and black pepper, to taste
- 120ml double cream
- Fresh basil leaves, for garnish
- Croutons, for serving

Preparation instructions:
1. In the slow cooker, combine canned whole tomatoes (with their juices), chopped onion, minced garlic, vegetable broth, tomato paste, dried basil, dried oregano, salt, and black pepper.
2. Cover and cook on low for 4 hours.
3. Use an immersion blender to blend the soup until smooth.
4. Stir in the double cream and continue cooking for another 10 minutes.
5. Ladle the tomato basil soup into bowls. Garnish with fresh basil leaves and serve with croutons.

Crockpot Beef and Ale Stew

Serves: 4 Prep time: 15 minutes / Cook time: 6 hours

Ingredients:
- 600g stewing beef, diced   • 2 tbsp vegetable oil
- 1 onion, finely chopped   • 2 cloves garlic, minced
- 200g carrots, peeled and sliced
- 200g potatoes, peeled and diced
- 330ml ale   • 500ml beef stock
- 2 tbsp tomato paste   • 1 tbsp Worcestershire sauce
- 1 tsp dried thyme   • Salt and black pepper, to taste
- Fresh parsley, chopped, for garnish

Preparation instructions:
1. Heat the vegetable oil in a pan over medium heat. Brown the diced stewing beef on all sides. Transfer the beef to the crockpot.
2. In the same pan, add the chopped onion and minced garlic. Cook until softened, then transfer to the crockpot.
3. Add carrots, potatoes, ale, beef stock, tomato paste, Worcestershire sauce, dried thyme, salt, and black pepper to the crockpot. Stir well to combine.
4. Cover and cook on low for 6 hours or until the beef is tender and the flavours are well combined.
5. Ladle the beef and ale stew into bowls. Garnish with chopped fresh parsley before serving.

Slow Cooker Lentil Soup

Serves: 4 Prep time: 15 minutes / Cook time: 6 hours

Ingredients:

- 200g dried green or brown lentils, rinsed and drained
- 1 onion, finely chopped
- 2 cloves garlic, minced
- 200g carrots, peeled and diced
- 200g celery, diced
- 1.5 litres vegetable stock
- 400g canned chopped tomatoes
- 1 tsp ground cumin
- 1/2 tsp ground turmeric
- 1/2 tsp paprika
- Salt and black pepper, to taste
- Fresh parsley, chopped, for garnish

Preparation instructions:

1. In the slow cooker, combine rinsed lentils, chopped onion, minced garlic, carrots, celery, vegetable stock, canned chopped tomatoes, ground cumin, ground turmeric, paprika, salt, and black pepper. Stir well to combine.
2. Cover and cook on low for 6 hours or until the lentils and vegetables are tender.
3. Taste and adjust the seasoning if necessary.
4. Ladle the lentil soup into bowls. Garnish with chopped fresh parsley before serving.

Crockpot Potato Leek Soup

Serves: 4 Prep time: 15 minutes / Cook time: 6 hours

Ingredients:

- 500g potatoes, peeled and diced
- 2 leeks, washed and sliced
- 1 onion, finely chopped
- 2 cloves garlic, minced
- 1.5 litres vegetable stock
- 200ml double cream
- Salt and white pepper, to taste
- Fresh chives, chopped, for garnish

Preparation instructions:

1. In the crockpot, combine diced potatoes, sliced leeks, chopped onion, minced garlic, and vegetable stock. Stir well to combine.
2. Cover and cook on low for 6 hours or until the potatoes are tender.
3. Use an immersion blender to blend the soup until smooth.
4. Stir in the double cream and season with salt and white pepper. Continue cooking for another 10 minutes.
5. Ladle the potato leek soup into bowls. Garnish with chopped fresh chives before serving.

Slow Cooker Mushroom Soup

Serves: 4 Prep time: 15 minutes / Cook time: 4 hours

Ingredients:

- 500g button mushrooms, sliced
- 1 onion, finely chopped • 2 cloves garlic, minced
- 1 litre vegetable stock • 250ml double cream
- 30g unsalted butter • 30g plain flour
- Salt and black pepper, to taste
- Fresh parsley, chopped, for garnish

Preparation instructions:

1. In a frying pan, melt the butter over medium heat. Add the chopped onion and minced garlic, sauté until softened.
2. Add sliced mushrooms and continue cooking until they release their moisture and turn golden brown.
3. Transfer the mushroom mixture to the slow cooker. Add vegetable stock, cover, and cook on low for 3 hours.
4. In a small saucepan, melt the remaining butter over medium heat. Stir in the plain flour to create a roux. Cook for 2 minutes, stirring constantly.
5. Gradually whisk in the double cream until the mixture thickens, forming a smooth sauce.
6. Add the cream mixture to the slow cooker, stirring well to combine. Cover and cook for an additional hour.
7. Season with salt and black pepper. Ladle the mushroom soup into bowls and garnish with chopped fresh parsley before serving.

Crockpot Chicken and Rice Soup

Serves: 4 Prep time: 15 minutes / Cook time: 4 hours

Ingredients:

- 500g chicken breasts, diced
- 150g carrots, peeled and sliced
- 150g celery, sliced • 1 onion, finely chopped
- 2 cloves garlic, minced • 150g long-grain rice
- 1.5 litres chicken stock • 1 bay leaf
- Salt and black pepper, to taste
- Fresh parsley, chopped, for garnish

Preparation instructions:

1. In the crockpot, combine diced chicken breasts, sliced carrots, celery, chopped onion, minced garlic, long-grain rice, chicken stock, and bay leaf. Stir well to combine.
2. Cover and cook on low for 4 hours or until the chicken is cooked through, and the rice and vegetables are tender.
3. Remove the bay leaf and discard. Season the soup with salt and black pepper to taste.
4. Ladle the chicken and rice soup into bowls. Garnish with chopped fresh parsley before serving.

Slow Cooker Moroccan Lentil Soup

Serves: 4 Prep time: 15 minutes / Cook time: 6 hours

Ingredients:

- 250g red lentils, rinsed and drained
- 1 onion, finely chopped
- 2 cloves garlic, minced
- 150g carrots, peeled and diced
- 400g canned chopped tomatoes
- 1.5 litres vegetable stock
- 1 tsp ground cumin
- 1/2 tsp ground turmeric
- 1/2 tsp paprika
- Salt and black pepper, to taste
- Fresh coriander, chopped, for garnish

Preparation instructions:

1. In the slow cooker, combine rinsed red lentils, chopped onion, minced garlic, diced carrots, canned chopped

tomatoes, vegetable stock, ground cumin, ground turmeric, and paprika. Stir well to combine.
2. Cover and cook on low for 6 hours or until the lentils and vegetables are tender.
3. Taste and adjust the seasoning with salt and black pepper.
4. Ladle the Moroccan lentil soup into bowls. Garnish with chopped fresh coriander before serving.

Crockpot Carrot and Coriander Soup

Serves: 4 Prep time: 10 minutes / Cook time: 4 hours

Ingredients:
- 500g carrots, peeled and chopped
- 1 onion, chopped
- 2 cloves garlic, minced
- 1 litre vegetable stock
- 1 tsp ground coriander
- Salt and black pepper, to taste
- 60ml double cream
- Fresh coriander leaves, chopped, for garnish

Preparation instructions:
1. In the crockpot, combine chopped carrots, chopped onion, minced garlic, vegetable stock, and ground coriander. Stir well to combine.
2. Cover and cook on low for 4 hours or until the carrots are tender.
3. Use an immersion blender to blend the soup until smooth.
4. Season with salt and black pepper to taste. Stir in the double cream and mix well.
5. Ladle the carrot and coriander soup into bowls. Garnish with chopped fresh coriander before serving.

Slow Cooker Chicken Noodle Soup

Serves: 4 Prep time: 15 minutes / Cook time: 6 hours

Ingredients:
- 500g boneless, skinless chicken thighs, diced
- 1 onion, chopped
- 2 carrots, peeled and sliced
- 2 celery stalks, sliced
- 2 cloves garlic, minced
- 2 litres chicken stock
- 150g dried egg noodles
- 1 tsp dried thyme
- Salt and black pepper, to taste
- Fresh parsley, chopped, for garnish

Preparation instructions:
1. In the slow cooker, combine diced chicken thighs, chopped onion, sliced carrots, sliced celery, minced garlic, chicken stock, dried egg noodles, and dried thyme. Stir well to combine.
2. Cover and cook on low for 6 hours or until the chicken is cooked through, and the vegetables are tender.
3. Season with salt and black pepper to taste.
4. Ladle the chicken noodle soup into bowls. Garnish with chopped fresh parsley before serving.

Crockpot Spiced Pumpkin Soup

Serves: 4 Prep time: 15 minutes / Cook time: 4 hours

Ingredients:
- 500g pumpkin, peeled and diced
- 1 onion, chopped
- 2 cloves garlic, minced
- 1 litre vegetable stock
- 1 tsp ground cinnamon
- 1/2 tsp ground nutmeg

- Salt and black pepper, to taste
- 60ml double cream
- Roasted pumpkin seeds, for garnish

Preparation instructions:
1. In the crockpot, combine diced pumpkin, chopped onion, minced garlic, vegetable stock, ground cinnamon, and ground nutmeg. Stir well to combine.
2. Cover and cook on low for 4 hours or until the pumpkin is tender.
3. Use an immersion blender to blend the soup until smooth.
4. Season with salt and black pepper to taste. Stir in the double cream and mix well.
5. Ladle the spiced pumpkin soup into bowls. Garnish with roasted pumpkin seeds before serving.

Slow Cooker Beef Stew

Serves: 4 Prep time: 15 minutes / Cook time: 6 hours

Ingredients:
- 500g beef stew meat, cubed
- 400g potatoes, peeled and diced
- 250g carrots, peeled and sliced
- 1 onion, chopped
- 2 cloves garlic, minced
- 600ml beef stock
- 2 tbsp tomato paste
- 1 tsp dried thyme
- Salt and black pepper, to taste
- 60g frozen peas
- Fresh parsley, chopped, for garnish

Preparation instructions:
1. In the slow cooker, combine cubed beef stew meat, diced potatoes, sliced carrots, chopped onion, minced garlic, beef stock, tomato paste, and dried thyme. Stir well to combine.
2. Cover and cook on low for 6 hours or until the beef is tender.
3. Season with salt and black pepper to taste. Stir in the frozen peas and cook for an additional 30 minutes.
4. Ladle the beef stew into bowls. Garnish with chopped fresh parsley before serving.

Crockpot Split Pea Soup

Serves: 4 Prep time: 15 minutes / Cook time: 6 hours

Ingredients:
- 250g dried split peas, rinsed and drained
- 1 onion, chopped
- 2 carrots, peeled and sliced
- 2 celery stalks, sliced
- 2 cloves garlic, minced
- 1.5 litres vegetable stock
- 1 bay leaf
- Salt and black pepper, to taste
- 60ml double cream
- Croutons, for garnish

Preparation instructions:
1. In the crockpot, combine dried split peas, chopped onion, sliced carrots, sliced celery, minced garlic, vegetable stock, and bay leaf. Stir well to combine.
2. Cover and cook on low for 6 hours or until the split peas are tender and the soup has thickened.
3. Remove the bay leaf and discard. Use an immersion blender to blend the soup until smooth.
4. Season with salt and black pepper to taste. Stir in the

double cream and mix well.

5. Ladle the split pea soup into bowls. Garnish with croutons before serving.

Slow Cooker Vegetable Soup

Serves: 4 Prep time: 15 minutes / Cook time: 6 hours

Ingredients:
- 500g mixed vegetables (such as carrots, potatoes, peas, corn), peeled and diced
- 1 onion, chopped   • 2 cloves garlic, minced
- 1.5 litres vegetable stock • 1 tsp dried basil
- 1/2 tsp dried oregano
- Salt and black pepper, to taste
- 60g green beans, trimmed and chopped
- Fresh parsley, chopped, for garnish

Preparation instructions:
1. In the slow cooker, combine diced mixed vegetables, chopped onion, minced garlic, vegetable stock, dried basil, and dried oregano. Stir well to combine.
2. Cover and cook on low for 6 hours or until the vegetables are tender.
3. Season with salt and black pepper to taste. Stir in the chopped green beans and cook for an additional 30 minutes.
4. Ladle the vegetable soup into bowls. Garnish with chopped fresh parsley before serving.

Crockpot Broccoli and Cheddar Soup

Serves: 4 Prep time: 15 minutes / Cook time: 4 hours

Ingredients:
- 500g broccoli, florets chopped
- 1 onion, chopped   • 2 cloves garlic, minced
- 500ml vegetable stock • 250ml double cream
- 200g shredded cheddar cheese
- Salt and black pepper, to taste
- Fresh chives, chopped, for garnish

Preparation instructions:
1. In the crockpot, combine chopped broccoli, chopped onion, minced garlic, and vegetable stock. Cook on low for 3 hours until the vegetables are tender.
2. Use an immersion blender to blend the soup until smooth.
3. Stir in double cream and shredded cheddar cheese. Cover and cook for an additional 1 hour on low until the cheese is melted and the soup is creamy.
4. Season with salt and black pepper to taste. Garnish with chopped fresh chives before serving.

Slow Cooker Lamb Stew

Serves: 4 Prep time: 20 minutes / Cook time: 6 hours

Ingredients:
- 500g lamb stew meat, cubed
- 400g potatoes, peeled and diced
- 250g carrots, peeled and sliced
- 1 onion, chopped   • 2 cloves garlic, minced
- 600ml lamb or vegetable stock

- 2 tbsp tomato paste
- 1 tsp dried rosemary
- Salt and black pepper, to taste
- Fresh parsley, chopped, for garnish

Preparation instructions:
1. In the slow cooker, combine cubed lamb stew meat, diced potatoes, sliced carrots, chopped onion, minced garlic, lamb or vegetable stock, tomato paste, and dried rosemary. Stir well to combine.
2. Cover and cook on low for 6 hours or until the lamb is tender.
3. Season with salt and black pepper to taste. Garnish with chopped fresh parsley before serving.

Crockpot Butternut Squash Soup

Serves: 4 Prep time: 15 minutes / Cook time: 4 hours

Ingredients:
- 1 butternut squash, peeled, seeded, and diced
- 1 onion, chopped   • 2 cloves garlic, minced
- 500ml vegetable stock • 250ml coconut milk
- 1 tsp curry powder
- Salt and black pepper, to taste
- Fresh oregano, chopped, for garnish

Preparation instructions:
1. In the crockpot, combine diced butternut squash, chopped onion, minced garlic, and vegetable stock. Cook on low for 3 hours or until the squash is tender.
2. Use an immersion blender to blend the soup until smooth.
3. Stir in coconut milk and curry powder. Cover and cook for an additional 1 hour on low until the soup is heated through and flavorful.
4. Season with salt and black pepper to taste. Garnish with chopped fresh oregano before serving.

Slow Cooker Irish Stew

Crockpot Spinach and Chickpea Soup
Serves: 4 Prep time: 15 minutes / Cook time: 4 hours

Ingredients:
- 200g fresh spinach, chopped
- 400g canned chickpeas, drained and rinsed
- 1 onion, finely chopped • 2 cloves garlic, minced
- 1 litre vegetable stock
- 200ml passata (sieved tomatoes)
- 1 tsp ground cumin   • 1/2 tsp paprika
- Salt and black pepper, to taste
- 30ml olive oil
- Fresh parsley, chopped, for garnish

Preparation instructions:
1. In the crockpot, combine chopped fresh spinach, drained chickpeas, finely chopped onion, minced garlic, vegetable stock, passata, ground cumin, paprika, salt, and black pepper. Stir well to combine.
2. Drizzle olive oil over the top. Cover and cook on low for 4 hours.
3. Stir the soup well before serving. Garnish with chopped fresh parsley.

Slow Cooker Cauliflower Cheese Soup

Serves: 4 Prep time: 15 minutes / Cook time: 4 hours

Ingredients:

- 1 medium cauliflower, chopped into florets
- 1 onion, chopped
- 2 cloves garlic, minced
- 500ml vegetable stock
- 200ml double cream
- 200g shredded cheddar cheese
- Salt and black pepper, to taste
- Fresh chives, chopped, for garnish

Preparation instructions:

1. In the slow cooker, combine chopped cauliflower, chopped onion, minced garlic, and vegetable stock. Cook on low for 3 hours or until the cauliflower is tender.
2. Use an immersion blender to blend the soup until smooth.
3. Stir in double cream and shredded cheddar cheese. Cover and cook for an additional 1 hour on low until the cheese is melted and the soup is creamy.
4. Season with salt and black pepper to taste. Garnish with chopped fresh chives before serving.

Crockpot Chicken and Sweetcorn Soup

Serves: 4 Prep time: 15 minutes / Cook time: 4 hours

Ingredients:

- 2 chicken breasts, cooked and shredded
- 200g sweetcorn kernels
- 1 carrot, diced
- 1 onion, chopped
- 2 cloves garlic, minced
- 1 litre chicken stock
- 60ml soy sauce
- 1 tsp ground ginger
- 2 spring onions, chopped, for garnish
- 1 red chilli, sliced, for garnish

Preparation instructions:

1. In the crockpot, combine shredded cooked chicken, sweetcorn kernels, diced carrot, chopped onion, minced garlic, chicken stock, soy sauce, and ground ginger. Stir well to combine.
2. Cover and cook on low for 4 hours.
3. Stir the soup well before serving. Garnish with chopped spring onions and sliced red chilli.

Slow Cooker Mulligatawny Soup

Serves: 4 Prep time: 15 minutes / Cook time: 6 hours

Ingredients:

- 200g red lentils, rinsed and drained
- 1 onion, finely chopped
- 2 carrots, diced
- 2 celery sticks, diced
- 1 apple, peeled, cored, and chopped
- 1 tbsp curry powder
- 1/2 tsp ground turmeric
- 1/4 tsp cayenne pepper
- 1.5 litres vegetable stock
- 400g canned chopped tomatoes
- 60ml coconut milk
- Salt and black pepper, to taste
- Fresh oregano, chopped, for garnish

Preparation instructions:

1. In the slow cooker, combine red lentils, finely chopped onion, diced carrots, diced celery sticks, chopped apple, curry powder, ground turmeric, cayenne pepper, vegetable stock, and canned chopped tomatoes. Stir well to combine.
2. Cover and cook on low for 6 hours or until the lentils and vegetables are tender.
3. Stir in coconut milk and season with salt and black pepper to taste. Cook for an additional 10 minutes.
4. Garnish with chopped fresh oregano before serving.

Crockpot Spicy Tomato Soup

Serves: 4 Prep time: 15 minutes / Cook time: 4 hours

Ingredients:

- 800g canned tomatoes
- 1 onion, chopped
- 2 cloves garlic, minced
- 1 red chilli, deseeded and chopped
- 500ml vegetable stock
- 1 tsp paprika
- 1/2 tsp cumin powder
- Salt and black pepper, to taste
- 60ml double cream
- Fresh basil leaves, torn, for garnish

Preparation instructions:

1. In the crockpot, combine canned tomatoes, chopped onion, minced garlic, chopped red chilli, vegetable stock, paprika, cumin powder, salt, and black pepper. Stir well to combine.
2. Cover and cook on low for 4 hours.
3. Use an immersion blender to blend the soup until smooth.
4. Stir in double cream and cook for an additional 10 minutes.
5. Garnish with torn fresh basil leaves before serving.

Slow Cooker Vegetable and Lentil Stew

Serves: 4 Prep time: 15 minutes / Cook time: 6 hours

Ingredients:

- 200g green lentils, rinsed and drained
- 2 carrots, diced
- 2 potatoes, peeled and diced
- 1 leek, sliced
- 2 cloves garlic, minced
- 1.5 litres vegetable stock
- 1 tsp dried thyme
- Salt and black pepper, to taste
- Fresh parsley, chopped, for garnish

Preparation instructions:

1. In the slow cooker, combine green lentils, diced carrots, diced potatoes, sliced leek, minced garlic, vegetable stock, and dried thyme. Stir well to combine.
2. Cover and cook on low for 6 hours or until the lentils and vegetables are tender.
3. Season with salt and black pepper to taste. Cook for an additional 10 minutes.
4. Garnish with chopped fresh parsley before serving.

Crockpot Thai Coconut Soup

Serves: 4 Prep time: 15 minutes / Cook time: 4 hours

Ingredients:

- 400g chicken breast, thinly sliced
- 400ml coconut milk
- 500ml chicken stock
- 200g button mushrooms, sliced
- 2 stalks lemongrass, bruised and chopped
- 3 kaffir lime leaves
- 1 red chilli, sliced

- 2 cloves garlic, minced
- 1 thumb-sized piece of ginger, grated
- 60ml fish sauce   • 30ml lime juice
- 15ml soy sauce   • 15g brown sugar
- Fresh oregano leaves, for garnish
- Cooked rice, for serving

Preparation instructions:

1. In the crockpot, combine thinly sliced chicken breast, coconut milk, chicken stock, sliced mushrooms, lemongrass, kaffir lime leaves, sliced red chilli, minced garlic, and grated ginger. Stir well to combine.
2. Cover and cook on low for 4 hours.
3. Remove lemongrass and kaffir lime leaves from the soup.
4. Stir in fish sauce, lime juice, soy sauce, and brown sugar. Cook for an additional 10 minutes.
5. Serve the soup over cooked rice, garnished with fresh oregano leaves.

Slow Cooker Chicken Curry Soup

Serves: 4 Prep time: 15 minutes / Cook time: 4 hours

Ingredients:

- 400g boneless, skinless chicken thighs, diced
- 400ml coconut milk
- 500ml chicken stock
- 1 onion, finely chopped
- 2 cloves garlic, minced
- 1 red chilli, sliced
- 1 tbsp curry powder
- 1 tsp turmeric powder
- Salt and black pepper, to taste
- 200g baby spinach leaves
- Fresh coriander leaves, for garnish
- Cooked rice or naan bread, for serving

Preparation instructions:

1. In the slow cooker, combine diced chicken thighs, coconut milk, chicken stock, finely chopped onion, minced garlic, sliced red chilli, curry powder, turmeric powder, salt, and black pepper. Stir well to combine.
2. Cover and cook on low for 4 hours.
3. Stir in baby spinach leaves and cook for an additional 10 minutes or until the spinach wilts.
4. Serve the soup over cooked rice or with naan bread, garnished with fresh coriander leaves.

Crockpot Broccoli and Stilton Soup

Serves: 4 Prep time: 15 minutes / Cook time: 4 hours

Ingredients:

- 500g broccoli florets
- 1 onion, chopped
- 2 cloves garlic, minced
- 500ml vegetable stock
- 200ml double cream
- 200g Stilton cheese, crumbled
- Salt and black pepper, to taste
- Chopped chives, for garnish

Preparation instructions:

1. In the crockpot, combine broccoli florets, chopped onion, minced garlic, and vegetable stock. Stir well to combine.
2. Cover and cook on low for 4 hours or until the broccoli is tender.
3. Use an immersion blender to blend the soup until smooth.
4. Stir in double cream and crumbled Stilton cheese. Cook for an additional 10 minutes or until the cheese melts and the soup is creamy.
5. Season with salt and black pepper to taste. Garnish with chopped chives before serving.

Slow Cooker Chickpea and Spinach Stew

Serves: 4 Prep time: 15 minutes / Cook time: 4 hours

Ingredients:

- 400g canned chickpeas, drained and rinsed
- 200g fresh spinach leaves
- 1 onion, finely chopped
- 2 cloves garlic, minced
- 400g canned chopped tomatoes
- 500ml vegetable stock
- 1 tsp ground cumin
- 1 tsp ground coriander
- 1/2 tsp smoked paprika
- Salt and black pepper, to taste
- Fresh parsley, for garnish

Preparation instructions:

1. In the slow cooker, combine chickpeas, fresh spinach leaves, finely chopped onion, minced garlic, canned chopped tomatoes, vegetable stock, ground cumin, ground coriander, smoked paprika, salt, and black pepper. Stir well to combine.
2. Cover and cook on low for 4 hours.
3. Adjust the seasoning with salt and black pepper if necessary.
4. Serve the stew hot, garnished with fresh parsley.

Crockpot Pea and Ham Soup

Serves: 4 Prep time: 15 minutes / Cook time: 4 hours

Ingredients:

- 400g frozen peas
- 200g cooked ham, diced
- 1 onion, chopped
- 2 cloves garlic, minced
- 1.2 litres vegetable stock
- 250ml double cream
- Salt and black pepper, to taste
- Fresh mint leaves, for garnish

Preparation instructions:

1. In the crockpot, combine frozen peas, diced cooked ham, chopped onion, minced garlic, and vegetable stock. Stir well to combine.
2. Cover and cook on low for 4 hours.
3. Use an immersion blender to blend the soup until smooth.
4. Stir in double cream and season with salt and black pepper.
5. Cook for an additional 10 minutes.
6. Serve the soup hot, garnished with fresh mint leaves.

Slow Cooker Moroccan Vegetable Stew

Serves: 4 Prep time: 15 minutes / Cook time: 4 hours

Ingredients:

- 2 sweet potatoes, peeled and diced
- 2 carrots, peeled and sliced
- 1 onion, chopped
- 2 cloves garlic, minced
- 400g canned chickpeas, drained and rinsed
- 400g canned chopped tomatoes
- 500ml vegetable stock
- 1 tsp ground cumin
- 1/2 tsp ground cinnamon
- 1/2 tsp ground turmeric
- Salt and black pepper, to taste
- Fresh coriander leaves, for garnish

Preparation instructions:

1. In the slow cooker, combine diced sweet potatoes, sliced carrots, chopped onion, minced garlic, chickpeas, canned chopped tomatoes, vegetable stock, ground cumin, ground cinnamon, ground turmeric, salt, and black pepper. Stir well to combine.
2. Cover and cook on low for 4 hours.
3. Adjust the seasoning with salt and black pepper if necessary.
4. Serve the stew hot, garnished with fresh coriander leaves.

Crockpot Italian Wedding Soup

Serves: 4 Prep time: 15 minutes / Cook time: 4 hours

Ingredients:

- 400g lean pork or beef meatballs, cooked and sliced
- 1 onion, finely chopped
- 2 cloves garlic, minced
- 100g acini di pepe pasta or small pasta of your choice
- 1 litre chicken broth
- 200g fresh spinach leaves, chopped
- 60g grated Parmesan cheese
- Salt and black pepper, to taste
- Fresh basil leaves, for garnish

Preparation instructions:

1. In the crockpot, combine sliced cooked meatballs, finely chopped onion, minced garlic, acini di pepe pasta, and chicken broth. Stir well to combine.
2. Cover and cook on low for 4 hours.
3. Add chopped fresh spinach leaves and grated Parmesan cheese to the soup. Stir until the spinach wilts and the cheese melts.
4. Season with salt and black pepper to taste.
5. Serve the soup hot, garnished with fresh basil leaves.

Slow Cooker Pumpkin and Sweet Potato Soup

Serves: 4 Prep time: 15 minutes / Cook time: 4 hours

Ingredients:

- 500g pumpkin, peeled and diced
- 500g sweet potatoes, peeled and diced
- 1 onion, chopped
- 2 cloves garlic, minced
- 1 litre vegetable stock
- 250ml coconut milk
- 1 tsp ground cumin
- 1/2 tsp ground ginger
- Salt and black pepper, to taste
- Fresh coriander leaves, for garnish

Preparation instructions:

1. In the slow cooker, combine diced pumpkin, diced sweet potatoes, chopped onion, minced garlic, vegetable stock, coconut milk, ground cumin, and ground ginger. Stir well to combine.
2. Cover and cook on low for 4 hours.
3. Use an immersion blender to blend the soup until smooth.
4. Season with salt and black pepper to taste.
5. Serve the soup hot, garnished with fresh coriander leaves.

Crockpot Beetroot Soup

Serves: 4 Prep time: 15 minutes / Cook time: 4 hours

Ingredients:

- 500g beetroots, peeled and diced
- 1 onion, chopped
- 2 cloves garlic, minced
- 1 litre vegetable stock
- 250ml sour cream
- 1 tbsp balsamic vinegar
- Salt and black pepper, to taste
- Fresh dill, for garnish

Preparation instructions:

1. In the crockpot, combine diced beetroots, chopped onion, minced garlic, vegetable stock, sour cream, and balsamic vinegar. Stir well to combine.
2. Cover and cook on low for 4 hours.
3. Use an immersion blender to blend the soup until smooth.
4. Season with salt and black pepper to taste.
5. Serve the soup hot, garnished with fresh dill.

Slow Cooker Chicken and Rice Stew

Serves: 4 Prep time: 15 minutes / Cook time: 4 hours

Ingredients:

- 500g boneless, skinless chicken thighs, diced
- 200g carrots, peeled and sliced
- 200g celery, sliced
- 1 onion, chopped
- 2 cloves garlic, minced
- 150g long-grain white rice
- 1 litre chicken broth
- 1 tsp dried thyme
- Salt and black pepper, to taste
- Fresh parsley, for garnish

Preparation instructions:

1. In the slow cooker, combine diced chicken thighs, sliced carrots, sliced celery, chopped onion, minced garlic, long-grain white rice, chicken broth, and dried thyme. Stir well

to combine.

2. Cover and cook on low for 4 hours.
3. Season with salt and black pepper to taste.
4. Serve the stew hot, garnished with fresh parsley.

Crockpot Spicy Lentil Soup

Serves: 4 Prep time: 15 minutes / Cook time: 6 hours

Ingredients:

- 250g dried red lentils
- 1 onion, chopped
- 2 cloves garlic, minced
- 1 can (400g) chopped tomatoes
- 1.2 litres vegetable broth
- 1 tsp ground cumin
- 1/2 tsp paprika
- 1/4 tsp cayenne pepper
- Salt and black pepper, to taste
- Fresh coriander, for garnish

Preparation instructions:

1. In the crockpot, combine dried red lentils, chopped onion, minced garlic, chopped tomatoes, vegetable broth, ground cumin, paprika, and cayenne pepper. Stir well to combine.
2. Cover and cook on low for 6 hours.
3. Use an immersion blender to blend the soup until smooth.
4. Season with salt and black pepper to taste.
5. Serve the soup hot, garnished with fresh coriander.

Slow Cooker Potato and Chive Soup

Serves: 4 Prep time: 15 minutes / Cook time: 4 hours

Ingredients:

- 500g potatoes, peeled and diced
- 1 onion, chopped
- 2 cloves garlic, minced
- 1 litre vegetable broth
- 250ml whole milk
- 2 tbsp chopped fresh chives
- Salt and black pepper, to taste
- Grated cheddar cheese, for garnish

Preparation instructions:

1. In the slow cooker, combine diced potatoes, chopped onion, minced garlic, vegetable broth, and whole milk. Stir well to combine.
2. Cover and cook on low for 4 hours.
3. Use an immersion blender to blend the soup until smooth.
4. Stir in chopped fresh chives and season with salt and black pepper to taste.
5. Serve the soup hot, garnished with grated cheddar cheese.

Crockpot Leek and Potato Soup

Serves: 4 Prep time: 15 minutes / Cook time: 4 hours

Ingredients:

- 500g potatoes, peeled and diced
- 300g leeks, washed and sliced
- 1 onion, chopped
- 2 cloves garlic, minced

- 1 litre vegetable broth
- 250ml whole milk
- Salt and black pepper, to taste
- Fresh chives, for garnish

Preparation instructions:

1. In the crockpot, combine diced potatoes, sliced leeks, chopped onion, minced garlic, vegetable broth, and whole milk. Stir well to combine.
2. Cover and cook on low for 4 hours.
3. Use an immersion blender to blend the soup until smooth.
4. Season with salt and black pepper to taste.
5. Serve the soup hot, garnished with fresh chives.

Slow Cooker Black Bean Soup

Serves: 4 Prep time: 15 minutes / Cook time: 6 hours

Ingredients:

- 400g black beans, soaked and drained
- 1 onion, chopped
- 2 cloves garlic, minced
- 1 red pepper, chopped
- 1 can (400g) chopped tomatoes
- 1.2 litres vegetable broth
- 1 tsp ground cumin
- 1/2 tsp chilli powder
- Salt and black pepper, to taste
- Fresh oregano, for garnish

Preparation instructions:

1. In the slow cooker, combine soaked black beans, chopped onion, minced garlic, chopped red pepper, chopped tomatoes, vegetable broth, ground cumin, and chilli powder. Stir well to combine.
2. Cover and cook on low for 6 hours.
3. Use an immersion blender to blend a portion of the soup for a thicker texture, if desired.
4. Season with salt and black pepper to taste.
5. Serve the soup hot, garnished with fresh oregano.

Crockpot Mediterranean Vegetable Stew

Serves: 4 Prep time: 15 minutes / Cook time: 4 hours

Ingredients:

- 2 aubergines, diced
- 2 courgettes, diced
- 2 red onions, chopped
- 2 cloves garlic, minced
- 1 can (400g) chopped tomatoes
- 1 can (400g) chickpeas, drained and rinsed
- 1 tsp dried oregano
- 1/2 tsp dried thyme
- Salt and black pepper, to taste
- Fresh parsley, for garnish

Preparation instructions:

1. In the crockpot, combine diced aubergines, diced courgettes, chopped red onions, minced garlic, chopped tomatoes, and chickpeas. Stir well to combine.
2. Season with dried oregano, dried thyme, salt, and black

pepper. Stir again to distribute the seasonings.

3. Cover and cook on low for 4 hours.

4. Serve the stew hot, garnished with fresh parsley.

Slow Cooker Chestnut Soup

Serves: 4 Prep time: 15 minutes / Cook time: 4 hours

Ingredients:

- 400g chestnuts, peeled and cooked
- 1 onion, chopped
- 2 cloves garlic, minced
- 1 celery stalk, chopped
- 1 litre vegetable broth
- 250ml whole milk
- 60ml double cream
- Salt and black pepper, to taste
- Fresh parsley, for garnish

Preparation instructions:

1. In the slow cooker, combine peeled and cooked chestnuts, chopped onion, minced garlic, chopped celery, vegetable broth, and whole milk. Stir well to combine.

2. Cover and cook on low for 4 hours.

3. Use an immersion blender to blend the soup until smooth.

4. Stir in double cream and season with salt and black pepper to taste.

5. Serve the soup hot, garnished with fresh parsley.

Crockpot Mexican Chicken Soup

Serves: 4 Prep time: 15 minutes / Cook time: 6 hours

Ingredients:

- 500g chicken breast, cooked and shredded
- 1 onion, chopped
- 2 cloves garlic, minced
- 1 red pepper, chopped
- 1 can (400g) black beans, drained and rinsed
- 1 can (400g) sweetcorn, drained
- 1 can (400g) chopped tomatoes
- 1 litre chicken broth
- 1 tsp ground cumin
- 1/2 tsp chilli powder
- Salt and black pepper, to taste
- Fresh coriander, for garnish

Preparation instructions:

1. In the crockpot, combine cooked and shredded chicken breast, chopped onion, minced garlic, chopped red pepper, black beans, sweetcorn, chopped tomatoes, chicken broth, ground cumin, and chilli powder. Stir well to combine.

2. Cover and cook on low for 6 hours.

3. Season with salt and black pepper to taste.

4. Serve the soup hot, garnished with fresh coriander.

Slow Cooker Courgette and Parmesan Soup

Serves: 4 Prep time: 15 minutes / Cook time: 4 hours

Ingredients:

- 500g courgettes, chopped
- 1 onion, chopped

- 2 cloves garlic, minced
- 1 litre vegetable broth
- 60g grated Parmesan cheese
- 250ml whole milk
- Salt and black pepper, to taste
- Fresh basil, for garnish

Preparation instructions:

1. In the slow cooker, combine chopped courgettes, chopped onion, minced garlic, vegetable broth, grated Parmesan cheese, and whole milk. Stir well to combine.

2. Cover and cook on low for 4 hours.

3. Use an immersion blender to blend the soup until smooth.

4. Season with salt and black pepper to taste.

5. Serve the soup hot, garnished with fresh basil.

Crockpot Cabbage Soup

Serves: 4 Prep time: 15 minutes / Cook time: 4 hours

Ingredients:

- 400g green cabbage, shredded
- 2 carrots, peeled and diced
- 1 onion, chopped
- 2 cloves garlic, minced
- 1 litre vegetable broth
- 250ml passata (strained tomatoes)
- 1 tsp dried thyme
- Salt and black pepper, to taste
- Fresh parsley, for garnish

Preparation instructions:

1. In the crockpot, combine shredded green cabbage, diced carrots, chopped onion, minced garlic, vegetable broth, passata, and dried thyme. Stir well to combine.

2. Cover and cook on low for 4 hours.

3. Season with salt and black pepper to taste.

4. Serve the soup hot, garnished with fresh parsley.

Slow Cooker Pea and Mint Soup

Serves: 4 Prep time: 10 minutes / Cook time: 4 hours

Ingredients:

- 400g frozen peas
- 1 onion, chopped
- 2 cloves garlic, minced
- 1 litre vegetable broth
- 60ml double cream
- 1 tbsp fresh mint leaves, chopped
- Salt and black pepper, to taste
- Croutons, for garnish

Preparation instructions:

1. In the slow cooker, combine frozen peas, chopped onion, minced garlic, and vegetable broth. Stir well to combine.

2. Cover and cook on low for 4 hours.

3. Use an immersion blender to blend the soup until smooth.

4. Stir in double cream and chopped mint leaves. Season with salt and black pepper to taste.

5. Serve the soup hot, garnished with croutons.

Crockpot Corn Chowder

Serves: 4 Prep time: 15 minutes / Cook time: 4 hours

Ingredients:

- 400g corn kernels, fresh or frozen
- 2 potatoes, peeled and diced
- 1 onion, chopped
- 2 cloves garlic, minced
- 1 litre vegetable broth
- 250ml whole milk
- 2 tbsp butter
- 2 tbsp plain flour
- Salt and black pepper, to taste
- Fresh chives, for garnish

Preparation instructions:

1. In the crockpot, combine corn kernels, diced potatoes, chopped onion, minced garlic, and vegetable broth. Stir well to combine.
2. Cover and cook on low for 4 hours.
3. In a small saucepan, melt butter over medium heat. Stir in flour and cook, stirring constantly, for 2-3 minutes until golden brown.
4. Slowly whisk in whole milk until the mixture thickens.
5. Pour the milk mixture into the crockpot and stir to combine. Season with salt and black pepper to taste.
6. Serve the chowder hot, garnished with fresh chives.

Slow Cooker Spicy Sweet Potato Soup

Serves: 4 Prep time: 15 minutes / Cook time: 4 hours

Ingredients:

- 500g sweet potatoes, peeled and diced
- 1 onion, chopped
- 2 cloves garlic, minced
- 1 litre vegetable broth
- 1 tsp ground cumin
- 1/2 tsp paprika
- 1/4 tsp cayenne pepper
- 250ml coconut milk
- Salt and black pepper, to taste
- Fresh coriander, for garnish

Preparation instructions:

1. In the slow cooker, combine diced sweet potatoes, chopped onion, minced garlic, vegetable broth, ground cumin, paprika, and cayenne pepper. Stir well to combine.
2. Cover and cook on low for 4 hours.
3. Use an immersion blender to blend the soup until smooth.
4. Stir in coconut milk and season with salt and black pepper to taste.
5. Serve the soup hot, garnished with fresh coriander.

Crockpot Creamy Mushroom Soup

Serves: 4 Prep time: 15 minutes / Cook time: 4 hours

Ingredients:

- 400g button mushrooms, sliced
- 1 onion, finely chopped
- 2 cloves garlic, minced
- 1 litre vegetable broth
- 250ml double cream
- 2 tbsp butter
- 2 tbsp plain flour
- Salt and black pepper, to taste
- Fresh parsley, for garnish

Preparation instructions:

1. In the crockpot, combine sliced mushrooms, chopped onion, minced garlic, and vegetable broth. Stir well to combine.
2. Cover and cook on low for 4 hours.
3. In a small saucepan, melt butter over medium heat. Stir in flour and cook, stirring constantly, for 2-3 minutes until golden brown.
4. Slowly whisk in double cream until the mixture thickens.
5. Pour the cream mixture into the crockpot and stir to combine. Season with salt and black pepper to taste.
6. Serve the soup hot, garnished with fresh parsley.

Slow Cooker Asparagus Soup

Serves: 4 Prep time: 15 minutes / Cook time: 4 hours

Ingredients:

- 400g asparagus, trimmed and chopped
- 1 onion, chopped
- 2 cloves garlic, minced
- 1 litre vegetable broth
- 250ml double cream
- 2 tbsp butter
- 2 tbsp plain flour
- Salt and black pepper, to taste
- Lemon zest, for garnish

Preparation instructions:

1. In the slow cooker, combine chopped asparagus, chopped onion, minced garlic, and vegetable broth. Stir well to combine.
2. Cover and cook on low for 4 hours.
3. In a small saucepan, melt butter over medium heat. Stir in flour and cook, stirring constantly, for 2-3 minutes until golden brown.
4. Slowly whisk in double cream until the mixture thickens.
5. Pour the cream mixture into the slow cooker and stir to combine. Season with salt and black pepper to taste.
6. Serve the soup hot, garnished with lemon zest.

Crockpot Turkey and Vegetable Stew

Serves: 4 Prep time: 20 minutes / Cook time: 6 hours

Ingredients:

- 400g turkey breast, diced
- 2 carrots, peeled and diced
- 2 potatoes, peeled and diced
- 1 onion, chopped
- 2 cloves garlic, minced
- 1 litre chicken broth
- 2 tbsp tomato paste
- 1 tsp dried thyme
- Salt and black pepper, to taste
- Fresh parsley, for garnish

Preparation instructions:

1. In the crockpot, combine diced turkey breast, diced carrots, diced potatoes, chopped onion, minced garlic, chicken broth, tomato paste, and dried thyme. Stir well to combine.
2. Cover and cook on low for 6 hours.
3. Season with salt and black pepper to taste.
4. Serve the stew hot, garnished with fresh parsley.

Chapter 8: Fish and Seafood

Slow Cooker Fish Stew

Serves: 4 Prep time: 15 minutes / Cook time: 4 hours

Ingredients:
- 500g mixed white fish fillets, cut into chunks
- 250g prawns, peeled and deveined
- 2 onions, finely chopped • 2 cloves garlic, minced
- 400g canned chopped tomatoes
- 500ml fish stock • 200ml double cream
- 2 tbsp olive oil • 1 tsp paprika
- Salt and black pepper, to taste
- Fresh parsley, for garnish

Preparation instructions:
1. In a pan, heat olive oil over medium heat. Add onions and garlic, cooking until softened.
2. Transfer the cooked onions and garlic to the crockpot. Add fish chunks, prawns, chopped tomatoes, fish stock, paprika, salt, and black pepper. Stir well.
3. Cover and cook on low for 4 hours.
4. Stir in double cream and let it cook for an additional 10-15 minutes.
5. Serve the fish stew hot, garnished with fresh parsley.

Crockpot Seafood Chowder

Serves: 4 Prep time: 15 minutes / Cook time: 4 hours

Ingredients:
- 300g white fish fillets, cut into chunks
- 200g smoked salmon, chopped
- 250g prawns, peeled and deveined
- 2 potatoes, peeled and diced
- 1 onion, finely chopped • 2 cloves garlic, minced
- 500ml fish stock • 200ml double cream
- 2 tbsp butter • Salt and black pepper, to taste
- Fresh dill, for garnish

Preparation instructions:
1. In a pan, melt butter over medium heat. Add onions and garlic, cooking until softened.
2. Transfer the cooked onions and garlic to the crockpot. Add fish chunks, smoked salmon, prawns, diced potatoes, fish stock, salt, and black pepper. Stir well.
3. Cover and cook on low for 4 hours.
4. Stir in double cream and let it cook for an additional 10-15 minutes.
5. Serve the seafood chowder hot, garnished with fresh dill.

Slow Cooker Salmon Curry

Serves: 4 Prep time: 15 minutes / Cook time: 3 hours

Ingredients:
- 4 salmon fillets • 1 onion, finely chopped
- 2 cloves garlic, minced• 400ml coconut milk
- 2 tbsp curry paste • 1 tbsp olive oil
- 1 tsp turmeric powder
- Salt and black pepper, to taste
- Fresh coriander, for garnish

Preparation instructions:
1. In a pan, heat olive oil over medium heat. Add onions and garlic, cooking until softened.
2. Transfer the cooked onions and garlic to the crockpot. Add curry paste, turmeric powder, coconut milk, salt, and black pepper. Stir well.
3. Add salmon fillets to the crockpot, ensuring they are submerged in the curry mixture.
4. Cover and cook on low for 3 hours.
5. Serve the salmon curry hot, garnished with fresh coriander.

Crockpot Coconut Shrimp

Serves: 4 Prep time: 15 minutes / Cook time: 2 hours

Ingredients:
- 400g large shrimp, peeled and deveined
- 200ml coconut milk • 2 cloves garlic, minced
- 1 tbsp ginger, minced • 1 tbsp soy sauce
- 1 tbsp honey • 1/2 tsp red chilli flakes
- Salt and black pepper, to taste
- Fresh coriander, for garnish

Preparation instructions:
1. In a bowl, mix coconut milk, minced garlic, ginger, soy sauce, honey, red chilli flakes, salt, and black pepper.
2. Place the peeled and deveined shrimp into the crockpot. Pour the coconut milk mixture over the shrimp, ensuring they are well-coated.
3. Cover and cook on low for 2 hours.
4. Stir well before serving, garnished with fresh coriander. Serve the coconut shrimp hot over rice or noodles.

Slow Cooker Fisherman's Pie

Serves: 4 Prep time: 20 minutes / Cook time: 4 hours

Ingredients:
- 400g mixed white fish fillets, cut into chunks
- 200g salmon fillet, cut into chunks
- 250g prawns, peeled and deveined
- 2 onions, finely chopped
- 2 cloves garlic, minced
- 500ml fish stock
- 200ml double cream
- 2 tbsp olive oil
- 2 tbsp plain flour
- Salt and black pepper, to taste
- 800g mashed potatoes, for topping
- Fresh parsley, for garnish

Preparation instructions:
1. In a pan, heat olive oil over medium heat. Add onions and garlic, cooking until softened.

2. Add plain flour to the pan, stirring to form a roux. Slowly pour in the fish stock, stirring continuously until the sauce thickens.
3. Transfer the sauce to the crockpot. Add fish chunks, salmon chunks, prawns, salt, and black pepper. Stir well.
4. Cover and cook on low for 4 hours.
5. Stir in double cream and let it cook for an additional 10 minutes.
6. Preheat the oven to 200°C. Transfer the fish mixture to a baking dish. Spread the mashed potatoes over the top.
7. Bake in the oven for 20-25 minutes or until the potato topping is golden brown.
8. Garnish with fresh parsley before serving.

Crockpot Clam Chowder

Serves: 4 Prep time: 20 minutes / Cook time: 4 hours

Ingredients:
- 500g clams, cleaned and scrubbed
- 200g bacon, chopped
- 2 onions, finely chopped
- 2 cloves garlic, minced
- 500ml fish stock
- 200ml double cream
- 3 potatoes, peeled and diced
- 2 tbsp butter
- Salt and black pepper, to taste
- Fresh chives, for garnish

Preparation instructions:
1. In a pan, cook chopped bacon until crispy. Remove excess fat and transfer the bacon to the crockpot.
2. In the same pan, melt butter over medium heat. Add onions and garlic, cooking until softened.
3. Transfer the cooked onions and garlic to the crockpot. Add diced potatoes, fish stock, salt, and black pepper. Stir well.
4. Cover and cook on low for 4 hours.
5. Stir in double cream and cleaned clams. Let it cook for an additional 10-15 minutes.
6. Garnish with fresh chives before serving.

Slow Cooker Garlic Butter Shrimp

Serves: 4 Prep time: 15 minutes / Cook time: 2 hours

Ingredients:
- 500g large shrimp, peeled and deveined
- 1/2 cup unsalted butter, melted
- 4 cloves garlic, minced
- 1/4 tsp red pepper flakes
- Salt and black pepper, to taste
- 2 tbsp fresh parsley, chopped
- 1 lemon, sliced
- Cooked rice, for serving

Preparation instructions:
1. In a bowl, mix melted butter, minced garlic, red pepper flakes, salt, and black pepper.
2. Place the peeled and deveined shrimp into the crockpot. Pour the garlic butter mixture over the shrimp, ensuring

they are well-coated.
3. Cover and cook on low for 2 hours.
4. Stir well before serving, garnished with fresh parsley and lemon slices. Serve the garlic butter shrimp over cooked rice.

Crockpot Crab Bisque

Serves: 4 Prep time: 15 minutes / Cook time: 3 hours

Ingredients:
- 500g crab meat, cooked and shredded
- 1 onion, finely chopped
- 2 cloves garlic, minced
- 500ml fish stock
- 250ml double cream
- 2 tbsp butter
- 2 tbsp plain flour
- 60ml brandy
- Salt and black pepper, to taste
- Fresh parsley, for garnish

Preparation instructions:
1. In a pan, melt butter over medium heat. Add chopped onions and minced garlic, cooking until softened.
2. Add plain flour to the pan, stirring to form a roux. Slowly pour in the fish stock, stirring continuously until the sauce thickens.
3. Transfer the sauce to the crockpot. Add crab meat, salt, and black pepper. Stir well.
4. Cover and cook on low for 3 hours.
5. Stir in double cream and brandy. Let it cook for an additional 15 minutes.
6. Garnish with fresh parsley before serving.

Slow Cooker Lemon Herb Fish

Serves: 4 Prep time: 10 minutes / Cook time: 2 hours

Ingredients:
- 500g white fish fillets (such as cod or haddock)
- 2 lemons, thinly sliced
- 4 tbsp olive oil
- 2 cloves garlic, minced
- 1 tsp dried mixed herbs (such as thyme, rosemary, and parsley)
- Salt and black pepper, to taste
- Fresh dill, for garnish

Preparation instructions:
1. Drizzle 2 tablespoons of olive oil in the bottom of the crockpot.
2. Place the fish fillets in the crockpot. Season with minced garlic, dried mixed herbs, salt, and black pepper.
3. Arrange lemon slices on top of the fish fillets.
4. Drizzle the remaining 2 tablespoons of olive oil over the lemon slices.
5. Cover and cook on low for 2 hours or until the fish is cooked through and flakes easily with a fork.
6. Garnish with fresh dill before serving.

Crockpot Seafood Paella

Serves: 4 Prep time: 20 minutes / Cook time: 3 hours

Ingredients:
- 300g arborio rice
- 500ml fish stock
- 200g prawns, peeled and deveined
- 200g mussels, cleaned and debearded
- 200g squid, cleaned and sliced into rings
- 1 onion, finely chopped
- 2 cloves garlic, minced
- 1 red pepper, diced
- 1 yellow pepper, diced
- 1 tsp smoked paprika
- 1/2 tsp saffron threads (optional)
- Salt and black pepper, to taste
- Fresh parsley, for garnish
- Lemon wedges, for serving

Preparation instructions:
1. In a bowl, mix saffron threads (if using) with a tablespoon of warm water. Let it steep.
2. In the crockpot, combine arborio rice, fish stock, chopped onions, minced garlic, diced peppers, smoked paprika, saffron mixture (if using), salt, and black pepper. Stir well.
3. Cover and cook on low for 2 hours.
4. Add prawns, mussels, and squid to the crockpot. Stir gently.
5. Cover and continue cooking on low for an additional hour or until the seafood is cooked through and the rice is tender.
6. Garnish with fresh parsley and serve with lemon wedges.

Slow Cooker Thai Fish Curry

Serves: 4 Prep time: 15 minutes / Cook time: 3 hours

Ingredients:
- 500g white fish fillets (such as cod or haddock), cut into chunks
- 400ml coconut milk
- 2 tbsp Thai red curry paste
- 1 onion, finely chopped
- 2 cloves garlic, minced
- 1 red chilli, thinly sliced (remove seeds for less heat)
- 1 tbsp fish sauce
- 1 tbsp brown sugar
- Juice of 1 lime
- Fresh coriander, for garnish
- Cooked jasmine rice, for serving

Preparation instructions:
1. In the crockpot, combine coconut milk, Thai red curry paste, chopped onions, minced garlic, sliced red chilli, fish sauce, and brown sugar. Stir well.
2. Add fish chunks to the crockpot, ensuring they are submerged in the curry mixture.
3. Cover and cook on low for 3 hours or until the fish is cooked through and tender.
4. Stir in lime juice before serving.
5. Garnish with fresh coriander and serve the Thai fish curry over cooked jasmine rice.

Crockpot Scallops in Cream Sauce

Serves: 4 Prep time: 10 minutes / Cook time: 2 hours

Ingredients:
- 400g fresh scallops
- 250ml double cream
- 50ml white wine
- 2 cloves garlic, minced
- 1 shallot, finely chopped
- 2 tbsp butter
- 1 tbsp chopped fresh parsley
- Salt and black pepper, to taste
- Fresh chives, for garnish

Preparation instructions:
1. In a pan, melt the butter over medium heat. Add minced garlic and finely chopped shallot, cooking until softened.
2. Add scallops to the pan, cooking briefly on each side until lightly browned.
3. Transfer the scallops, garlic, and shallot mixture to the crockpot.
4. Pour in the white wine and double cream. Season with salt and black pepper. Stir well.
5. Cover and cook on low for 2 hours or until the scallops are tender and the sauce is creamy.
6. Garnish with chopped fresh parsley and chives before serving.

Slow Cooker Lobster Bisque

Serves: 4 Prep time: 15 minutes / Cook time: 3 hours

Ingredients:
- 500g lobster meat, cooked and chopped
- 1 onion, finely chopped
- 2 cloves garlic, minced
- 250ml fish stock
- 250ml double cream
- 2 tbsp brandy
- 2 tbsp tomato paste
- 2 tbsp butter
- 1 tsp paprika
- Salt and black pepper, to taste
- Fresh chives, for garnish

Preparation instructions:
1. In a pan, melt butter over medium heat. Add chopped onions and minced garlic, cooking until softened.
2. Add lobster meat to the pan, cooking briefly to combine the flavours.
3. Transfer the lobster mixture to the crockpot. Add fish stock, double cream, brandy, tomato paste, paprika, salt, and black pepper. Stir well.
4. Cover and cook on low for 3 hours.
5. Adjust seasoning if necessary before serving.
6. Garnish with fresh chives before serving.

Crockpot Smoked Salmon Dip

Serves: 4 Prep time: 10 minutes / Chill time: 1 hour

Ingredients:

- 200g smoked salmon, finely chopped
- 250g cream cheese, softened
- 150ml sour cream
- 1 lemon, juiced and zested
- 1 tbsp chopped fresh dill
- Salt and black pepper, to taste
- Fresh chives, for garnish
- Crackers, for serving

Preparation instructions:

1. In a bowl, combine chopped smoked salmon, softened cream cheese, sour cream, lemon juice, lemon zest, and chopped fresh dill. Mix well.
2. Season with salt and black pepper. Adjust lemon juice and dill to taste.
3. Transfer the mixture to the crockpot. Cover and chill in the refrigerator for at least 1 hour.
4. Garnish with fresh chives before serving.
5. Serve the smoked salmon dip with crackers.

Slow Cooker Mediterranean Fish Stew

Serves: 4 Prep time: 15 minutes / Cook time: 3 hours

Ingredients:

- 500g mixed white fish fillets (such as cod, haddock, or snapper), cut into chunks
- 200g prawns, peeled and deveined
- 1 onion, finely chopped
- 2 cloves garlic, minced
- 1 red pepper, diced
- 1 yellow pepper, diced
- 400g canned chopped tomatoes
- 250ml fish stock
- 120ml white wine
- 2 tbsp olive oil
- 1 tsp dried oregano
- 1 tsp dried basil
- Salt and black pepper, to taste
- Fresh basil, for garnish
- Cooked couscous or crusty bread, for serving

Preparation instructions:

1. In a pan, heat olive oil over medium heat. Add chopped onions and minced garlic, cooking until softened.
2. Add diced peppers to the pan, cooking briefly until slightly tender.
3. Transfer the onion and pepper mixture to the crockpot. Add chopped tomatoes, fish stock, white wine, dried oregano, dried basil, salt, and black pepper. Stir well.
4. Add fish chunks and prawns to the crockpot, ensuring they are submerged in the liquid.
5. Cover and cook on low for 3 hours or until the fish is cooked through and tender.
6. Garnish with fresh basil before serving.
7. Serve the Mediterranean fish stew over cooked couscous

or with crusty bread.

Crockpot Garlic Herb Mussels

Serves: 4 Prep time: 15 minutes / Cook time: 2 hours

Ingredients:

- 1 kg fresh mussels, cleaned and debearded
- 2 cloves garlic, minced
- 1 shallot, finely chopped
- 60ml white wine
- 120ml fish stock
- 2 tbsp butter
- 2 tbsp fresh parsley, chopped
- Salt and black pepper, to taste
- Crusty bread, for serving

Preparation instructions:

1. In a pan, melt the butter over medium heat. Add minced garlic and chopped shallot, cooking until softened.
2. Pour in the white wine and fish stock. Bring to a gentle simmer.
3. Add cleaned mussels to the pan, cover, and steam for a few minutes until the mussels open.
4. Transfer the mussels and cooking liquid to the crockpot. Season with salt and black pepper. Sprinkle fresh parsley on top.
5. Cover and cook on low for 2 hours.
6. Serve the garlic herb mussels with crusty bread.

Slow Cooker Fish Tacos

Serves: 4 Prep time: 20 minutes / Cook time: 2 hours

Ingredients:

- 500g white fish fillets (such as cod or haddock), cut into strips
- 1 onion, finely chopped
- 2 cloves garlic, minced
- 1 red pepper, sliced
- 1 yellow pepper, sliced
- 1 tsp ground cumin
- 1 tsp paprika
- 1/2 tsp chilli powder
- Salt and black pepper, to taste
- 250ml fish stock
- 60ml lime juice
- Fresh coriander, chopped, for garnish
- Corn tortillas, for serving
- Shredded lettuce, diced tomatoes, and sour cream, for toppings

Preparation instructions:

1. In the crockpot, layer the fish strips, chopped onion, minced garlic, and sliced peppers.
2. In a small bowl, mix ground cumin, paprika, chilli powder, salt, and black pepper. Sprinkle the spice mix over the fish and vegetables.
3. Pour fish stock and lime juice over the Ingredients in the crockpot.
4. Cover and cook on low for 2 hours or until the fish is

cooked through and the vegetables are tender.

5. Warm the corn tortillas according to the package instructions.

6. Serve the fish tacos on warm tortillas, garnished with fresh coriander. Offer shredded lettuce, diced tomatoes, and sour cream as toppings.

Crockpot Coconut Curry Shrimp

Serves: 4 Prep time: 15 minutes / Cook time: 2 hours

Ingredients:

- 500g large shrimp, peeled and deveined
- 1 onion, finely chopped
- 2 cloves garlic, minced
- 1 red chilli, sliced (seeds removed for milder curry)
- 1 tbsp curry powder
- 400ml coconut milk
- 250ml fish stock
- 2 tbsp vegetable oil
- Salt and black pepper, to taste
- Fresh oregano, chopped, for garnish
- Cooked basmati rice, for serving

Preparation instructions:

1. In a pan, heat vegetable oil over medium heat. Add chopped onion, minced garlic, and sliced red chilli. Cook until softened.

2. Add curry powder to the pan, stirring to release its aroma.

3. Transfer the onion mixture to the crockpot. Add shrimp, coconut milk, fish stock, salt, and black pepper. Stir well.

4. Cover and cook on low for 2 hours or until the shrimp is cooked through and the curry is flavorful.

5. Serve the coconut curry shrimp over cooked basmati rice, garnished with fresh oregano.

Slow Cooker Cioppino (Italian Seafood Stew)

Serves: 4 Prep time: 20 minutes / Cook time: 3 hours

Ingredients:

- 500g mixed seafood (such as fish, mussels, clams, and shrimp), cleaned and prepared
- 1 onion, finely chopped
- 2 cloves garlic, minced
- 2 tbsp tomato paste
- 400g canned chopped tomatoes
- 250ml fish stock
- 250ml white wine
- 1 tsp dried oregano
- Salt and black pepper, to taste
- Fresh basil, chopped, for garnish
- Crusty bread, for serving

Preparation instructions:

1. In the crockpot, combine chopped onion, minced garlic, tomato paste, chopped tomatoes, fish stock, white wine, dried oregano, salt, and black pepper.

2. Stir well to mix the Ingredients.

3. Add mixed seafood to the crockpot, ensuring it is submerged in the liquid.

4. Cover and cook on low for 3 hours or until the seafood is cooked through and tender.

5. Adjust seasoning if necessary before serving.

6. Garnish with fresh basil and serve the Cioppino with crusty bread.

Crockpot Creamy Garlic Prawns

Serves: 4 Prep time: 15 minutes / Cook time: 2 hours

Ingredients:

- 500g large prawns, peeled and deveined
- 2 cloves garlic, minced
- 1 onion, finely chopped
- 250ml heavy cream
- 60ml chicken stock
- 2 tbsp butter
- 1 tbsp fresh parsley, chopped
- Salt and black pepper, to taste
- Cooked rice or crusty bread, for serving

Preparation instructions:

1. In the crockpot, combine minced garlic, chopped onion, heavy cream, chicken stock, butter, salt, and black pepper.

2. Stir well to mix the Ingredients.

3. Add the peeled and deveined prawns to the crockpot, ensuring they are submerged in the liquid.

4. Cover and cook on low for 2 hours or until the prawns are cooked through and the sauce is creamy and flavorful.

5. Garnish with fresh parsley before serving.

6. Serve the creamy garlic prawns over cooked rice or with crusty bread.

Slow Cooker Shrimp and Grits

Serves: 4 Prep time: 20 minutes / Cook time: 3 hours

Ingredients:

- 500g large shrimp, peeled and deveined
- 200g quick-cooking grits
- 1 litre chicken stock
- 1 onion, finely chopped
- 2 cloves garlic, minced
- 120ml heavy cream
- 60g shredded cheddar cheese
- 2 tbsp butter
- Salt and black pepper, to taste
- Fresh parsley, chopped, for garnish

Preparation instructions:

1. In the crockpot, combine quick-cooking grits, chicken stock, chopped onion, minced garlic, heavy cream, shredded cheddar cheese, butter, salt, and black pepper.

2. Stir well to mix the Ingredients.

3. Add peeled and deveined shrimp to the crockpot, ensuring they are submerged in the liquid.

4. Cover and cook on low for 3 hours or until the shrimp are cooked through and the grits are creamy.

5. Adjust seasoning if necessary before serving.

6. Garnish with fresh parsley before serving.

Crockpot Tuscan Seafood Stew

Serves: 4 Prep time: 20 minutes / Cook time: 3 hours

Ingredients:

- 500g mixed seafood (such as fish, mussels, clams, and shrimp), cleaned and prepared
- 1 onion, finely chopped
- 2 cloves garlic, minced
- 2 tbsp tomato paste
- 400g canned chopped tomatoes
- 250ml fish stock
- 250ml white wine
- 1 tsp dried oregano
- Salt and black pepper, to taste
- Fresh basil, chopped, for garnish
- Crusty bread, for serving

Preparation instructions:

1. In the crockpot, combine chopped onion, minced garlic, tomato paste, chopped tomatoes, fish stock, white wine, dried oregano, salt, and black pepper.
2. Stir well to mix the Ingredients.
3. Add mixed seafood to the crockpot, ensuring it is submerged in the liquid.
4. Cover and cook on low for 3 hours or until the seafood is cooked through and tender.
5. Adjust seasoning if necessary before serving.
6. Garnish with fresh basil and serve the Tuscan seafood stew with crusty bread.

Slow Cooker Lemon Garlic Scallops

Serves: 4 Prep time: 15 minutes / Cook time: 2 hours

Ingredients:

- 500g fresh scallops
- 2 cloves garlic, minced
- Zest and juice of 1 lemon
- 60ml white wine
- 60ml chicken stock
- 2 tbsp butter
- Fresh parsley, chopped, for garnish
- Salt and black pepper, to taste
- Cooked pasta or rice, for serving

Preparation instructions:

1. In the crockpot, combine minced garlic, lemon zest, lemon juice, white wine, chicken stock, butter, salt, and black pepper.
2. Stir well to mix the Ingredients.
3. Add fresh scallops to the crockpot, ensuring they are submerged in the liquid.
4. Cover and cook on low for 2 hours or until the scallops are cooked through and tender.
5. Adjust seasoning if necessary before serving.
6. Garnish with fresh parsley and serve the lemon garlic scallops over cooked pasta or rice.

Crockpot Thai Shrimp Soup

Serves: 4 Prep time: 15 minutes / Cook time: 3 hours

Ingredients:

- 500g large shrimp, peeled and deveined
- 1 onion, finely chopped
- 2 cloves garlic, minced
- 1 red pepper, thinly sliced
- 1 carrot, julienned
- 400ml coconut milk
- 500ml chicken stock
- 2 tbsp red curry paste
- 2 tbsp fish sauce
- 1 tbsp brown sugar
- Juice of 1 lime
- Fresh oregano, chopped, for garnish
- Red chilli flakes, for garnish
- Cooked rice, for serving

Preparation instructions:

1. In the crockpot, combine chopped onion, minced garlic, sliced red pepper, julienned carrot, coconut milk, chicken stock, red curry paste, fish sauce, and brown sugar.
2. Stir well to mix the Ingredients.
3. Add peeled and deveined shrimp to the crockpot, ensuring they are submerged in the liquid.
4. Cover and cook on low for 3 hours or until the shrimp are cooked through and the vegetables are tender.
5. Adjust seasoning with lime juice and additional fish sauce if necessary before serving.
6. Serve the Thai shrimp soup over cooked rice, garnished with fresh oregano and red chilli flakes.

Slow Cooker Seafood Gumbo

Serves: 4 Prep time: 20 minutes / Cook time: 4 hours

Ingredients:

- 500g mixed seafood (such as shrimp, fish, mussels, and crab), cleaned and prepared
- 1 onion, finely chopped
- 2 cloves garlic, minced
- 1 green pepper, chopped
- 1 celery stalk, chopped
- 400g canned diced tomatoes
- 500ml chicken stock
- 2 tbsp vegetable oil
- 3 tbsp all-purpose flour
- 1 tsp dried thyme
- 1 tsp smoked paprika
- Salt and black pepper, to taste
- Fresh parsley, chopped, for garnish
- Cooked rice, for serving

Preparation instructions:

1. In the crockpot, combine chopped onion, minced garlic, chopped green pepper, chopped celery, diced tomatoes, and chicken stock.
2. Stir well to mix the Ingredients.
3. In a separate pan, make a roux by heating vegetable oil over medium heat. Whisk in flour and cook, stirring constantly, until the roux becomes golden brown.
4. Add the roux to the crock pot and stir to combine.

5. Add mixed seafood, dried thyme, smoked paprika, salt, and black pepper to the crockpot, ensuring they are submerged in the liquid.
6. Cover and cook on low for 4 hours or until the seafood is cooked through and the gumbo thickens.
7. Adjust seasoning if necessary before serving.
8. Serve the seafood gumbo over cooked rice, garnished with fresh parsley.

Crockpot Fish and Chips

Serves: 4 Prep time: 20 minutes / Cook time: 3 hours

Ingredients:
- 500g white fish fillets (such as cod or haddock)
- 200g all-purpose flour
- 2 tsp baking powder
- 1/2 tsp salt
- 1/4 tsp black pepper
- 300ml milk
- 2 large potatoes, peeled and cut into thick fries
- Vegetable oil, for frying
- Lemon wedges, for serving
- Tartar sauce, for serving

Preparation instructions:
1. In a bowl, combine all-purpose flour, baking powder, salt, and black pepper.
2. Gradually whisk in milk until the batter is smooth and thick enough to coat the back of a spoon.
3. Dip fish fillets into the batter, ensuring they are well-coated, and place them in the crockpot.
4. In a separate bowl, toss potato fries with a little vegetable oil until evenly coated.
5. Place the potato fries around the fish in the crockpot.
6. Cover and cook on low for 3 hours or until the fish is cooked through and the fries are crispy.
7. While the fish and chips are cooking, heat vegetable oil in a deep fryer or large pan over medium-high heat. Fry the potato fries until golden brown and crispy. Remove and drain on paper towels.
8. Serve the crockpot fish and chips with lemon wedges and tartar sauce.

Slow Cooker New England Clam Chowder

Serves: 4 Prep time: 15 minutes / Cook time: 4 hours

Ingredients:
- 500g clams, shucked, juices reserved
- 1 onion, finely chopped
- 2 cloves garlic, minced
- 2 potatoes, peeled and diced
- 500ml chicken stock
- 250ml heavy cream
- 2 tbsp butter
- 2 tbsp all-purpose flour
- Salt and black pepper, to taste
- Fresh parsley, chopped, for garnish
- Oyster crackers, for serving

Preparation instructions:
1. In the crockpot, combine chopped onion, minced garlic, diced potatoes, reserved clam juices, and chicken stock.
2. Stir well to mix the Ingredients.
3. Cover and cook on low for 4 hours or until the potatoes are tender.
4. In a separate pan, melt butter over medium heat. Whisk in all-purpose flour and cook, stirring constantly, until the mixture becomes golden brown.
5. Gradually whisk in heavy cream until the chowder thickens.
6. Add the creamy mixture to the crock pot and stir to combine.
7. Add shucked clams to the crockpot and season with salt and black pepper. Cover and cook for an additional 30 minutes.
8. Adjust seasoning if necessary before serving.
9. Garnish with fresh parsley and serve the New England clam chowder with oyster crackers.

Crockpot Teriyaki Salmon

Serves: 4 Prep time: 10 minutes / Cook time: 2 hours

Ingredients:
- 4 salmon fillets, about 150g each
- 60ml soy sauce
- 60ml mirin
- 30ml sake
- 30g brown sugar
- 2 cloves garlic, minced
- 1 tsp grated fresh ginger
- Sesame seeds and sliced green onions, for garnish
- Steamed rice, for serving

Preparation instructions:
1. In a small saucepan, combine soy sauce, mirin, sake, brown sugar, minced garlic, and grated ginger. Heat over medium heat until the sugar has dissolved and the mixture slightly thickens. Remove from heat.
2. Place the salmon fillets in the crockpot.
3. Pour the teriyaki sauce over the salmon fillets, ensuring they are well coated.
4. Cover and cook on low for 2 hours or until the salmon is cooked through and flakes easily with a fork.
5. Garnish with sesame seeds and sliced green onions.
6. Serve the teriyaki salmon over steamed rice.

Slow Cooker Coconut Fish Curry

Serves: 4 Prep time: 15 minutes / Cook time: 3 hours

Ingredients:
- 500g white fish fillets, cut into chunks
- 1 onion, finely chopped
- 2 cloves garlic, minced
- 1 red chilli, finely chopped
- 400ml coconut milk
- 250ml fish stock
- 1 tbsp curry powder
- 1 tsp ground turmeric
- 1 tsp ground cumin
- 1 tsp paprika

- Salt and black pepper, to taste
- Fresh oregano, chopped, for garnish
- Cooked basmati rice, for serving

Preparation instructions:

1. In the crockpot, combine chopped onion, minced garlic, chopped red chilli, coconut milk, fish stock, curry powder, ground turmeric, ground cumin, and paprika. Stir well to mix the Ingredients.
2. Add fish chunks to the crockpot, ensuring they are submerged in the liquid.
3. Cover and cook on low for 3 hours or until the fish is cooked through and the curry is flavorful.
4. Season with salt and black pepper to taste.
5. Garnish with fresh oregano.
6. Serve the coconut fish curry over cooked basmati rice.

Crockpot Seafood Risotto

Serves: 4 Prep time: 15 minutes / Cook time: 2 hours

Ingredients:

- 300g Arborio rice
- 500ml fish stock
- 200g mixed seafood (such as shrimp, mussels, and squid), cleaned and prepared
- 1 onion, finely chopped
- 2 cloves garlic, minced
- 120ml white wine
- 60ml heavy cream
- 30g grated Parmesan cheese
- 2 tbsp butter
- Salt and black pepper, to taste
- Fresh parsley, chopped, for garnish

Preparation instructions:

1. In the crockpot, combine Arborio rice, fish stock, chopped onion, minced garlic, and white wine. Stir well to mix the Ingredients.
2. Cover and cook on low for 1.5 hours, stirring occasionally.
3. Add mixed seafood to the crockpot and continue cooking for another 30 minutes or until the seafood is cooked through and the rice is creamy.
4. Stir in heavy cream, grated Parmesan cheese, and butter until well combined.
5. Season with salt and black pepper to taste.
6. Garnish with fresh parsley.
7. Serve the seafood risotto immediately.

Slow Cooker Cajun Shrimp

Serves: 4 Prep time: 10 minutes / Cook time: 2 hours

Ingredients:

- 500g large shrimp, peeled and deveined
- 1 onion, finely chopped
- 2 cloves garlic, minced
- 1 red pepper, thinly sliced
- 1 green pepper, thinly sliced
- 400g canned diced tomatoes
- 120ml chicken stock

- 2 tbsp Cajun seasoning
- 1 tsp smoked paprika
- Salt and black pepper, to taste
- Fresh parsley, chopped, for garnish
- Cooked rice, for serving

Preparation instructions:

1. In the crockpot, combine chopped onion, minced garlic, sliced red pepper, sliced green pepper, diced tomatoes, chicken stock, Cajun seasoning, and smoked paprika. Stir well to mix the Ingredients.
2. Add peeled and deveined shrimp to the crockpot, ensuring they are submerged in the liquid.
3. Cover and cook on low for 2 hours or until the shrimp is cooked through and the peppers are tender.
4. Adjust seasoning with salt and black pepper to taste.
5. Garnish with fresh parsley.
6. Serve the Cajun shrimp over cooked rice.

Crockpot Garlic Butter Lobster Tails

Serves: 4 Prep time: 10 minutes / Cook time: 2 hours

Ingredients:

- 4 lobster tails, shells removed and deveined
- 100g unsalted butter, melted
- 4 cloves garlic, minced
- 2 tbsp fresh parsley, chopped
- Salt and black pepper, to taste
- Lemon wedges, for serving
- Steamed rice or crusty bread, for serving

Preparation instructions:

1. In a bowl, mix melted butter, minced garlic, chopped parsley, salt, and black pepper.
2. Place lobster tails in the crockpot.
3. Pour the garlic butter mixture over the lobster tails, ensuring they are well coated.
4. Cover and cook on low for 2 hours or until the lobster tails are opaque and cooked through.
5. Serve the garlic butter lobster tails with lemon wedges and your choice of steamed rice or crusty bread.

Slow Cooker Mediterranean Salmon

Serves: 4 Prep time: 10 minutes / Cook time: 2 hours

Ingredients:

- 4 salmon fillets, about 150g each
- 1 lemon, thinly sliced
- 2 tbsp olive oil
- 2 cloves garlic, minced
- 1 tsp dried oregano
- 1 tsp dried basil
- Salt and black pepper, to taste
- Fresh parsley, chopped, for garnish
- Cooked couscous or quinoa, for serving

Preparation instructions:

1. Place salmon fillets in the crockpot.
2. In a small bowl, mix olive oil, minced garlic, dried oregano, dried basil, salt, and black pepper.

3. Drizzle the olive oil mixture over the salmon fillets.
4. Arrange lemon slices on top of the salmon.
5. Cover and cook on low for 2 hours or until the salmon is cooked through and flakes easily with a fork.
6. Garnish with fresh parsley.
7. Serve the Mediterranean salmon over cooked couscous or quinoa.

Crockpot Creamy Shrimp Pasta

Serves: 4 Prep time: 15 minutes / Cook time: 2 hours

Ingredients:
- 300g linguine or spaghetti
- 500g large shrimp, peeled and deveined
- 1 onion, finely chopped
- 2 cloves garlic, minced
- 250ml chicken broth
- 250ml heavy cream
- 50g grated Parmesan cheese
- 2 tbsp chopped fresh basil
- Salt and black pepper, to taste
- Fresh basil leaves, for garnish

Preparation instructions:
1. Cook linguine or spaghetti according to package instructions until al dente. Drain and set aside.
2. In the crockpot, combine chopped onion, minced garlic, chicken broth, heavy cream, and grated Parmesan cheese. Stir well to mix the Ingredients.
3. Add peeled and deveined shrimp to the crockpot.
4. Cover and cook on low for 2 hours or until the shrimp is cooked through and the sauce is creamy.
5. Season with salt and black pepper to taste.
6. Stir in chopped fresh basil.
7. Serve the creamy shrimp pasta over cooked linguine or spaghetti.
8. Garnish with fresh basil leaves.

Slow Cooker Seafood Alfredo

Serves: 4 Prep time: 15 minutes / Cook time: 2 hours

Ingredients:
- 300g fettuccine
- 300g mixed seafood (such as shrimp, scallops, and calamari), cleaned and prepared
- 1 onion, finely chopped
- 2 cloves garlic, minced
- 250ml heavy cream
- 50g grated Parmesan cheese
- 2 tbsp chopped fresh parsley
- Salt and black pepper, to taste
- Fresh parsley leaves, for garnish

Preparation instructions:
1. Cook fettuccine according to package instructions until al dente. Drain and set aside.
2. In the crockpot, combine chopped onion, minced garlic, heavy cream, and grated Parmesan cheese. Stir well to mix the Ingredients.

3. Add mixed seafood to the crockpot.
4. Cover and cook on low for 2 hours or until the seafood is cooked through and the sauce is creamy.
5. Season with salt and black pepper to taste.
6. Stir in chopped fresh parsley.
7. Serve the seafood Alfredo over cooked fettuccine.
8. Garnish with fresh parsley leaves.

Crockpot Crab Dip

Serves: 4 Prep time: 10 minutes / Cook time: 2 hours

Ingredients:
- 250g cream cheese, softened
- 120g crab meat, drained and flaked
- 60g shredded mozzarella cheese
- 60ml mayonnaise
- 1 clove garlic, minced
- 1/2 tsp Worcestershire sauce
- 1/2 tsp hot sauce (optional)
- Salt and black pepper, to taste
- Fresh parsley, chopped, for garnish
- Crusty bread or crackers, for serving

Preparation instructions:
1. In a mixing bowl, combine softened cream cheese, crab meat, shredded mozzarella cheese, mayonnaise, minced garlic, Worcestershire sauce, hot sauce (if using), salt, and black pepper. Mix until well combined.
2. Transfer the mixture to a Crock Pot.
3. Cover and cook on low for 2 hours, stirring occasionally, until the dip is hot and bubbly.
4. Garnish with chopped fresh parsley.
5. Serve the crab dip with slices of crusty bread or crackers.

Slow Cooker Lemon Butter Scallops

Serves: 4 Prep time: 10 minutes / Cook time: 2 hours

Ingredients:
- 400g fresh scallops
- 60g unsalted butter, melted
- Zest and juice of 1 lemon
- 2 cloves garlic, minced
- 1 tbsp fresh parsley, chopped
- Salt and black pepper, to taste
- Lemon wedges, for serving
- Cooked rice or pasta, for serving

Preparation instructions:
1. Rinse the scallops and pat them dry with paper towels.
2. In a small bowl, mix melted butter, lemon zest, lemon juice, minced garlic, chopped parsley, salt, and black pepper.
3. Place the scallops in the Crock Pot.
4. Pour the lemon butter mixture over the scallops.
5. Cover and cook on low for 2 hours or until the scallops are opaque and cooked through.
6. Serve the lemon butter scallops over cooked rice or pasta.
7. Garnish with lemon wedges.

Crockpot Salmon with Dill Sauce

Serves: 4 Prep time: 10 minutes / Cook time: 2 hours

Ingredients:
- 4 salmon fillets, about 150g each
- 60ml olive oil
- 2 cloves garlic, minced
- Zest and juice of 1 lemon
- 1 tbsp fresh dill, chopped
- Salt and black pepper, to taste
- Fresh dill sprigs, for garnish
- Steamed vegetables, for serving

Preparation instructions:
1. In a small bowl, mix olive oil, minced garlic, lemon zest, lemon juice, chopped dill, salt, and black pepper.
2. Place salmon fillets in the Crock Pot.
3. Drizzle the olive oil mixture over the salmon.
4. Cover and cook on low for 2 hours or until the salmon is cooked through and flakes easily with a fork.
5. Garnish with fresh dill sprigs.
6. Serve the salmon with steamed vegetables.

Slow Cooker Lobster Mac and Cheese

Serves: 4 Prep time: 10 minutes / Cook time: 2 hours

Ingredients:
- 250g macaroni or pasta of your choice
- 2 lobster tails, shells removed and chopped into bite-sized pieces
- 60g unsalted butter   • 60g all-purpose flour
- 500ml whole milk
- 150g shredded sharp cheddar cheese
- 150g shredded Gruyere cheese
- Salt and black pepper, to taste
- Fresh chives, chopped, for garnish

Preparation instructions:
1. Cook macaroni or pasta according to package instructions until al dente. Drain and set aside.
2. In a saucepan, melt butter over medium heat. Stir in flour to create a roux. Cook for 1-2 minutes, stirring constantly.
3. Gradually whisk in whole milk until the sauce thickens.
4. Remove the saucepan from heat and stir in shredded cheddar cheese and shredded Gruyere cheese until melted and smooth. Season with salt and black pepper to taste.
5. In the Crock Pot, combine cooked macaroni or pasta, chopped lobster tails, and the cheese sauce. Stir well to coat the pasta and lobster with the sauce.
6. Cover and cook on low for 2 hours or until the lobster is cooked through and the mac and cheese is hot and creamy.
7. Garnish with chopped fresh chives.
8. Serve the lobster mac and cheese hot.

Crockpot Shrimp and Broccoli

Serves: 4 Prep time: 10 minutes / Cook time: 2 hours

Ingredients:
- 400g large shrimp, peeled and deveined
- 400g broccoli florets
- 1 red pepper, sliced
- 1 yellow pepper, sliced
- 60ml low-sodium soy sauce
- 30ml oyster sauce
- 2 cloves garlic, minced
- 1 tsp fresh ginger, grated
- 1 tbsp cornstarch
- 60ml water
- Salt and black pepper, to taste
- Cooked rice, for serving

Preparation instructions:
1. In the Crock Pot, combine shrimp, broccoli florets, sliced red pepper, and sliced yellow pepper.
2. In a small bowl, whisk together low-sodium soy sauce, oyster sauce, minced garlic, grated ginger, cornstarch, and water to create a sauce.
3. Pour the sauce over the shrimp and vegetables in the Crock Pot. Season with salt and black pepper to taste.
4. Cover and cook on low for 2 hours or until the shrimp is cooked through and the vegetables are tender.
5. Serve the shrimp and broccoli over cooked rice.

Slow Cooker Seafood Pilaf

Serves: 4 Prep time: 10 minutes / Cook time: 2.5 hours

Ingredients:
- 300g mixed seafood (such as shrimp, mussels, and squid), cleaned and chopped if necessary
- 200g basmati rice, rinsed and drained
- 1 onion, finely chopped
- 2 cloves garlic, minced
- 1 red pepper, diced
- 1 yellow pepper, diced
- 400ml fish or vegetable broth
- 1 tsp paprika
- 1/2 tsp turmeric
- Salt and black pepper, to taste
- Fresh parsley, chopped, for garnish

Preparation instructions:
1. In the Crock Pot, combine mixed seafood, rinsed basmati rice, finely chopped onion, minced garlic, diced red pepper, and diced yellow pepper.
2. Add fish or vegetable broth, paprika, turmeric, salt, and black pepper. Stir well to combine all Ingredients.
3. Cover and cook on low for 2.5 hours or until the rice is cooked through and the seafood is tender.
4. Garnish with chopped fresh parsley before serving.

Crockpot Garlic Butter Shrimp Pasta

Serves: 4 Prep time: 10 minutes / Cook time: 2 hours

Ingredients:
- 400g large shrimp, peeled and deveined
- 250g linguine or spaghetti
- 60g unsalted butter
- 4 cloves garlic, minced

- 240ml chicken or vegetable broth
- 120ml heavy cream
- 60g grated Parmesan cheese
- Salt and black pepper, to taste
- Fresh parsley, chopped, for garnish

Preparation instructions:

1. In the Crock Pot, combine large shrimp and linguine or spaghetti.
2. In a saucepan, melt unsalted butter over medium heat. Add minced garlic and cook until fragrant.
3. Pour in chicken or vegetable broth, then add heavy cream and grated Parmesan cheese. Stir until the cheese is melted and the sauce is smooth.
4. Pour the garlic butter sauce over the shrimp and pasta in the Crock Pot. Season with salt and black pepper to taste. Stir well to coat the shrimp and pasta with the sauce.
5. Cover and cook on low for 2 hours or until the shrimp is cooked through and the pasta is tender.
6. Garnish with chopped fresh parsley before serving.

Slow Cooker Salmon Chowder

Serves: 4 Prep time: 10 minutes / Cook time: 2.5 hours

Ingredients:
- 400g salmon fillets, skin removed, chopped into bite-sized pieces
- 300g potatoes, peeled and diced
- 1 onion, finely chopped
- 2 cloves garlic, minced
- 2 celery stalks, diced
- 400ml fish or vegetable broth
- 240ml heavy cream
- 1 bay leaf
- Salt and black pepper, to taste
- Fresh dill, chopped, for garnish

Preparation instructions:

1. In the Crock Pot, combine chopped salmon fillets, diced potatoes, finely chopped onion, minced garlic, and diced celery stalks.
2. Add fish or vegetable broth, heavy cream, and a bay leaf. Season with salt and black pepper to taste. Stir to combine all Ingredients.
3. Cover and cook on low for 2.5 hours or until the salmon is cooked through, and the potatoes are tender.
4. Remove the bay leaf before serving.
5. Garnish with chopped fresh dill before serving.

Crockpot Scallop and Bacon Skewers

Serves: 4 Prep time: 15 minutes / Cook time: 2 hours

Ingredients:
- 400g scallops, cleaned
- 200g bacon, cut into strips
- 1 lemon, zest and juice
- 60ml olive oil
- 2 cloves garlic, minced
- 1 tsp smoked paprika

- Salt and black pepper, to taste
- Fresh parsley, chopped, for garnish

Preparation instructions:

1. In a bowl, combine scallops, bacon strips, lemon zest, lemon juice, olive oil, minced garlic, smoked paprika, salt, and black pepper. Toss to coat the scallops and bacon evenly.
2. Thread the marinated scallops and bacon onto skewers.
3. Place the skewers in the Crock Pot.
4. Cover and cook on low for 2 hours or until the scallops are opaque and cooked through.
5. Garnish with chopped fresh parsley before serving.

Slow Cooker Thai Coconut Shrimp Soup

Serves: 4 Prep time: 15 minutes / Cook time: 2 hours

Ingredients:
- 400g large shrimp, peeled and deveined
- 1 can (400ml) coconut milk
- 500ml chicken or vegetable broth
- 1 red pepper, thinly sliced
- 1 onion, thinly sliced
- 2 cloves garlic, minced
- 1 thumb-sized piece of ginger, grated
- 2 tbsp red curry paste
- 2 tbsp fish sauce
- 1 tbsp brown sugar
- Juice of 1 lime
- Fresh oregano, chopped, for garnish
- Red chilli flakes, for garnish (optional)

Preparation instructions:

1. In the Crock Pot, combine large shrimp, coconut milk, chicken or vegetable broth, thinly sliced red pepper, thinly sliced onion, minced garlic, grated ginger, red curry paste, fish sauce, and brown sugar. Stir to combine.
2. Cover and cook on low for 2 hours.
3. Stir in the lime juice before serving.
4. Garnish with chopped fresh oregano and red chilli flakes (if using) before serving.

Crockpot Shrimp and Spinach

Serves: 4 Prep time: 10 minutes / Cook time: 2 hours

Ingredients:
- 400g large shrimp, peeled and deveined
- 200g fresh spinach leaves
- 2 cloves garlic, minced
- 60ml chicken or vegetable broth
- 60ml heavy cream
- 30g grated Parmesan cheese
- Salt and black pepper, to taste
- 1 tbsp olive oil
- Lemon wedges, for serving

Preparation instructions:

1. In a pan, heat olive oil over medium heat. Add minced garlic and cook until fragrant.
2. Add fresh spinach leaves and sauté until wilted.

3. In the Crock Pot, combine large shrimp, sautéed spinach, chicken or vegetable broth, heavy cream, and grated Parmesan cheese. Stir to combine.
4. Cover and cook on low for 2 hours or until the shrimp is cooked through and the sauce is creamy.
5. Season with salt and black pepper to taste.
6. Serve with lemon wedges.

Slow Cooker Seafood Curry

Serves: 4 Prep time: 15 minutes / Cook time: 2.5 hours

Ingredients:
- 400g mixed seafood (such as shrimp, mussels, and squid), cleaned and chopped if necessary
- 1 can (400ml) coconut milk
- 1 onion, finely chopped
- 2 cloves garlic, minced
- 1 thumb-sized piece of ginger, grated
- 2 tbsp curry powder
- 1 tbsp fish sauce
- 1 tbsp vegetable oil
- Fresh oregano, chopped, for garnish
- Cooked rice, for serving

Preparation instructions:
1. In a pan, heat vegetable oil over medium heat. Add finely chopped onion, minced garlic, and grated ginger. Cook until the onion is translucent.
2. Add curry powder and cook until fragrant.
3. In the Crock Pot, combine mixed seafood, sautéed onion mixture, coconut milk, and fish sauce. Stir to combine.
4. Cover and cook on low for 2.5 hours or until the seafood is cooked through.
5. Serve the seafood curry over cooked rice, garnished with chopped fresh oregano.

Crockpot Tuna Casserole

Serves: 4 Prep time: 15 minutes / Cook time: 2 hours

Ingredients:
- 300g canned tuna, drained
- 200g elbow macaroni, cooked al dente and drained
- 400ml whole milk
- 100g shredded cheddar cheese
- 1 onion, finely chopped
- 2 cloves garlic, minced
- 60ml chicken or vegetable broth
- 30g butter
- 30g all-purpose flour
- 1/4 tsp garlic powder
- 1/4 tsp onion powder
- Salt and black pepper, to taste
- Fresh parsley, chopped, for garnish

Preparation instructions:
1. In a pan, melt butter over medium heat. Add finely chopped onion and minced garlic. Cook until the onion is translucent.
2. Stir in the all-purpose flour to create a roux. Cook for a minute, stirring constantly.

3. Gradually whisk in whole milk and chicken or vegetable broth. Cook until the sauce thickens.
4. Add drained tuna, cooked macaroni, shredded cheddar cheese, garlic powder, onion powder, salt, and black pepper. Stir to combine.
5. Transfer the mixture into the Crock Pot.
6. Cover and cook on low for 2 hours.
7. Garnish with chopped fresh parsley before serving.

Slow Cooker Lemon Herb Crab Legs

Serves: 4 Prep time: 10 minutes / Cook time: 2 hours

Ingredients:
- 800g crab legs, thawed if frozen
- 60ml olive oil
- Juice of 1 lemon
- 2 cloves garlic, minced
- 1 tbsp fresh parsley, chopped
- 1 tbsp fresh dill, chopped
- Salt and black pepper, to taste
- Lemon wedges, for serving

Preparation instructions:
1. In a bowl, combine olive oil, lemon juice, minced garlic, chopped fresh parsley, chopped fresh dill, salt, and black pepper.
2. Place crab legs in the Crock Pot.
3. Pour the olive oil and lemon herb mixture over the crab legs, ensuring they are well coated.
4. Cover and cook on low for 2 hours or until the crab legs are heated through.
5. Serve with lemon wedges.

Crockpot Mediterranean Octopus Stew

Serves: 4 Prep time: 20 minutes / Cook time: 3 hours

Ingredients:
- 600g octopus, cleaned and chopped into bite-sized pieces
- 400g canned diced tomatoes
- 1 onion, finely chopped
- 2 cloves garlic, minced
- 1 red pepper, sliced
- 1 yellow pepper, sliced
- 60ml white wine
- 30ml olive oil
- 1 tsp dried oregano
- Salt and black pepper, to taste
- Fresh basil, chopped, for garnish

Preparation instructions:
1. In a pan, heat olive oil over medium heat. Add finely chopped onion and minced garlic. Cook until the onion is translucent.
2. Add chopped octopus and cook until it turns opaque.
3. Transfer the octopus mixture into the Crock Pot.
4. Add canned diced tomatoes, sliced red pepper, sliced yellow pepper, white wine, dried oregano, salt, and black pepper. Stir to combine.
5. Cover and cook on low for 3 hours or until the octopus is tender.
6. Garnish with chopped fresh basil before serving.

Chapter 9: Beef, Pork and Lamb Recipes

Slow Cooker Beef Stew

Serves: 4 Prep time: 15 minutes / Cook time: 6 hours

Ingredients:
- 600g beef stew meat, diced
- 400g potatoes, peeled and cubed
- 200g carrots, peeled and sliced
- 1 onion, chopped
- 2 cloves garlic, minced
- 500ml beef broth
- 60ml tomato paste
- 30g all-purpose flour
- 1 tsp Worcestershire sauce
- 1/2 tsp dried thyme
- Salt and black pepper, to taste
- Fresh parsley, chopped, for garnish

Preparation instructions:
1. In a bowl, toss diced beef stew meat with all-purpose flour until well coated.
2. Place coated beef, potatoes, carrots, chopped onion, and minced garlic into the Crock Pot.
3. In another bowl, whisk together beef broth, tomato paste, Worcestershire sauce, dried thyme, salt, and black pepper.
4. Pour the broth mixture over the beef and vegetables in the Crock Pot.
5. Cover and cook on low for 6 hours or until the beef and vegetables are tender.
6. Garnish with chopped fresh parsley before serving.

Crockpot Beef Curry

Serves: 4 Prep time: 15 minutes / Cook time: 6 hours

Ingredients:
- 600g beef stew meat, diced
- 1 onion, chopped
- 2 cloves garlic, minced
- 400ml coconut milk
- 60ml beef broth
- 2 tbsp curry powder
- 1 tsp ground turmeric
- 1/2 tsp ground cumin
- 1/2 tsp paprika
- Salt and black pepper, to taste
- Fresh coriander, chopped, for garnish

Preparation instructions:
1. In the Crock Pot, combine diced beef stew meat, chopped onion, and minced garlic.
2. In a bowl, mix together coconut milk, beef broth, curry powder, ground turmeric, ground cumin, paprika, salt, and black pepper.
3. Pour the coconut milk mixture over the beef in the Crock Pot.
4. Cover and cook on low for 6 hours or until the beef is tender and the flavours are well blended.
5. Garnish with chopped fresh coriander before serving.

Slow Cooker Beef and Ale Casserole

Serves: 4 Prep time: 15 minutes / Cook time: 6 hours

Ingredients:
- 600g beef stew meat, diced
- 1 onion, chopped
- 2 cloves garlic, minced
- 250ml beef broth
- 2 tbsp all-purpose flour
- Salt and black pepper, to taste
- Fresh thyme, chopped, for garnish
- 400ml ale or stout beer
- 2 tbsp tomato paste
- 1 tsp dried rosemary

Preparation instructions:
1. In the Crock Pot, combine diced beef stew meat, chopped onion, and minced garlic.
2. In a bowl, whisk together ale or stout beer, beef broth, tomato paste, all-purpose flour, dried rosemary, salt, and black pepper.
3. Pour the beer mixture over the beef in the Crock Pot.
4. Cover and cook on low for 6 hours or until the beef is tender and the sauce has thickened.
5. Garnish with chopped fresh thyme before serving.

Crockpot Beef Bourguignon

Serves: 4 Prep time: 20 minutes / Cook time: 6 hours

Ingredients:
- 600g beef stew meat, diced
- 200g pearl onions, peeled
- 200g mushrooms, sliced
- 2 cloves garlic, minced
- 500ml red wine (Burgundy or any dry red wine)
- 250ml beef broth
- 2 tbsp tomato paste
- 2 tbsp all-purpose flour
- 2 tbsp butter
- 1 tsp dried thyme
- Salt and black pepper, to taste
- Fresh parsley, chopped, for garnish

Preparation instructions:
1. In a pan, melt butter over medium heat. Add pearl onions and sliced mushrooms. Cook until the onions are caramelised and mushrooms are golden brown. Add minced garlic and cook for an additional minute.
2. Transfer the onion and mushroom mixture into the Crock Pot. Add diced beef stew meat.
3. In a bowl, whisk together red wine, beef broth, tomato paste, all-purpose flour, dried thyme, salt, and black pepper.
4. Pour the wine mixture over the beef, onions, and mushrooms in the Crock Pot.
5. Cover and cook on low for 6 hours or until the beef is tender and the sauce is rich and flavorful.
6. Garnish with chopped fresh parsley before serving.

Slow Cooker Beef and Guinness Stew

Serves: 4 Prep time: 15 minutes / Cook time: 6 hours

Ingredients:
- 600g stewing beef, diced
- 2 onions, chopped
- 2 carrots, peeled and sliced
- 2 cloves garlic, minced
- 400ml Guinness beer
- 500ml beef broth
- 2 tbsp tomato paste
- 2 tbsp all-purpose flour
- 1 tsp dried thyme
- Salt and black pepper, to taste

- Fresh parsley, chopped, for garnish

Preparation instructions:

1. In the Crock Pot, combine diced stewing beef, chopped onions, sliced carrots, and minced garlic.
2. In a bowl, whisk together Guinness beer, beef broth, tomato paste, all-purpose flour, dried thyme, salt, and black pepper.
3. Pour the beer mixture over the beef and vegetables in the Crock Pot.
4. Cover and cook on low for 6 hours or until the beef is tender and the sauce has thickened.
5. Garnish with chopped fresh parsley before serving.

Crockpot Beef and Mushroom Pie

Serves: 4 Prep time: 15 minutes / Cook time: 6 hours

Ingredients:

- 600g stewing beef, diced
- 2 onions, chopped
- 2 cloves garlic, minced
- 200g mushrooms, sliced
- 500ml beef broth
- 2 tbsp tomato paste
- 2 tbsp all-purpose flour
- 1 tsp dried thyme
- Salt and black pepper, to taste
- 400g puff pastry, thawed
- 1 egg, beaten, for egg wash

Preparation instructions:

1. In the Crock Pot, combine diced stewing beef, chopped onions, minced garlic, and sliced mushrooms.
2. In a bowl, whisk together beef broth, tomato paste, all-purpose flour, dried thyme, salt, and black pepper.
3. Pour the broth mixture over the beef and vegetables in the Crock Pot.
4. Cover and cook on low for 6 hours or until the beef is tender and the flavours are well blended.
5. Preheat the oven to 200°C.
6. Roll out the puff pastry on a floured surface and cut into 4 circles slightly larger than the top of the Crock Pot.
7. Ladle the beef and mushroom mixture into 4 individual oven-safe dishes.
8. Place the pastry circles on top of each dish, pressing the edges to seal. Brush with beaten egg for a golden finish.
9. Bake in the preheated oven for 20-25 minutes or until the pastry is golden brown and puffed.
10. Serve hot, garnished with fresh parsley if desired.

Slow Cooker Beef Rendang

Serves: 4 Prep time: 15 minutes / Cook time: 6 hours

Ingredients:

- 600g stewing beef, diced
- 2 onions, chopped
- 4 cloves garlic, minced
- 2 lemongrass stalks, bruised
- 400ml coconut milk
- 250ml beef broth
- 2 tbsp tamarind paste
- 2 tbsp palm sugar
- 2 tbsp vegetable oil
- 1 tsp ground turmeric
- 1 tsp ground coriander
- Salt, to taste
- Fresh oregano, chopped, for garnish

Preparation instructions:

1. In a pan, heat vegetable oil over medium heat. Add chopped onions and minced garlic. Cook until the onions are translucent.
2. Add diced stewing beef to the pan and cook until browned on all sides.
3. Transfer the beef, onions, and garlic into the Crock Pot. Add bruised lemongrass stalks.
4. In a bowl, whisk together coconut milk, beef broth, tamarind paste, palm sugar, ground turmeric, ground coriander, and salt.
5. Pour the coconut milk mixture over the beef in the Crock Pot.
6. Cover and cook on low for 6 hours or until the beef is tender and the sauce has thickened.
7. Remove lemongrass stalks before serving.
8. Garnish with chopped fresh oregano before serving.

Crockpot Beef and Broccoli

Serves: 4 Prep time: 15 minutes / Cook time: 4 hours

Ingredients:

- 600g sirloin steak, thinly sliced
- 200g broccoli florets
- 1 onion, sliced
- 4 cloves garlic, minced
- 250ml beef broth
- 4 tbsp soy sauce
- 2 tbsp oyster sauce
- 2 tbsp brown sugar
- 2 tbsp cornstarch
- 2 tbsp water
- Sesame seeds, for garnish
- Sliced green onions, for garnish

Preparation instructions:

1. In the Crock Pot, combine thinly sliced sirloin steak, broccoli florets, sliced onion, and minced garlic.
2. In a bowl, whisk together beef broth, soy sauce, oyster sauce, and brown sugar. Pour the sauce over the beef and vegetables in the Crock Pot.
3. Cover and cook on low for 4 hours or until the beef is cooked through and the broccoli is tender.
4. In a small bowl, mix cornstarch with water to create a slurry. Stir the slurry into the Crock Pot to thicken the sauce.
5. Serve hot over cooked rice, garnished with sesame seeds and sliced green onions.

Slow Cooker Beef and Red Wine Casserole

Serves: 4 Prep time: 15 minutes / Cook time: 6 hours

Ingredients:

- 600g beef stewing meat, cubed
- 2 onions, chopped
- 2 carrots, peeled and sliced
- 2 cloves garlic, minced
- 250ml red wine
- 500ml beef broth
- 2 tbsp tomato paste
- 2 tbsp all-purpose flour
- 1 tsp dried thyme
- Salt and black pepper, to taste
- Fresh parsley, chopped, for garnish

Preparation instructions:

1. In the Crock Pot, combine beef stewing meat, chopped onions, sliced carrots, and minced garlic.
2. In a bowl, whisk together red wine, beef broth, tomato

paste, all-purpose flour, dried thyme, salt, and black pepper.

3. Pour the wine mixture over the beef and vegetables in the Crock Pot.

4. Cover and cook on low for 6 hours or until the beef is tender and the sauce has thickened.

5. Garnish with chopped fresh parsley before serving.

Crockpot Beef and Vegetable Stir-Fry

Serves: 4 Prep time: 15 minutes / Cook time: 4 hours

Ingredients:

- 600g beef sirloin, thinly sliced
- 1 onion, sliced
- 2 peppers, sliced (assorted colours)
- 200g broccoli florets
- 2 tbsp oyster sauce
- 2 cloves garlic, minced
- 2 tbsp vegetable oil
- 4 tbsp water
- 4 tbsp soy sauce
- 2 tbsp brown sugar
- 1 tsp ginger, grated
- 2 tbsp cornstarch
- Sesame seeds, for garnish
- Sliced green onions, for garnish

Preparation instructions:

1. In the Crock Pot, combine thinly sliced beef sirloin, sliced onion, peppers, broccoli florets, minced garlic, and grated ginger.

2. In a bowl, mix together soy sauce, oyster sauce, and brown sugar. Pour the sauce over the beef and vegetables in the Crock Pot.

3. Cover and cook on low for 4 hours or until the beef is cooked through and the vegetables are tender.

4. In a small bowl, mix cornstarch with water to create a slurry. Stir the slurry into the Crock Pot to thicken the sauce.

5. Heat vegetable oil in a pan over medium heat. Add the beef and vegetable mixture from the Crock Pot and stir-fry for 2-3 minutes until heated through.

6. Serve hot over cooked rice, garnished with sesame seeds and sliced green onions.

Slow Cooker Beef and Barley Soup

Serves: 4 Prep time: 15 minutes / Cook time: 6 hours

Ingredients:

- 600g stewing beef, cubed
- 2 carrots, peeled and sliced
- 2 cloves garlic, minced
- 2 litres beef broth
- Salt and black pepper, to taste
- Fresh parsley, chopped, for garnish
- 1 onion, chopped
- 150g pearl barley
- 2 bay leaves

Preparation instructions:

1. In the Crock Pot, combine cubed stewing beef, chopped onion, sliced carrots, minced garlic, pearl barley, beef broth, and bay leaves.

2. Cover and cook on low for 6 hours or until the beef is tender and the barley is cooked through.

3. Season with salt and black pepper to taste. Remove bay leaves before serving.

4. Garnish with chopped fresh parsley before serving.

Crockpot Beef Tacos

Serves: 4 Prep time: 15 minutes / Cook time: 6 hours

Ingredients:

- 600g beef brisket, sliced
- 2 cloves garlic, minced
- 1 tbsp chilli powder
- 1 tsp paprika
- Salt and black pepper, to taste
- 250ml beef broth
- 2 tbsp fresh oregano, chopped
- Corn or flour tortillas, for serving
- Shredded lettuce, diced tomatoes, grated cheese, sour cream, for toppings
- 1 onion, chopped
- 2 tbsp tomato paste
- 1 tsp ground cumin
- 1/2 tsp cayenne pepper

Preparation instructions:

1. In the Crock Pot, combine sliced beef brisket, chopped onion, minced garlic, tomato paste, chilli powder, ground cumin, paprika, cayenne pepper, salt, black pepper, and beef broth.

2. Cover and cook on low for 6 hours or until the beef is tender and flavorful.

3. Shred the beef using two forks and mix it back into the sauce in the Crock Pot.

4. Warm the tortillas according to package instructions.

5. Serve the shredded beef in warm tortillas, topped with shredded lettuce, diced tomatoes, grated cheese, sour cream, and chopped fresh oregano.

Slow Cooker Beef Stroganoff

Serves: 4 Prep time: 15 minutes / Cook time: 6 hours

Ingredients:

- 500g beef sirloin, thinly sliced
- 1 onion, finely chopped
- 250g mushrooms, sliced
- 200ml sour cream
- 2 tbsp Worcestershire sauce
- Salt and black pepper, to taste
- Fresh parsley, chopped, for garnish
- 300g cooked egg noodles, for serving
- 2 cloves garlic, minced
- 300ml beef broth
- 2 tbsp all-purpose flour

Preparation instructions:

1. In the Crock Pot, combine thinly sliced beef sirloin, chopped onion, minced garlic, and sliced mushrooms.

2. In a bowl, whisk together beef broth, sour cream, all-purpose flour, Worcestershire sauce, salt, and black pepper. Pour the mixture over the beef and vegetables in the Crock Pot.

3. Cover and cook on low for 6 hours or until the beef is tender and the sauce has thickened.

4. Serve the beef stroganoff over cooked egg noodles, garnished with chopped fresh parsley.

Crockpot Beef and Potato Curry

Serves: 4 Prep time: 15 minutes / Cook time: 6 hours

Ingredients:

- 600g beef stewing meat, cubed

- 4 potatoes, peeled and diced
- 1 onion, finely chopped
- 3 cloves garlic, minced
- 400ml coconut milk
- 2 tbsp curry powder
- 1 tbsp tomato paste
- 1 tbsp vegetable oil
- Salt and black pepper, to taste
- Fresh coriander, chopped, for garnish
- Cooked rice, for serving

Preparation instructions:

1. In the Crock Pot, combine cubed beef stewing meat, diced potatoes, chopped onion, and minced garlic.
2. In a bowl, mix together coconut milk, curry powder, and tomato paste. Pour the mixture over the beef and vegetables in the Crock Pot.
3. Cover and cook on low for 6 hours or until the beef is cooked through and the potatoes are tender.
4. Season with salt and black pepper to taste.
5. Heat vegetable oil in a pan over medium heat. Add the curry mixture from the Crock Pot and stir-fry for 2-3 minutes until heated through.
6. Serve the beef and potato curry over cooked rice, garnished with chopped fresh coriander.

Slow Cooker Beef and Pepper Casserole

Serves: 4 Prep time: 15 minutes / Cook time: 6 hours

Ingredients:

- 600g beef chuck, cubed
- 2 red peppers, sliced
- 2 yellow peppers, sliced
- 1 onion, sliced
- 3 cloves garlic, minced
- 400ml beef broth
- 2 tbsp tomato paste
- 1 tbsp balsamic vinegar
- 1 tbsp brown sugar
- 1 tsp dried thyme
- Salt and black pepper, to taste
- Fresh parsley, chopped, for garnish
- Mashed potatoes, for serving

Preparation instructions:

1. In the Crock Pot, combine cubed beef chuck, sliced red and yellow peppers, sliced onion, and minced garlic.
2. In a bowl, whisk together beef broth, tomato paste, balsamic vinegar, brown sugar, dried thyme, salt, and black pepper. Pour the mixture over the beef and vegetables in the Crock Pot.
3. Cover and cook on low for 6 hours or until the beef is tender and the peppers are cooked through.
4. Serve the beef and pepper casserole over mashed potatoes, garnished with chopped fresh parsley.

Crockpot Beef and Sweet Potato Stew

Serves: 4 Prep time: 15 minutes / Cook time: 6 hours

Ingredients:

- 600g beef stewing meat, cubed
- 2 sweet potatoes, peeled and diced
- 2 carrots, peeled and sliced
- 1 onion, chopped
- 3 cloves garlic, minced
- 400ml beef broth
- 2 tbsp tomato paste

- 1 tbsp Worcestershire sauce
- 1 tsp dried rosemary
- Salt and black pepper, to taste
- Fresh parsley, chopped, for garnish
- Crusty bread, for serving

Preparation instructions:

1. In the Crock Pot, combine cubed beef stewing meat, diced sweet potatoes, sliced carrots, chopped onion, and minced garlic.
2. In a bowl, mix together beef broth, tomato paste, Worcestershire sauce, dried rosemary, salt, and black pepper. Pour the mixture over the beef and vegetables in the Crock Pot.
3. Cover and cook on low for 6 hours or until the beef is cooked through and the sweet potatoes are tender.
4. Serve the beef and sweet potato stew in bowls, garnished with chopped fresh parsley. Enjoy with crusty bread on the side.

Slow Cooker Beef and Kidney Bean Chili

Serves: 4 Prep time: 15 minutes / Cook time: 6 hours

Ingredients:

- 500g lean beef mince
- 2 cans (400g each) kidney beans, drained and rinsed
- 1 onion, finely chopped
- 3 cloves garlic, minced
- 2 cans (400g each) chopped tomatoes
- 250ml beef broth
- 2 tbsp tomato paste
- 1 tbsp chilli powder
- 1 tsp ground cumin
- 1/2 tsp paprika
- Salt and black pepper, to taste
- Fresh coriander, chopped, for garnish
- Grated cheddar cheese, for serving

Preparation instructions:

1. In a pan, brown the lean beef mince over medium heat. Drain excess fat and transfer the mince to the Crock Pot.
2. Add drained kidney beans, finely chopped onion, minced garlic, chopped tomatoes, beef broth, tomato paste, chilli powder, ground cumin, paprika, salt, and black pepper to the Crock Pot. Stir to combine.
3. Cover and cook on low for 6 hours, allowing the flavours to meld together.
4. Serve the beef and kidney bean chilli hot, garnished with chopped fresh coriander and a sprinkle of grated cheddar cheese.

Crockpot Beef Ragu

Serves: 4 Prep time: 15 minutes / Cook time: 6 hours

Ingredients:

- 600g beef stewing meat, cubed
- 2 cans (400g each) crushed tomatoes
- 1 onion, finely chopped
- 3 cloves garlic, minced
- 2 tbsp tomato paste

- 250ml beef broth
- 1 tsp dried oregano
- 1/2 tsp dried basil
- Salt and black pepper, to taste
- Fresh parsley, chopped, for garnish
- Cooked pasta, for serving

Preparation instructions:

1. In the Crock Pot, combine cubed beef stewing meat, crushed tomatoes, finely chopped onion, minced garlic, tomato paste, beef broth, dried oregano, dried basil, salt, and black pepper.
2. Cover and cook on low for 6 hours or until the beef is tender and the sauce is rich and flavorful.
3. Serve the beef ragu over cooked pasta, garnished with chopped fresh parsley.

Slow Cooker Beef and Vegetable Soup

Serves: 4 Prep time: 15 minutes / Cook time: 6 hours

Ingredients:

- 500g beef stewing meat, cubed
- 2 carrots, peeled and sliced
- 2 potatoes, peeled and diced
- 1 onion, chopped
- 2 cloves garlic, minced
- 1 can (400g) diced tomatoes
- 1.2 litres beef broth
- 1 tsp dried thyme
- Salt and black pepper, to taste
- Fresh parsley, chopped, for garnish
- Crusty bread, for serving

Preparation instructions:

1. In the Crock Pot, combine cubed beef stewing meat, sliced carrots, diced potatoes, chopped onion, minced garlic, diced tomatoes, beef broth, dried thyme, salt, and black pepper.
2. Cover and cook on low for 6 hours or until the beef is cooked through and the vegetables are tender.
3. Serve the beef and vegetable soup in bowls, garnished with chopped fresh parsley. Enjoy with crusty bread on the side.

Crockpot Beef and Black Bean Stir-Fry

Serves: 4 Prep time: 15 minutes / Cook time: 6 hours

Ingredients:

- 600g beef sirloin, thinly sliced
- 1 can (400g) black beans, drained and rinsed
- 1 red pepper, sliced
- 1 yellow pepper, sliced
- 1 onion, sliced
- 3 cloves garlic, minced
- 60ml soy sauce
- 2 tbsp honey
- 1 tbsp sesame oil
- 1 tsp grated fresh ginger
- Sesame seeds, for garnish
- Cooked rice, for serving

Preparation instructions:

1. In the Crock Pot, combine thinly sliced beef sirloin, drained black beans, sliced red and yellow peppers, sliced onion, and minced garlic.

2. In a bowl, whisk together soy sauce, honey, sesame oil, and grated fresh ginger. Pour the sauce over the beef and vegetables in the Crock Pot.
3. Cover and cook on low for 6 hours or until the beef is tender and the flavours are well combined.
4. Serve the beef and black bean stir-fry over cooked rice, garnished with sesame seeds. Enjoy this delicious and savoury stir-fry meal.

Slow Cooker Beef and Guinness Pie

Serves: 4 Prep time: 15 minutes / Cook time: 6 hours

Ingredients:

- 500g beef stewing meat, cubed
- 1 onion, finely chopped
- 2 carrots, peeled and diced
- 2 potatoes, peeled and diced
- 2 cloves garlic, minced
- 250ml Guinness stout
- 250ml beef broth
- 2 tbsp tomato paste
- 1 tbsp Worcestershire sauce
- 1 tsp dried thyme
- Salt and black pepper, to taste
- 400g puff pastry, thawed if frozen
- 1 egg, beaten, for egg wash

Preparation instructions:

1. In the Crock Pot, combine beef stewing meat, finely chopped onion, diced carrots, diced potatoes, minced garlic, Guinness stout, beef broth, tomato paste, Worcestershire sauce, dried thyme, salt, and black pepper. Stir well to combine.
2. Cover and cook on low for 6 hours or until the beef is tender and the flavours meld together.
3. Preheat the oven to 200°C. Transfer the beef stew mixture to a pie dish.
4. Roll out the puff pastry on a floured surface and cover the pie dish with the pastry, trimming any excess. Make a few slits in the pastry to allow steam to escape.
5. Brush the pastry with the beaten egg for a golden finish.
6. Bake in the preheated oven for 25-30 minutes or until the pastry is golden brown and cooked through.
7. Serve the Beef and Guinness Pie hot, accompanied by your favourite vegetables.

Crockpot Pulled Pork

Serves: 4 Prep time: 10 minutes / Cook time: 8 hours

Ingredients:

- 1.2kg pork shoulder, boneless
- 1 onion, finely chopped
- 4 cloves garlic, minced
- 250ml barbecue sauce
- 60ml apple cider vinegar
- 2 tbsp brown sugar
- 1 tsp paprika
- 1/2 tsp cayenne pepper
- Salt and black pepper, to taste

- Burger buns, coleslaw, and pickles, for serving

Preparation instructions:

1. Place the pork shoulder in the Crock Pot. In a bowl, mix together finely chopped onion, minced garlic, barbecue sauce, apple cider vinegar, brown sugar, paprika, cayenne pepper, salt, and black pepper.
2. Pour the sauce mixture over the pork, ensuring it is well coated.
3. Cover and cook on low for 8 hours or until the pork is tender and easily shredded.
4. Shred the pork using two forks, mixing it with the sauce in the Crock Pot.
5. Serve the pulled pork on burger buns, topped with coleslaw and pickles, creating a delicious and satisfying pulled pork sandwich.

Slow Cooker Pork Roast with Apple Sauce

Serves: 4 Prep time: 15 minutes / Cook time: 6 hours

Ingredients:

- 1.2kg pork loin roast
- 2 apples, peeled, cored, and sliced
- 1 onion, sliced
- 250ml apple juice
- 1 tbsp honey
- 1 tsp ground cinnamon
- 1/2 tsp ground nutmeg
- Salt and black pepper, to taste
- Fresh parsley, chopped, for garnish

Preparation instructions:

1. Place the pork loin roast in the Crock Pot. Arrange sliced apples and onions around the roast.
2. In a bowl, mix together apple juice, honey, ground cinnamon, ground nutmeg, salt, and black pepper.
3. Pour the apple juice mixture over the pork roast and apples.
4. Cover and cook on low for 6 hours or until the pork is cooked through and tender.
5. Transfer the pork roast to a serving platter, garnish with chopped fresh parsley, and serve with the cooked apples and onions.
6. Spoon the delicious apple sauce from the Crock Pot over the pork slices before serving.

Crockpot Pork and Bean Stew

Serves: 4 Prep time: 15 minutes / Cook time: 6 hours

Ingredients:

- 500g pork shoulder, diced
- 2 cans (400g each) mixed beans, drained and rinsed
- 1 onion, finely chopped
- 2 cloves garlic, minced
- 2 carrots, peeled and diced
- 1 can (400g) chopped tomatoes
- 500ml vegetable broth
- 1 tsp smoked paprika
- 1/2 tsp ground cumin
- Salt and black pepper, to taste
- Fresh parsley, chopped, for garnish

Preparation instructions:

1. In the Crock Pot, combine diced pork shoulder, drained mixed beans, finely chopped onion, minced garlic, diced carrots, chopped tomatoes, vegetable broth, smoked paprika, ground cumin, salt, and black pepper.
2. Stir well to combine all the Ingredients.
3. Cover and cook on low for 6 hours, allowing the flavours to meld together.
4. Serve the pork and bean stew hot, garnished with chopped fresh parsley. Enjoy this hearty and flavorful stew on a chilly evening.

Slow Cooker Pork and Cider Casserole

Serves: 4 Prep time: 15 minutes / Cook time: 6 hours

Ingredients:

- 500g pork shoulder, diced
- 2 apples, peeled, cored, and sliced
- 1 onion, finely chopped
- 2 carrots, peeled and sliced
- 500ml dry cider
- 250ml vegetable broth
- 2 tbsp whole grain mustard
- 1 tbsp honey
- Salt and black pepper, to taste
- Fresh parsley, chopped, for garnish

Preparation instructions:

1. In the Crock Pot, combine diced pork shoulder, sliced apples, finely chopped onion, sliced carrots, dry cider, vegetable broth, whole grain mustard, honey, salt, and black pepper.
2. Stir well to combine all the Ingredients.
3. Cover and cook on low for 6 hours or until the pork is tender and infused with the flavours.
4. Serve the pork and cider casserole hot, garnished with chopped fresh parsley. This hearty and comforting dish pairs perfectly with crusty bread or mashed potatoes.

Crockpot Pork and Apricot Curry

Serves: 4 Prep time: 15 minutes / Cook time: 6 hours

Ingredients:

- 500g pork loin, diced
- 1 onion, finely chopped
- 2 cloves garlic, minced
- 250ml coconut milk
- 125ml apricot nectar
- 2 tbsp curry powder
- 1 tsp ground turmeric
- 1 tsp ground cumin
- Salt and black pepper, to taste
- Fresh coriander, chopped, for garnish

Preparation instructions:

1. Place diced pork loin, finely chopped onion, minced garlic, coconut milk, apricot nectar, curry powder, ground turmeric, ground cumin, salt, and black pepper in the Crock Pot.

2. Stir well to ensure the pork is coated with the flavorful mixture.
3. Cover and cook on low for 6 hours or until the pork is tender and the curry has thickened.
4. Garnish the pork and apricot curry with chopped fresh coriander before serving. Serve this aromatic curry with steamed rice or naan bread for a delightful meal.

Slow Cooker Pork and Pineapple Stir-Fry

Serves: 4 Prep time: 15 minutes / Cook time: 6 hours

Ingredients:
- 500g pork tenderloin, thinly sliced
- 1 red pepper, sliced
- 1 yellow pepper, sliced
- 1 onion, thinly sliced
- 250g pineapple chunks, drained
- 4 tbsp soy sauce
- 2 tbsp honey
- 2 cloves garlic, minced
- 1 tsp ginger, grated
- 1 tbsp cornstarch, mixed with 2 tbsp water
- Sesame seeds, for garnish
- Spring onions, sliced, for garnish

Preparation instructions:
1. In the Crock Pot, combine thinly sliced pork tenderloin, sliced red pepper, sliced yellow pepper, thinly sliced onion, and pineapple chunks.
2. In a bowl, mix together soy sauce, honey, minced garlic, and grated ginger. Pour the sauce over the pork and vegetables in the Crock Pot.
3. Stir well to coat the Ingredients with the sauce.
4. Cover and cook on low for 6 hours or until the pork is cooked through and the vegetables are tender.
5. During the last 30 minutes of cooking, stir in the cornstarch mixture to thicken the sauce.
6. Serve the pork and pineapple stir-fry hot, garnished with sesame seeds and sliced spring onions. Enjoy this flavorful stir-fry with steamed rice or noodles.

Crockpot Pork and Sweet Potato Stew

Serves: 4 Prep time: 15 minutes / Cook time: 6 hours

Ingredients:
- 500g pork shoulder, diced
- 2 sweet potatoes, peeled and diced
- 1 onion, finely chopped
- 2 cloves garlic, minced
- 500ml vegetable broth
- 2 tbsp tomato paste
- 1 tsp dried thyme
- 1 tsp paprika
- Salt and black pepper, to taste
- Fresh parsley, chopped, for garnish

Preparation instructions:
1. In the Crock Pot, combine diced pork shoulder, diced sweet potatoes, finely chopped onion, minced garlic,

vegetable broth, tomato paste, dried thyme, paprika, salt, and black pepper.
2. Stir well to combine all the Ingredients.
3. Cover and cook on low for 6 hours or until the pork is tender and the sweet potatoes are cooked through.
4. Garnish the pork and sweet potato stew with chopped fresh parsley before serving. This comforting stew is perfect for chilly evenings and can be enjoyed with crusty bread or a side salad.

Slow Cooker Pork and Mushroom Pie

Serves: 4 Prep time: 15 minutes / Cook time: 6 hours

Ingredients:
- 500g pork loin, diced
- 250g mushrooms, sliced
- 1 onion, finely chopped
- 2 cloves garlic, minced
- 250ml vegetable broth
- 125ml double cream
- 2 tbsp plain flour
- 1 tsp dried thyme
- Salt and black pepper, to taste
- 1 sheet puff pastry
- 1 egg, beaten, for egg wash

Preparation instructions:
1. In the Crock Pot, combine diced pork loin, sliced mushrooms, finely chopped onion, minced garlic, vegetable broth, double cream, plain flour, dried thyme, salt, and black pepper.
2. Stir well to combine all the Ingredients.
3. Cover and cook on low for 6 hours or until the pork is tender and the sauce has thickened.
4. Preheat the oven to 200°C (180°C fan). Transfer the cooked pork and mushroom filling into a baking dish.
5. Roll out the puff pastry sheet and place it over the filling. Trim any excess pastry and press the edges to seal the pie.
6. Brush the pastry with beaten egg for a golden finish.
7. Bake in the preheated oven for 20-25 minutes or until the pastry is puffed up and golden brown.
8. Remove from the oven and let it cool for a few minutes before serving. This hearty pork and mushroom pie is perfect for a comforting dinner.

Crockpot Pork and Black Bean Chili

Serves: 4 Prep time: 15 minutes / Cook time: 6 hours

Ingredients:
- 500g pork shoulder, diced
- 2 cans (400g each) black beans, drained and rinsed
- 1 onion, finely chopped
- 2 cloves garlic, minced
- 1 red pepper, diced
- 1 green pepper, diced
- 1 can (400g) diced tomatoes
- 250ml vegetable broth
- 2 tbsp chilli powder
- 1 tsp ground cumin

- 1/2 tsp paprika
- Salt and black pepper, to taste
- Fresh coriander, chopped, for garnish
- Grated cheddar cheese, for topping

Preparation instructions:

1. In the Crock Pot, combine diced pork shoulder, black beans, finely chopped onion, minced garlic, diced red pepper, diced green pepper, diced tomatoes, vegetable broth, chilli powder, ground cumin, paprika, salt, and black pepper.
2. Stir well to combine all the Ingredients.
3. Cover and cook on low for 6 hours, allowing the flavours to meld together.
4. Serve the pork and black bean chilli hot, garnished with chopped fresh coriander and a sprinkle of grated cheddar cheese. This chilli pairs well with rice, tortilla chips, or crusty bread.

Slow Cooker Pork and Leek Casserole

Serves: 4 Prep time: 15 minutes / Cook time: 6 hours

Ingredients:

- 500g pork tenderloin, sliced
- 2 leeks, sliced
- 1 onion, finely chopped
- 250ml chicken broth
- 125ml double cream
- 2 tbsp plain flour
- 1 tbsp Dijon mustard
- Salt and black pepper, to taste
- Fresh parsley, chopped, for garnish

Preparation instructions:

1. In the Crock Pot, combine sliced pork tenderloin, sliced leeks, finely chopped onion, chicken broth, double cream, plain flour, Dijon mustard, salt, and black pepper.
2. Stir well to combine all the Ingredients.
3. Cover and cook on low for 6 hours or until the pork is cooked through and the leeks are tender.
4. Garnish the pork and leek casserole with chopped fresh parsley before serving. This creamy and flavorful casserole is excellent when served with mashed potatoes or crusty bread.

Slow Cooker Pork and Red Pepper Curry

Serves: 4 Prep time: 15 minutes / Cook time: 6 hours

Ingredients:

- 500g pork loin, diced
- 2 red peppers, sliced
- 1 onion, finely chopped
- 2 cloves garlic, minced
- 400ml coconut milk
- 2 tbsp red curry paste
- 1 tbsp fish sauce
- 1 tsp brown sugar
- Juice of 1 lime
- Fresh coriander, chopped, for garnish

- Cooked rice, for serving

Preparation instructions:

1. In the Crock Pot, combine diced pork loin, sliced red peppers, finely chopped onion, minced garlic, coconut milk, red curry paste, fish sauce, brown sugar, and lime juice.
2. Stir well to combine all the Ingredients.
3. Cover and cook on low for 6 hours or until the pork is tender and infused with the curry flavours.
4. Serve the pork and red pepper curry hot, garnished with chopped fresh coriander. Enjoy this aromatic curry with cooked rice for a satisfying meal.

Crockpot Pork and Apple Casserole

Serves: 4 Prep time: 15 minutes / Cook time: 6 hours

Ingredients:

- 500g pork shoulder, diced
- 2 apples, peeled, cored, and sliced
- 1 onion, finely chopped
- 2 cloves garlic, minced
- 250ml chicken broth
- 125ml double cream
- 2 tbsp plain flour
- 1 tsp dried sage
- Salt and black pepper, to taste
- Fresh parsley, chopped, for garnish

Preparation instructions:

1. In the Crock Pot, combine diced pork shoulder, sliced apples, finely chopped onion, minced garlic, chicken broth, double cream, plain flour, dried sage, salt, and black pepper.
2. Stir well to combine all the Ingredients.
3. Cover and cook on low for 6 hours or until the pork is tender and the sauce has thickened.
4. Garnish the pork and apple casserole with chopped fresh parsley before serving. This dish pairs wonderfully with mashed potatoes or rice.

Slow Cooker Pork and Vegetable Stir-Fry

Serves: 4 Prep time: 15 minutes / Cook time: 6 hours

Ingredients:

- 500g pork loin, thinly sliced
- 1 yellow pepper, sliced
- 1 carrot, julienned
- 3 tbsp soy sauce
- 2 tbsp honey
- 1 tsp fresh ginger, grated
- 1 tbsp cornflour
- 125ml chicken broth
- Sesame seeds, for garnish
- Spring onions, sliced, for garnish
- 1 red pepper, sliced
- 1 courgette, sliced
- 1 onion, thinly sliced
- 2 tbsp oyster sauce
- 2 cloves garlic, minced

Preparation instructions:

1. In the Crock Pot, combine thinly sliced pork loin, sliced red pepper, sliced yellow pepper, sliced courgette, julienned carrot, thinly sliced onion, soy sauce, oyster sauce, honey, minced garlic, grated fresh ginger, cornflour,

and chicken broth.

2.Stir well to combine all the Ingredients.

3.Cover and cook on low for 6 hours or until the pork is cooked through and the vegetables are tender.

4.Garnish the pork and vegetable stir-fry with sesame seeds and sliced spring onions before serving. Serve this delicious stir-fry over steamed rice or noodles.

Crockpot Pork and Chickpea Curry

Serves: 4 Prep time: 15 minutes / Cook time: 6 hours

Ingredients:

- 500g pork tenderloin, diced
- 2 cans (400g each) chickpeas, drained and rinsed
- 1 onion, finely chopped
- 2 cloves garlic, minced
- 1 can (400ml) coconut milk
- 3 tbsp curry paste   • 1 tbsp vegetable oil
- 250ml chicken broth
- Salt and black pepper, to taste
- Fresh coriander, chopped, for garnish
- Cooked basmati rice, for serving

Preparation instructions:

1.In a pan, heat vegetable oil over medium heat. Add diced pork tenderloin and cook until browned on all sides. Transfer the pork to the Crock Pot.

2.To the Crock Pot, add drained and rinsed chickpeas, finely chopped onion, minced garlic, coconut milk, curry paste, chicken broth, salt, and black pepper.

3.Stir well to combine all the Ingredients.

4.Cover and cook on low for 6 hours or until the pork is tender and the curry is flavorful.

5.Garnish the pork and chickpea curry with chopped fresh coriander and serve over cooked basmati rice for a satisfying meal.

Slow Cooker Pork and Green Bean Stir-Fry

Serves: 4 Prep time: 15 minutes / Cook time: 6 hours

Ingredients:

- 500g pork loin, thinly sliced
- 400g green beans, trimmed and halved
- 1 red pepper, sliced
- 1 yellow pepper, sliced
- 3 tbsp soy sauce
- 2 tbsp hoisin sauce
- 1 tbsp honey
- 2 cloves garlic, minced
- 1 tsp fresh ginger, grated
- 1 tbsp cornflour
- 125ml chicken broth
- Sesame seeds, for garnish
- Spring onions, sliced, for garnish

Preparation instructions:

1.In the Crock Pot, combine thinly sliced pork loin, halved green beans, sliced red pepper, sliced yellow pepper, soy sauce, hoisin sauce, honey, minced garlic, grated fresh

ginger, cornflour, and chicken broth.

2.Stir well to combine all the Ingredients.

3.Cover and cook on low for 6 hours or until the pork is cooked through and the vegetables are tender.

4.Garnish the pork and green bean stir-fry with sesame seeds and sliced spring onions before serving. Serve this flavorful stir-fry over steamed rice for a delightful meal.

Crockpot Pork and Coconut Curry

Serves: 4 Prep time: 15 minutes / Cook time: 6 hours

Ingredients:

- 500g pork loin, diced   • 1 onion, finely chopped
- 2 cloves garlic, minced
- 1 red chilli, deseeded and finely chopped
- 400ml coconut milk   • 2 tbsp red curry paste
- 2 tbsp soy sauce   • 1 tbsp vegetable oil
- 1 tbsp brown sugar
- Salt and black pepper, to taste
- Fresh coriander, chopped, for garnish
- Cooked jasmine rice, for serving

Preparation instructions:

1.In a pan, heat vegetable oil over medium heat. Add diced pork loin and cook until browned on all sides. Transfer the pork to the Crock Pot.

2.To the Crock Pot, add finely chopped onion, minced garlic, finely chopped red chilli, coconut milk, red curry paste, soy sauce, brown sugar, salt, and black pepper.

3.Stir well to combine all the Ingredients.

4.Cover and cook on low for 6 hours or until the pork is tender and the curry is flavorful.

5.Garnish the pork and coconut curry with chopped fresh coriander and serve over cooked jasmine rice for a delicious meal.

Slow Cooker Pork and Spinach Soup

Serves: 4 Prep time: 15 minutes / Cook time: 6 hours

Ingredients:

- 500g pork shoulder, diced
- 1 onion, finely chopped
- 2 cloves garlic, minced
- 1 litre chicken broth
- 200g fresh spinach, chopped
- 2 carrots, peeled and diced
- 1 potato, peeled and diced
- 1 tsp ground cumin
- 1/2 tsp ground turmeric
- Salt and black pepper, to taste
- Fresh parsley, chopped, for garnish

Preparation instructions:

1.In the Crock Pot, combine diced pork shoulder, finely chopped onion, minced garlic, chicken broth, chopped fresh spinach, diced carrots, diced potato, ground cumin, ground turmeric, salt, and black pepper.

2.Stir well to combine all the Ingredients.

3.Cover and cook on low for 6 hours or until the pork is

tender and the vegetables are cooked through.

4. Garnish the pork and spinach soup with chopped fresh parsley before serving. This hearty soup is perfect for a comforting meal.

Crockpot Pork and Rice Casserole

Serves: 4 Prep time: 15 minutes / Cook time: 6 hours

Ingredients:
- 500g pork tenderloin, diced
- 1 onion, finely chopped
- 2 cloves garlic, minced
- 250g long-grain white rice
- 500ml chicken broth
- 1 can (400g) diced tomatoes
- 1 tsp paprika
- 1/2 tsp dried thyme
- Salt and black pepper, to taste
- Fresh parsley, chopped, for garnish

Preparation instructions:
1. In the Crock Pot, combine diced pork tenderloin, finely chopped onion, minced garlic, long-grain white rice, chicken broth, diced tomatoes, paprika, dried thyme, salt, and black pepper.
2. Stir well to combine all the Ingredients.
3. Cover and cook on low for 6 hours or until the pork is tender and the rice is cooked through.
4. Garnish the pork and rice casserole with chopped fresh parsley before serving. This flavorful casserole is a complete meal in one pot.

Slow Cooker Pork and Mango Curry

Serves: 4 Prep time: 15 minutes / Cook time: 6 hours

Ingredients:
- 500g pork loin, diced
- 1 onion, finely chopped
- 2 cloves garlic, minced
- 1 ripe mango, peeled, pitted, and diced
- 400ml coconut milk
- 2 tbsp mango chutney
- 2 tbsp curry powder
- 1 tbsp vegetable oil
- Salt and black pepper, to taste
- Fresh coriander, chopped, for garnish
- Cooked basmati rice, for serving

Preparation instructions:
1. In a pan, heat vegetable oil over medium heat. Add diced pork loin and cook until browned on all sides. Transfer the pork to the Crock Pot.
2. To the Crock Pot, add finely chopped onion, minced garlic, diced ripe mango, coconut milk, mango chutney, curry powder, salt, and black pepper.
3. Stir well to combine all the Ingredients.
4. Cover and cook on low for 6 hours or until the pork is tender and the curry is flavorful.
5. Garnish the pork and mango curry with chopped fresh

coriander and serve over cooked basmati rice for a delightful meal.

Crockpot Pork and Pea Risotto

Serves: 4 Prep time: 15 minutes / Cook time: 3 hours

Ingredients:
- 400g pork loin, diced
- 1 onion, finely chopped
- 2 cloves garlic, minced
- 300g Arborio rice
- 1 litre chicken broth
- 150g frozen peas
- 60ml white wine
- 60ml double cream
- 50g grated Parmesan cheese
- 2 tbsp butter
- Salt and black pepper, to taste
- Fresh parsley, chopped, for garnish

Preparation instructions:
1. In a pan, heat butter over medium heat. Add diced pork loin and cook until browned on all sides. Transfer the pork to the Crock Pot.
2. To the Crock Pot, add finely chopped onion, minced garlic, Arborio rice, chicken broth, frozen peas, white wine, double cream, grated Parmesan cheese, salt, and black pepper.
3. Stir well to combine all the Ingredients.
4. Cover and cook on low for 3 hours or until the risotto is creamy and the rice is tender.
5. Garnish the pork and pea risotto with chopped fresh parsley before serving. This rich and comforting dish is perfect for a hearty meal.

Slow Cooker Lamb Stew

Serves: 4 Prep time: 20 minutes / Cook time: 6 hours

Ingredients:
- 500g lamb shoulder, diced
- 2 carrots, peeled and sliced
- 2 potatoes, peeled and diced
- 1 onion, finely chopped
- 2 cloves garlic, minced
- 500ml lamb or beef broth
- 2 tbsp tomato paste
- 1 tsp dried rosemary
- 1 tsp dried thyme
- Salt and black pepper, to taste
- Fresh mint, chopped, for garnish

Preparation instructions:
1. In the Crock Pot, combine diced lamb shoulder, sliced carrots, diced potatoes, finely chopped onion, minced garlic, lamb or beef broth, tomato paste, dried rosemary, dried thyme, salt, and black pepper.
2. Stir well to combine all the Ingredients.
3. Cover and cook on low for 6 hours or until the lamb is tender and the vegetables are cooked through.
4. Garnish the lamb stew with chopped fresh mint before serving. This hearty stew is a comforting meal for any occasion.

Crockpot Lamb Curry

Serves: 4 Prep time: 20 minutes / Cook time: 4 hours

Ingredients:

- 500g lamb leg, diced
- 2 cloves garlic, minced
- 2 tbsp curry powder
- 1 tsp ground cumin
- 1 onion, finely chopped
- 400ml coconut milk
- 1 tsp ground turmeric
- 1 tsp paprika
- Salt and black pepper, to taste
- Fresh coriander, chopped, for garnish
- Cooked basmati rice, for serving

Preparation instructions:

1. In a pan, heat vegetable oil over medium heat. Add diced lamb leg and cook until browned on all sides. Transfer the lamb to the Crock Pot.
2. To the Crock Pot, add finely chopped onion, minced garlic, coconut milk, curry powder, ground turmeric, ground cumin, paprika, salt, and black pepper.
3. Stir well to combine all the Ingredients.
4. Cover and cook on low for 4 hours or until the lamb is tender and the curry is flavorful.
5. Garnish the lamb curry with chopped fresh coriander and serve over cooked basmati rice for a delicious meal.

Slow Cooker Lamb and Vegetable Soup

Serves: 4 Prep time: 20 minutes / Cook time: 6 hours

Ingredients:

- 500g lamb stew meat, diced
- 2 carrots, peeled and sliced
- 2 potatoes, peeled and diced
- 1 leek, trimmed and sliced
- 1 onion, finely chopped
- 2 cloves garlic, minced
- 1.5 litres lamb or vegetable broth
- 1 tsp dried thyme
- Salt and black pepper, to taste
- Fresh parsley, chopped, for garnish

Preparation instructions:

1. In the Crock Pot, combine diced lamb stew meat, sliced carrots, diced potatoes, sliced leek, finely chopped onion, minced garlic, lamb or vegetable broth, dried thyme, salt, and black pepper.
2. Stir well to combine all the Ingredients.
3. Cover and cook on low for 6 hours or until the lamb is tender and the vegetables are cooked through.
4. Garnish the lamb and vegetable soup with chopped fresh parsley before serving. This nourishing soup is a comforting option for a filling meal.

Crockpot Lamb and Apricot Tagine

Serves: 4 Prep time: 15 minutes / Cook time: 4 hours

Ingredients:

- 500g lamb shoulder, diced
- 1 onion, finely chopped
- 2 cloves garlic, minced
- 1 tsp ground cumin
- 1 tsp ground coriander
- 1/2 tsp ground cinnamon

- 1/4 tsp ground ginger
- 400g canned chickpeas, drained and rinsed
- 400g canned chopped tomatoes
- 250ml lamb or vegetable broth
- 100g dried apricots, chopped
- Salt and black pepper, to taste
- Fresh coriander, chopped, for garnish
- Cooked couscous, for serving

Preparation instructions:

1. In a pan, heat vegetable oil over medium heat. Add diced lamb shoulder and cook until browned on all sides. Transfer the lamb to the Crock Pot.
2. To the Crock Pot, add finely chopped onion, minced garlic, ground cumin, ground coriander, ground cinnamon, ground ginger, drained chickpeas, canned chopped tomatoes, lamb or vegetable broth, chopped dried apricots, salt, and black pepper.
3. Stir well to combine all the Ingredients.
4. Cover and cook on low for 4 hours or until the lamb is tender and the flavours are well blended.
5. Serve the lamb and apricot tagine over cooked couscous, garnished with chopped fresh coriander. This fragrant dish is a delightful taste of North African cuisine.

Slow Cooker Lamb and Lentil Soup

Serves: 4 Prep time: 15 minutes / Cook time: 6 hours

Ingredients:

- 500g lamb leg, diced
- 1 onion, finely chopped
- 2 carrots, peeled and diced
- 2 cloves garlic, minced
- 200g red lentils, rinsed and drained
- 1.5 litres lamb or vegetable broth
- 1 tsp ground cumin
- 1/2 tsp ground turmeric
- Salt and black pepper, to taste
- Fresh parsley, chopped, for garnish

Preparation instructions:

1. In the Crock Pot, combine diced lamb leg, finely chopped onion, diced carrots, minced garlic, rinsed red lentils, lamb or vegetable broth, ground cumin, ground turmeric, salt, and black pepper.
2. Stir well to combine all the Ingredients.
3. Cover and cook on low for 6 hours or until the lamb is tender and the lentils are cooked through, creating a hearty soup.
4. Garnish the lamb and lentil soup with chopped fresh parsley before serving. This nutritious soup is perfect for a filling meal.

Crockpot Lamb and Chickpea Stew

Serves: 4 Prep time: 15 minutes / Cook time: 4 hours

Ingredients:

- 500g lamb stew meat, diced
- 1 onion, finely chopped

- 2 cloves garlic, minced
- 2 carrots, peeled and sliced
- 2 potatoes, peeled and diced
- 400g canned chickpeas, drained and rinsed
- 400g canned chopped tomatoes
- 250ml lamb or vegetable broth
- 1 tsp ground cumin
- 1/2 tsp ground paprika
- Salt and black pepper, to taste
- Fresh mint, chopped, for garnish
- Cooked couscous, for serving

Preparation instructions:

1. In a pan, heat vegetable oil over medium heat. Add diced lamb stew meat and cook until browned on all sides. Transfer the lamb to the Crock Pot.
2. To the Crock Pot, add finely chopped onion, minced garlic, sliced carrots, diced potatoes, drained chickpeas, canned chopped tomatoes, lamb or vegetable broth, ground cumin, ground paprika, salt, and black pepper.
3. Stir well to combine all the Ingredients.
4. Cover and cook on low for 4 hours or until the lamb is tender and the stew is flavorful.
5. Serve the lamb and chickpea stew over cooked couscous, garnished with chopped fresh mint. This hearty stew is a taste of Middle Eastern cuisine.

Slow Cooker Lamb and Red Pepper Curry

Serves: 4 Prep time: 15 minutes / Cook time: 6 hours

Ingredients:
- 500g lamb shoulder, diced
- 1 onion, finely chopped
- 2 red peppers, sliced
- 3 cloves garlic, minced
- 400ml canned coconut milk
- 250ml lamb or vegetable broth
- 2 tbsp red curry paste
- 1 tbsp vegetable oil
- 1 tsp ground turmeric
- 1 tsp ground cumin
- Salt and black pepper, to taste
- Fresh oregano, chopped, for garnish
- Cooked basmati rice, for serving

Preparation instructions:

1. In a pan, heat vegetable oil over medium heat. Add diced lamb shoulder and cook until browned on all sides. Transfer the lamb to the Crock Pot.
2. To the Crock Pot, add sliced red peppers, finely chopped onion, minced garlic, canned coconut milk, lamb or vegetable broth, red curry paste, ground turmeric, ground cumin, salt, and black pepper.
3. Stir well to combine all the Ingredients.
4. Cover and cook on low for 6 hours or until the lamb is tender and the curry is aromatic and flavorful.
5. Serve the lamb and red pepper curry over cooked basmati rice, garnished with chopped fresh oregano. This rich and spicy curry is a delightful taste of Southeast Asian cuisine.

Crockpot Lamb and Potato Curry

Serves: 4 Prep time: 15 minutes / Cook time: 6 hours

Ingredients:
- 500g lamb leg, diced
- 3 potatoes, peeled and diced
- 1 onion, finely chopped
- 3 cloves garlic, minced
- 400ml canned coconut milk
- 250ml lamb or vegetable broth
- 2 tbsp curry powder
- 1 tbsp vegetable oil
- Salt and black pepper, to taste
- Fresh coriander, chopped, for garnish
- Cooked naan bread, for serving

Preparation instructions:

1. In a pan, heat vegetable oil over medium heat. Add diced lamb leg and cook until browned on all sides. Transfer the lamb to the Crock Pot.
2. To the Crock Pot, add diced potatoes, finely chopped onion, minced garlic, canned coconut milk, lamb or vegetable broth, curry powder, salt, and black pepper.
3. Stir well to combine all the Ingredients.
4. Cover and cook on low for 6 hours or until the lamb is tender and the potatoes are cooked through, creating a hearty and comforting curry.
5. Serve the lamb and potato curry with cooked naan bread, garnished with chopped fresh coriander. This flavorful curry is a classic Indian dish made easy in the Crock Pot.

Crockpot Lamb and Green Bean Stir-Fry

Serves: 4 Prep time: 15 minutes / Cook time: 4 hours

Ingredients:
- 500g lamb stir-fry strips
- 300g green beans, trimmed and halved
- 1 red pepper, sliced
- 1 yellow pepper, sliced
- 1 onion, thinly sliced
- 3 cloves garlic, minced
- 60ml soy sauce
- 2 tbsp oyster sauce
- 1 tbsp vegetable oil
- 1 tsp honey
- 1/2 tsp ground ginger
- Salt and black pepper, to taste
- Sesame seeds, for garnish
- Cooked jasmine rice, for serving

Preparation instructions:

1. In a pan, heat vegetable oil over medium heat. Add lamb stir-fry strips and cook until browned. Transfer the lamb to the Crock Pot.
2. To the Crock Pot, add halved green beans, sliced red pepper, sliced yellow pepper, thinly sliced onion, minced garlic, soy sauce, oyster sauce, honey, ground ginger, salt, and black pepper.
3. Stir well to combine all the Ingredients.
4. Cover and cook on low for 4 hours or until the lamb is tender and the vegetables are cooked yet crisp.
5. Serve the lamb and green bean stir-fry over cooked jasmine rice, garnished with sesame seeds. This vibrant stir-fry is a tasty fusion of flavours and textures.

Chapter 10: Dessert Recipes

Slow Cooker Chocolate Fondue

Serves: 4 Prep time: 10 minutes / Cook time: 1 hour

Ingredients:

- 200g dark chocolate, chopped
- 200ml double cream • 50g unsalted butter
- 1 tsp vanilla extract
- Assorted fruits (strawberries, bananas, pineapple) and marshmallows, for dipping

Preparation instructions:

1. In a slow cooker, combine the chopped dark chocolate, double cream, and unsalted butter.
2. Cover and cook on low for 1 hour, stirring occasionally until the chocolate is fully melted and the mixture is smooth.
3. Stir in the vanilla extract.
4. Serve the chocolate fondue warm in the slow cooker with assorted fruits and marshmallows for dipping. Enjoy this indulgent treat for dessert or a special occasion.

Crockpot Bread Pudding

Serves: 4 Prep time: 15 minutes / Cook time: 2 hours

Ingredients:

- 400g white bread, cubed   • 500ml whole milk
- 3 large eggs   • 100g granulated sugar
- 1 tsp vanilla extract   • 1/2 tsp ground cinnamon
- 1/4 tsp ground nutmeg • 50g raisins
- 50g unsalted butter, melted
- Custard or vanilla sauce, for serving

Preparation instructions:

1. In a large bowl, combine the cubed white bread and milk. Let it soak for 10-15 minutes until the bread absorbs the milk.
2. In another bowl, whisk together the large eggs, granulated sugar, vanilla extract, ground cinnamon, and ground nutmeg.
3. Add the egg mixture, raisins, and melted unsalted butter to the soaked bread. Stir well to combine.
4. Transfer the mixture to the greased crockpot.
5. Cover and cook on low for 2 hours or until the bread pudding is set and golden brown on top.
6. Serve the bread pudding warm, drizzled with custard or vanilla sauce, for a comforting and delightful dessert.

Slow Cooker Apple Crumble

Serves: 4 Prep time: 15 minutes / Cook time: 3 hours

Ingredients:

- 4 apples, peeled, cored, and sliced
- 50g granulated sugar   • 1/2 tsp ground cinnamon
- 1/4 tsp ground nutmeg • 100g plain flour
- 50g rolled oats
- 50g unsalted butter, cold and cubed
- Vanilla ice cream or custard, for serving

Preparation instructions:

1. In a bowl, combine the sliced apples, granulated sugar, ground cinnamon, and ground nutmeg. Toss until the apples are evenly coated.
2. Transfer the apple mixture to the slow cooker.
3. In another bowl, mix the plain flour and rolled oats. Add the cold, cubed unsalted butter and rub it into the flour-oat mixture until it resembles coarse crumbs.
4. Sprinkle the crumb mixture evenly over the apples in the slow cooker.
5. Cover and cook on low for 3 hours or until the apples are tender and the crumble topping is golden and crisp.
6. Serve the apple crumble warm, accompanied by a scoop of vanilla ice cream or custard for a comforting dessert.

Crockpot Sticky Toffee Pudding

Serves: 4 Prep time: 15 minutes / Cook time: 3 hours

Ingredients:

- 200g dates, pitted and chopped
- 250ml boiling water
- 1 tsp bicarbonate of soda
- 100g unsalted butter, softened
- 175g dark brown sugar
- 2 large eggs
- 250g self-raising flour
- 1 tsp vanilla extract
- 200ml double cream, for serving
- For the toffee sauce:
- 150g dark brown sugar
- 200ml double cream
- 50g unsalted butter

Preparation instructions:

1. In a bowl, combine the chopped dates, boiling water, and bicarbonate of soda. Let it sit for 10 minutes until the dates soften.
2. In another bowl, cream together the softened unsalted butter and dark brown sugar until light and fluffy. Beat in the large eggs, one at a time.
3. Fold in the self-raising flour and vanilla extract into the butter-sugar mixture. Stir in the soaked dates.
4. Grease the crockpot and pour the pudding batter into it.
5. Cover and cook on low for 3 hours or until the pudding is cooked through and springs back when lightly touched.
6. For the toffee sauce, combine the dark brown sugar, double cream, and unsalted butter in a saucepan. Heat over medium heat, stirring constantly until the sauce thickens.
7. Serve the sticky toffee pudding warm, drizzled with the toffee sauce and accompanied by a dollop of double cream. Enjoy this classic British dessert for a delightful treat.

Slow Cooker Rice Pudding

Serves: 4 Prep time: 10 minutes / Cook time: 2 hours

Ingredients:

- 100g pudding rice   • 600ml whole milk

- 50g granulated sugar • 1/2 tsp vanilla extract
- Ground cinnamon, for garnish

Preparation instructions:
1. In the slow cooker, combine the pudding rice, whole milk, and granulated sugar. Stir well.
2. Cover and cook on low for 2 hours, stirring occasionally, until the rice is tender and the mixture has thickened.
3. Stir in the vanilla extract.
4. Serve the rice pudding warm, sprinkled with a dash of ground cinnamon for a comforting dessert.

Crockpot Lemon Drizzle Cake

Serves: 4 Prep time: 15 minutes / Cook time: 2 hours

Ingredients:
- 175g unsalted butter, softened
- 175g granulated sugar • 3 large eggs
- 175g self-raising flour • Zest of 2 lemons
- 60ml lemon juice
- 50g icing sugar, for drizzling

Preparation instructions:
1. Grease and line the base of the crockpot.
2. In a bowl, cream together the softened unsalted butter and granulated sugar until pale and fluffy.
3. Beat in the large eggs, one at a time, adding a spoonful of self-raising flour with each egg.
4. Fold in the remaining self-raising flour and the lemon zest.
5. Spoon the batter into the crockpot and smooth the top.
6. Cover and cook on low for 2 hours or until a skewer inserted into the centre comes out clean.
7. While the cake is still warm, mix the lemon juice with icing sugar to make a thick, pourable glaze. Drizzle the lemon glaze over the cake.
8. Allow the cake to cool slightly before serving. Enjoy this zesty treat with a cup of tea.

Slow Cooker Chocolate Lava Cake

Serves: 4 Prep time: 15 minutes / Cook time: 2 hours

Ingredients:
- 100g dark chocolate, chopped
- 100g unsalted butter • 100g granulated sugar
- 2 large eggs • 50g plain flour
- 1/4 tsp salt • Vanilla ice cream, for serving

Preparation instructions:
1. Grease the base and sides of the crockpot.
2. In a heatproof bowl, melt the dark chocolate and unsalted butter together over a pan of simmering water, stirring until smooth. Remove from heat and let it cool slightly.
3. In another bowl, whisk the granulated sugar and large eggs until well combined.
4. Gradually add the melted chocolate mixture, stirring continuously.
5. Fold in the plain flour and salt until just combined.
6. Pour the batter into the crockpot and spread it out evenly.
7. Cover and cook on low for 2 hours or until the edges are set but the centre is still slightly gooey.

8. Serve the chocolate lava cake warm, topped with a scoop of vanilla ice cream for a decadent dessert.

Crockpot Berry Cobbler

Serves: 4 Prep time: 15 minutes / Cook time: 2 hours

Ingredients:
- 500g mixed berries (such as strawberries, blueberries, and raspberries)
- 75g granulated sugar • 1 tbsp cornstarch
- 1/2 tsp ground cinnamon • 150g self-raising flour
- 50g unsalted butter, cold and cubed
- 60ml whole milk • Vanilla custard, for serving

Preparation instructions:
1. In a bowl, combine the mixed berries, granulated sugar, cornstarch, and ground cinnamon. Toss until the berries are coated evenly.
2. Transfer the berry mixture to the greased crockpot.
3. In another bowl, rub the cold, cubed unsalted butter into the self-raising flour until it resembles breadcrumbs.
4. Stir in the whole milk to form a thick batter.
5. Drop spoonfuls of the batter over the berry mixture in the crockpot.
6. Cover and cook on low for 2 hours or until the berry mixture is bubbling, and the cobbler topping is golden and cooked through.
7. Serve the berry cobbler warm, accompanied by a generous drizzle of vanilla custard for a delightful dessert. Enjoy the combination of warm berries and tender cobbler topping.

Slow Cooker Banana Bread

Serves: 4 Prep time: 15 minutes / Cook time: 3 hours

Ingredients:
- 250g ripe bananas, mashed
- 100g unsalted butter, melted
- 150g granulated sugar
- 2 large eggs • 250g plain flour
- 1 tsp baking soda • 1/4 tsp salt
- 60ml whole milk • 1 tsp vanilla extract

Preparation instructions:
1. Grease and line the base of the slow cooker.
2. In a large bowl, combine the mashed ripe bananas, melted unsalted butter, and granulated sugar. Mix well.
3. Beat in the large eggs one at a time.
4. In another bowl, whisk together the plain flour, baking soda, and salt.
5. Gradually add the dry Ingredients to the banana mixture, alternating with the whole milk. Mix until just combined.
6. Stir in the vanilla extract.
7. Pour the batter into the prepared slow cooker, spreading it out evenly.
8. Cover and cook on low for 3 hours or until a toothpick inserted into the centre of the banana bread comes out clean.
9. Allow the banana bread to cool in the slow cooker for 10-15 minutes before transferring it to a wire rack to cool completely. Slice and enjoy this moist and flavourful banana bread.

Crockpot Rice Krispie Treats

Serves: 4 Prep time: 10 minutes / Cook time: 1 hour

Ingredients:

- 200g marshmallows
- 200g Rice Krispies cereal
- 60g unsalted butter

Preparation instructions:

1. Grease the base and sides of the crockpot.
2. In the crockpot, melt the unsalted butter over low heat.
3. Add the marshmallows and stir until completely melted and well combined with the butter.
4. Remove the crockpot from the heat and gently fold in the Rice Krispies cereal until evenly coated with the marshmallow mixture.
5. Press the mixture into the greased crockpot, smoothing the top with a spatula.
6. Cover and cook on low for 1 hour. This will help the Rice Krispie treats set.
7. Turn off the crockpot and let the treats cool completely before cutting them into squares. Enjoy these classic treats with your family and friends.

Slow Cooker Tiramisu

Serves: 4 Prep time: 20 minutes / Chill time: 4 hours

Ingredients:

- 250ml heavy cream
- 60g icing sugar
- 240ml strong brewed coffee, cooled
- 2 tbsp coffee liqueur (optional)
- 200g ladyfingers
- 250g mascarpone cheese
- 1 tsp vanilla extract
- Cocoa powder, for dusting

Preparation instructions:

1. In a bowl, whip the heavy cream until stiff peaks form.
2. In another bowl, combine the mascarpone cheese, icing sugar, and vanilla extract. Mix until smooth and creamy.
3. Gently fold the whipped cream into the mascarpone mixture until well incorporated.
4. In a shallow dish, mix the brewed coffee and coffee liqueur if using.
5. Quickly dip each ladyfinger into the coffee mixture, ensuring they are soaked but not soggy.
6. Arrange a layer of soaked ladyfingers in the bottom of the slow cooker.
7. Spread half of the mascarpone mixture over the ladyfingers.
8. Repeat with another layer of soaked ladyfingers and the remaining mascarpone mixture.
9. Cover and refrigerate the tiramisu in the slow cooker for at least 4 hours or overnight to allow the flavours to meld.
10. Before serving, dust the top with cocoa powder for an elegant finish. Slice and enjoy this delightful Italian dessert.

Crockpot Peach Crisp

Serves: 4 Prep time: 15 minutes / Cook time: 2 hours

Ingredients:

- 500g fresh peaches, peeled, pitted, and sliced
- 50g granulated sugar
- 1/2 tsp ground cinnamon
- 50g plain flour
- 60g unsalted butter, cold and cubed
- Vanilla ice cream, for serving
- 1 tbsp cornstarch
- 100g rolled oats
- 50g brown sugar

Preparation instructions:

1. In a bowl, combine the sliced peaches, granulated sugar, cornstarch, and ground cinnamon. Toss until the peaches are coated evenly.
2. Transfer the peach mixture to the greased crockpot.
3. In another bowl, mix the rolled oats, plain flour, brown sugar, and cold, cubed unsalted butter until it resembles coarse crumbs.
4. Sprinkle the oat mixture over the peach layer in the crockpot.
5. Cover and cook on low for 2 hours or until the peaches are tender and the crisp topping is golden and crispy.
6. Serve the peach crisp warm, topped with a scoop of vanilla ice cream for a comforting dessert. Enjoy the combination of sweet, juicy peaches and crispy, buttery oats.

Slow Cooker Sticky Ginger Pudding

Serves: 4 Prep time: 15 minutes / Cook time: 3 hours

Ingredients:

- 200g self-raising flour
- 100g unsalted butter, melted
- 100g golden syrup
- 2 large eggs
- 1 tbsp finely grated fresh ginger
- 1 tbsp hot water
- For the sticky toffee sauce:
- 100g dark brown sugar
- 50g unsalted butter
- 1 tsp ground ginger
- 100g black treacle
- 120ml whole milk
- 150ml double cream
- 1 tsp vanilla extract

Preparation instructions:

1. In a bowl, mix the self-raising flour and ground ginger.
2. In another bowl, whisk together the melted unsalted butter, golden syrup, black treacle, large eggs, whole milk, and finely grated fresh ginger.
3. Gradually add the wet Ingredients to the dry Ingredients, mixing until well combined.
4. Dissolve the hot water in the batter.
5. Grease the base and sides of the slow cooker.
6. Pour the batter into the slow cooker.
7. In a saucepan, combine the dark brown sugar, double cream, unsalted butter, and vanilla extract. Heat gently until the sugar is dissolved and the sauce is smooth.
8. Pour half of the sticky toffee sauce over the batter in the slow cooker.
9. Cover and cook on low for 3 hours or until the pudding is set and a skewer inserted into the middle comes out clean.
10. Serve the sticky ginger pudding warm, drizzled with the remaining sticky toffee sauce.

Crockpot Apple Cider

Serves: 4 Prep time: 10 minutes / Cook time: 3 hours

Ingredients:

- 1.5 litres apple juice
- 2-3 cinnamon sticks

- 4-5 cloves
- 1 lemon, thinly sliced
- 1 tsp ground nutmeg
- 1 orange, thinly sliced
- 50g brown sugar

Preparation instructions:
1. In the crockpot, combine the apple juice, cinnamon sticks, cloves, thinly sliced orange, thinly sliced lemon, brown sugar, and ground nutmeg.
2. Stir well to dissolve the sugar and mix the spices.
3. Cover and cook on low for 3 hours to allow the flavours to meld.
4. Before serving, strain the cider to remove the spices and fruit slices.
5. Ladle the warm cider into mugs and garnish with a cinnamon stick for a comforting, spiced apple drink.

Slow Cooker Chocolate Brownies

Serves: 4 Prep time: 15 minutes / Cook time: 2.5 hours

Ingredients:
- 200g dark chocolate, chopped
- 100g unsalted butter
- 150g granulated sugar
- 2 large eggs
- 1 tsp vanilla extract
- 100g plain flour
- 30g cocoa powder
- 1/4 tsp salt
- 100g chopped nuts (optional)

Preparation instructions:
1. Grease the base and sides of the slow cooker.
2. In a heatproof bowl, melt the dark chocolate and unsalted butter together, stirring until smooth. Allow it to cool slightly.
3. In another bowl, whisk together the granulated sugar, large eggs, and vanilla extract until well combined.
4. Gradually add the melted chocolate mixture to the egg mixture, stirring continuously.
5. In a separate bowl, sift together the plain flour, cocoa powder, and salt.
6. Gradually add the dry Ingredients to the wet Ingredients, mixing until just combined.
7. If desired, fold in the chopped nuts.
8. Pour the brownie batter into the slow cooker, spreading it out evenly.
9. Cover and cook on low for 2.5 hours or until the brownies are set around the edges but slightly gooey in the middle.
10. Let the brownies cool in the slow cooker before slicing them into squares. Serve these rich and indulgent chocolate brownies with a scoop of vanilla ice cream.

Crockpot Bread and Butter Pudding

Serves: 4 Prep time: 15 minutes / Cook time: 2.5 hours

Ingredients:
- 8 slices of day-old bread, crusts removed, buttered
- 50g raisins
- 300ml whole milk
- 50g granulated sugar
- 1/4 tsp ground cinnamon
- 1/4 tsp ground nutmeg
- 25g candied peel
- 2 large eggs
- 1 tsp vanilla extract
- 1/4 tsp salt

Preparation instructions:
1. Grease the base and sides of the crockpot.
2. Arrange the buttered bread slices in layers in the crockpot, sprinkling the raisins and candied peel between the layers.
3. In a bowl, whisk together the whole milk, large eggs, granulated sugar, vanilla extract, ground cinnamon, ground nutmeg, and salt.
4. Pour the milk mixture over the bread layers, ensuring the bread is well soaked.
5. Cover and cook on low for 2.5 hours or until the pudding is set and golden brown on top.
6. Serve the warm bread and butter pudding slices with custard or a dollop of whipped cream for a comforting dessert. Enjoy the delightful combination of soft, custard-soaked bread with hints of cinnamon and nutmeg.

Slow Cooker Spiced Apple Cake

Serves: 4 Prep time: 15 minutes / Cook time: 2.5 hours

Ingredients:
- 200g self-raising flour
- 1 tsp ground cinnamon
- 1/2 tsp ground nutmeg
- 150g unsalted butter, softened
- 150g light brown sugar
- 2 large eggs
- 1 tsp vanilla extract
- 200g peeled and diced apples
- 60ml whole milk
- For the topping:
- 2 tbsp demerara sugar
- 1/2 tsp ground cinnamon

Preparation instructions:
1. Grease the base and sides of the slow cooker.
2. In a bowl, mix the self-raising flour, ground cinnamon, and ground nutmeg.
3. In another large bowl, cream together the softened unsalted butter and light brown sugar until light and fluffy.
4. Beat in the large eggs, one at a time, and add the vanilla extract.
5. Gradually fold in the flour mixture, alternating with the diced apples, and mix well.
6. Add the whole milk to the batter, stirring until combined.
7. Pour the batter into the slow cooker, spreading it out evenly.
8. In a small bowl, combine the demerara sugar and ground cinnamon for the topping. Sprinkle this mixture over the cake batter.
9. Cover and cook on low for 2.5 hours or until a skewer inserted into the middle of the cake comes out clean.
10. Let the apple cake cool in the slow cooker for about 15 minutes before slicing. Serve warm with a dollop of whipped cream or a scoop of vanilla ice cream for a delightful dessert.

Crockpot Lemon Cheesecake

Serves: 4 Prep time: 15 minutes / Cook time: 2.5 hours +

Ingredients:

- 250g cream cheese, softened
- 100g granulated sugar • 2 large eggs
- 1 tsp vanilla extract • Zest and juice of 1 lemon
- 200g digestive biscuits, crushed
- 80g unsalted butter, melted

Preparation instructions:

1. Grease the base and sides of a springform pan that fits inside your crockpot.
2. In a large bowl, beat the softened cream cheese and granulated sugar until smooth and creamy.
3. Beat in the large eggs, one at a time, and add the vanilla extract.
4. Mix in the lemon zest and juice until well combined.
5. In another bowl, combine the crushed digestive biscuits with melted unsalted butter. Press this mixture into the bottom of the prepared springform pan to create the cheesecake crust.
6. Pour the cream cheese filling over the crust, spreading it out evenly.
7. Place a trivet or aluminium foil in the bottom of the crockpot to elevate the springform pan above the water.
8. Add hot water to the crockpot until it reaches halfway up the sides of the springform pan.
9. Cover and cook on low for 2.5 hours. After cooking, let the cheesecake cool in the crockpot for an hour.
10. Refrigerate the cheesecake for at least 4 hours or overnight before serving. When ready to serve, remove the sides of the springform pan and slice the lemon cheesecake into wedges.

Slow Cooker Berry Compote

Serves: 4 Prep time: 10 minutes / Cook time: 2 hours

Ingredients:

- 300g mixed berries (such as strawberries, blueberries, raspberries)
- 50g granulated sugar
- Juice of 1 lemon
- 1/2 tsp vanilla extract

Preparation instructions:

1. In the slow cooker, combine the mixed berries, granulated sugar, lemon juice, and vanilla extract. Stir well.
2. Cover and cook on low for 2 hours, stirring occasionally, until the berries have softened and released their juices, creating a flavorful compote.
3. Taste and adjust the sweetness by adding more sugar if desired.
4. Serve the warm berry compote over pancakes, waffles, ice cream, or yoghurt for a delightful fruity topping. Enjoy the vibrant flavours of the mixed berries in this versatile compote.

Crockpot Chocolate Fudge

Serves: 4 Prep time: 10 minutes / Cook time: 2 hours + chilling time

Ingredients:

- 300g dark chocolate, chopped
- 1 can (400g) sweetened condensed milk
- 60g unsalted butter
- 1 tsp vanilla extract
- Pinch of salt
- 100g chopped nuts (such as walnuts or pecans) (optional)

Preparation instructions:

1. Grease and line a small baking dish that fits inside your crockpot.
2. In a heatproof bowl, combine the chopped dark chocolate, sweetened condensed milk, and unsalted butter.
3. Place the bowl over a pot of simmering water (double boiler) and stir until the chocolate and butter are melted and the mixture is smooth.
4. Remove the bowl from the heat and stir in the vanilla extract, pinch of salt, and chopped nuts (if using).
5. Pour the chocolate fudge mixture into the prepared baking dish, spreading it out evenly.
6. Place the baking dish on a trivet inside the crockpot.
7. Cover and cook on low for 2 hours. After cooking, let the fudge cool in the crockpot for an hour.
8. Refrigerate the fudge for at least 4 hours or until set.
9. Once set, remove the fudge from the baking dish, cut it into squares, and serve. Enjoy the rich and creamy chocolate fudge as a decadent treat or a delightful homemade gift.

Slow Cooker Vanilla Custard

Serves: 4 Prep time: 10 minutes / Cook time: 2 hours

Ingredients:

- 500ml whole milk
- 4 large eggs
- 100g granulated sugar
- 1 tsp vanilla extract
- Freshly grated nutmeg, for garnish (optional)

Preparation instructions:

1. In a saucepan over medium heat, warm the whole milk until it steams but does not boil. Remove from heat and let it cool slightly.
2. In a mixing bowl, whisk the large eggs and granulated sugar until well combined and slightly thickened.
3. Gradually pour the warm milk into the egg mixture, whisking continuously to prevent curdling.
4. Stir in the vanilla extract, ensuring it's well incorporated into the custard mixture.
5. Pour the custard mixture into heatproof ramekins or jars, dividing it equally among them.
6. Place the ramekins or jars on a trivet inside the crockpot.
7. Add hot water to the crockpot until it reaches halfway up the sides of the ramekins or jars.
8. Cover and cook on low for 2 hours or until the custard is set but still slightly wobbly in the centre.
9. Carefully remove the ramekins or jars from the crockpot using tongs, as they will be hot.
10. Let the custard cool to room temperature before

refrigerating for at least 2 hours or until chilled.

11. Garnish with freshly grated nutmeg, if desired, before serving. Enjoy the smooth and creamy slow cooker vanilla custard as a delightful dessert.

Crockpot Coconut Rice Pudding

Serves: 4 Prep time: 10 minutes / Cook time: 2.5 hours

Ingredients:
- 150g arborio rice
- 800ml coconut milk
- 100g granulated sugar
- 1/2 tsp vanilla extract
- 1/4 tsp ground cinnamon
- 1/4 tsp salt
- Desiccated coconut, for garnish (optional)

Preparation instructions:
1. Rinse the arborio rice under cold water until the water runs clear. Drain well.
2. In the crockpot, combine the rinsed rice, coconut milk, granulated sugar, vanilla extract, ground cinnamon, and salt. Stir to mix well.
3. Cover and cook on low for 2.5 hours, stirring occasionally to prevent sticking and ensure even cooking.
4. After 2.5 hours, check the rice pudding for desired consistency. If it's too thick, you can add a bit more coconut milk to reach the desired creaminess.
5. Spoon the rice pudding into serving bowls or jars.
6. Let the rice pudding cool to room temperature before refrigerating for at least 2 hours or until chilled.
7. Garnish with desiccated coconut, if desired, before serving. Enjoy the rich and coconut-flavoured crockpot rice pudding as a comforting dessert.

Slow Cooker Carrot Cake

Serves: 4 Prep time: 20 minutes / Cook time: 3 hours

Ingredients:
- 200g plain flour
- 1/2 tsp baking powder
- 1/2 tsp baking soda
- 1/2 tsp salt
- 1/2 tsp ground cinnamon
- 1/4 tsp ground nutmeg
- 2 large eggs
- 100g light brown sugar
- 120ml vegetable oil
- 1 tsp vanilla extract
- 200g grated carrots
- 50g chopped walnuts (optional)
- Cream cheese frosting, for topping (store-bought or homemade)

Preparation instructions:
1. In a bowl, whisk together the plain flour, baking powder, baking soda, salt, ground cinnamon, and ground nutmeg.
2. In another bowl, beat the large eggs and light brown sugar until well combined and slightly thickened.

3. Gradually add the vegetable oil and vanilla extract to the egg mixture, stirring continuously.
4. Gradually fold in the dry Ingredients until just combined, then fold in the grated carrots and chopped walnuts (if using).
5. Grease the base and sides of the crock pot insert.
6. Pour the carrot cake batter into the crockpot insert, spreading it out evenly.
7. Cover and cook on low for 3 hours or until a toothpick inserted into the centre of the cake comes out clean.
8. Once the cake is cooked, let it cool in the crockpot for about 30 minutes before carefully removing it from the insert.
9. Let the carrot cake cool completely before spreading a layer of cream cheese frosting on top.
10. Slice and serve the slow cooker carrot cake as a delightful dessert or teatime treat.

Crockpot Butterscotch Pudding

Serves: 4 Prep time: 10 minutes / Cook time: 2 hours

Ingredients:
- 100g brown sugar
- 50g unsalted butter
- 300ml whole milk
- 2 large eggs
- 30g plain flour
- 1/4 tsp salt
- Whipped cream, for serving (optional)

Preparation instructions:
1. In a small saucepan over low heat, melt the unsalted butter. Add the brown sugar and stir until the sugar is dissolved and the mixture is smooth. Remove from heat and let it cool slightly.
2. In a mixing bowl, whisk the large eggs. Gradually add the plain flour and salt, whisking continuously to avoid lumps.
3. Slowly pour the warm butter and sugar mixture into the egg mixture, whisking constantly until well combined.
4. Heat the whole milk in the saucepan until it steams but does not boil.
5. Gradually add the warm milk to the egg mixture, whisking continuously.
6. Pour the pudding mixture back into the saucepan and cook over low heat, stirring constantly, until the mixture thickens and coats the back of a spoon.
7. Transfer the pudding mixture to the crockpot.
8. Cover and cook on low for 2 hours or until the pudding is set and has a creamy texture.
9. Stir the pudding occasionally during cooking to ensure even consistency.
10. Once cooked, remove from the crockpot and let it cool slightly before serving.
11. Serve the butterscotch pudding warm, optionally topped with whipped cream for extra indulgence.

Slow Cooker Pear Crumble

Serves: 4 Prep time: 15 minutes / Cook time: 3 hours

Ingredients:

- 4 ripe pears, peeled, cored, and sliced
- 1 tbsp lemon juice
- 50g granulated sugar
- 1/2 tsp ground cinnamon
- 100g plain flour
- 50g rolled oats
- 50g unsalted butter, chilled and cubed
- Vanilla ice cream, for serving (optional)

Preparation instructions:

1. In a bowl, combine the sliced pears, lemon juice, granulated sugar, and ground cinnamon. Toss to coat the pears evenly.
2. In another bowl, mix the plain flour and rolled oats together. Add the chilled, cubed unsalted butter and rub the mixture between your fingers until it resembles coarse breadcrumbs.
3. Grease the base and sides of the crock pot insert.
4. Spread the pear mixture evenly in the crockpot.
5. Sprinkle the flour and oats mixture over the pears to form a crumbly topping.
6. Cover and cook on low for 3 hours or until the pears are tender and the crumble topping is golden brown and crispy.
7. Serve the pear crumble warm, preferably with a scoop of vanilla ice cream for a delightful dessert.

Crockpot Pumpkin Pie

Serves: 4 Prep time: 15 minutes / Cook time: 2.5 hours

Ingredients:

- 400g canned pumpkin puree
- 200ml double cream
- 2 large eggs
- 100g brown sugar
- 1/2 tsp ground cinnamon
- 1/4 tsp ground ginger
- 1/4 tsp ground nutmeg
- 1/4 tsp salt
- 1/2 tsp vanilla extract
- 150g digestive biscuits, crushed
- 50g unsalted butter, melted

Preparation instructions:

1. In a bowl, combine the crushed digestive biscuits and melted unsalted butter. Press the mixture into the base of the crock pot insert to create the pie crust.
2. In another bowl, whisk together the canned pumpkin puree, double cream, large eggs, brown sugar, ground cinnamon, ground ginger, ground nutmeg, salt, and vanilla extract until well combined.
3. Pour the pumpkin mixture over the prepared crust in the crockpot.
4. Cover and cook on low for 2.5 hours or until the pumpkin pie is set and firm in the centre.
5. Once cooked, turn off the crockpot and let the pie cool to room temperature before refrigerating for at least 2 hours or until chilled.

6. Serve the chilled pumpkin pie slices, optionally topped with whipped cream, for a delightful autumn dessert.

Slow Cooker Raspberry Coulis

Makes: Approximately 300ml Prep time: 10 minutes / Cook time: 2 hours

Ingredients:

- 300g fresh raspberries
- 50g granulated sugar
- 1 tbsp lemon juice

Preparation instructions:

1. In a small saucepan, combine the fresh raspberries, granulated sugar, and lemon juice over medium heat.
2. Cook, stirring occasionally, until the raspberries break down and release their juices, and the mixture thickens slightly.
3. Remove from heat and let it cool for a few minutes.
4. Transfer the raspberry mixture to the crockpot.
5. Cover and cook on low for 2 hours, allowing the flavours to meld together and the coulis to thicken further.
6. Once cooked, use a fine mesh sieve or cheesecloth to strain the coulis, removing the seeds and pulp.
7. Let the coulis cool to room temperature before transferring it to a sterilised glass jar or bottle.
8. Refrigerate the raspberry coulis for up to a week. Serve drizzled over desserts like cheesecake, ice cream, or pancakes for a burst of fruity flavour.

Crockpot Chocolate Bread Pudding

Serves: 4 Prep time: 15 minutes / Cook time: 2 hours

Ingredients:

- 300g stale bread, cut into cubes
- 60g dark chocolate, chopped
- 400ml whole milk
- 3 large eggs
- 75g granulated sugar
- 1 tsp vanilla extract
- 1/4 tsp ground cinnamon
- Pinch of salt
- Whipped cream or custard, for serving (optional)

Preparation instructions:

1. Grease the base and sides of the crock pot insert.
2. Place the stale bread cubes and chopped dark chocolate in the crockpot.
3. In a mixing bowl, whisk together the whole milk, large eggs, granulated sugar, vanilla extract, ground cinnamon, and a pinch of salt until well combined.
4. Pour the egg mixture over the bread and chocolate in the crockpot, ensuring all the bread is soaked in the liquid.
5. Cover and cook on low for 2 hours or until the pudding is set and no longer runny in the middle.
6. Once cooked, let the pudding cool for a few minutes before serving.
7. Serve warm, optionally topped with whipped cream or custard for a delightful dessert.

Slow Cooker Mocha Pudding Cake

Serves: 4 Prep time: 15 minutes / Cook time: 2.5 hours

Ingredients:
- 100g plain flour
- 25g cocoa powder
- 150g granulated sugar
- 1 tsp instant coffee granules
- 1/2 tsp baking powder
- 1/4 tsp salt
- 120ml whole milk
- 30g unsalted butter, melted
- 1 tsp vanilla extract
- 50g dark chocolate, chopped
- 250ml boiling water

Preparation instructions:
1. Grease the base and sides of the crock pot insert.
2. In a mixing bowl, combine the plain flour, cocoa powder, 100g of granulated sugar, instant coffee granules, baking powder, and salt.
3. Stir in the whole milk, melted unsalted butter, and vanilla extract until a thick batter forms.
4. Fold in the chopped dark chocolate.
5. Spread the batter evenly in the crockpot.
6. In a separate bowl, mix the remaining 50g of granulated sugar with the boiling water until the sugar is dissolved.
7. Carefully pour the hot sugar-water mixture over the batter in the crockpot.
8. Cover and cook on low for 2.5 hours or until the pudding is set and springs back when gently touched.
9. Once cooked, let the pudding cool slightly before serving.
10. Serve warm, optionally with a scoop of vanilla ice cream for an indulgent treat.

Crockpot Apple Butter

Makes: Approximately 500g Prep time: 15 minutes / Cook time: 4 hours

Ingredients:
- 1kg apples, peeled, cored, and sliced
- 200g granulated sugar
- 1 tsp ground cinnamon
- 1/4 tsp ground cloves
- 1/4 tsp ground nutmeg
- 1/4 tsp salt
- 1 tbsp lemon juice

Preparation instructions:
1. In the crockpot, combine the sliced apples, granulated sugar, ground cinnamon, ground cloves, ground nutmeg, salt, and lemon juice. Stir to combine.
2. Cover and cook on low for 4 hours or until the apples are very soft and cooked down.
3. Use an immersion blender or transfer the mixture to a blender and blend until smooth.
4. Continue cooking, uncovered, for another 1-2 hours on low, stirring occasionally, until the apple butter thickens to your desired consistency.

5. Let the apple butter cool to room temperature before transferring it to sterilised jars.
6. Store the apple butter in the refrigerator for up to 2 weeks or preserve it using proper canning methods for longer shelf life.
7. Spread the apple butter on toast, pancakes, or use it as a filling for pastries.

Slow Cooker Rhubarb Crisp

Serves: 4 Prep time: 15 minutes / Cook time: 3 hours

Ingredients:
- 500g rhubarb, trimmed and sliced
- 50g granulated sugar
- 1 tbsp lemon juice
- 75g plain flour
- 50g rolled oats
- 50g light brown sugar
- 1/2 tsp ground cinnamon
- 50g unsalted butter, chilled and cubed
- Vanilla ice cream or custard, for serving (optional)

Preparation instructions:
1. In a bowl, combine the sliced rhubarb, granulated sugar, and lemon juice. Toss to coat the rhubarb evenly.
2. In another bowl, mix the plain flour, rolled oats, light brown sugar, and ground cinnamon together. Add the chilled, cubed unsalted butter and rub the mixture between your fingers until it resembles coarse breadcrumbs.
3. Grease the base and sides of the crock pot insert.
4. Spread the rhubarb mixture evenly in the crockpot.
5. Sprinkle the flour and oats mixture over the rhubarb to form a crumbly topping.
6. Cover and cook on low for 3 hours or until the rhubarb is tender and the crisp topping is golden brown and crispy.
7. Serve the rhubarb crisp warm, preferably with a scoop of vanilla ice cream or custard for a delightful dessert.

Crockpot Chocolate Covered Strawberries

Serves: 4 Prep time: 15 minutes / Cook time: 1 hour

Ingredients:
- 200g dark chocolate, chopped
- 250g fresh strawberries, washed and dried

Preparation instructions:
1. Place the chopped dark chocolate in a heatproof bowl.
2. Fill a saucepan with water and bring it to a gentle simmer over medium heat. Place the bowl with chocolate over the simmering water, ensuring the bowl doesn't touch the water. Stir until the chocolate is completely melted and smooth.
3. Dip each strawberry into the melted chocolate, covering it halfway. Place the chocolate-covered strawberries on a parchment-lined tray.
4. Carefully transfer the tray with the strawberries to the crockpot.
5. Cover the crockpot and cook on low for 1 hour or until the chocolate sets.

6. Once done, remove the chocolate-covered strawberries from the crockpot and let them cool slightly before serving.

Slow Cooker Figgy Pudding

Serves: 4 Prep time: 15 minutes / Cook time: 2.5 hours

Ingredients:

* 200g dried figs, chopped
* 100g dried dates, chopped
* 100g breadcrumbs
* 50g plain flour
* 1/2 tsp baking powder
* 1/2 tsp ground cinnamon
* 1/4 tsp ground nutmeg
* 75g unsalted butter, melted
* 75ml whole milk
* 2 large eggs
* Zest of 1 orange
* 2 tbsp orange juice
* 1 tbsp honey
* Butter or custard, for serving (optional)

Preparation instructions:

1. Grease the base and sides of the crock pot insert.
2. In a mixing bowl, combine the chopped dried figs, chopped dried dates, breadcrumbs, plain flour, baking powder, ground cinnamon, and ground nutmeg.
3. In another bowl, whisk together the melted unsalted butter, whole milk, large eggs, orange zest, orange juice, and honey.
4. Pour the wet Ingredients into the dry Ingredients and mix until well combined.
5. Transfer the mixture to the greased crockpot.
6. Cover and cook on low for 2.5 hours or until the pudding is set and springs back when gently touched.
7. Let the figgy pudding cool slightly before serving.
8. Serve warm, optionally with a dollop of butter or custard for added richness.

Crockpot Coconut Macaroons

Makes: Approximately 12 Prep time: 15 minutes / Cook time: 2 hours

Ingredients:

* 200g desiccated coconut
* 150g sweetened condensed milk
* 1 tsp vanilla extract
* 2 large egg whites
* Pinch of salt
* 150g dark chocolate, melted (for dipping)

Preparation instructions:

1. In a mixing bowl, combine the desiccated coconut, sweetened condensed milk, and vanilla extract.
2. In a separate clean, dry bowl, whisk the egg whites with a pinch of salt until stiff peaks form.
3. Gently fold the whipped egg whites into the coconut mixture until well combined.

4. Grease the base and sides of the crock pot insert.
5. Scoop tablespoon-sized portions of the coconut mixture and place them on the greased crockpot insert.
6. Cover and cook on low for 2 hours or until the coconut macaroons are set and lightly golden.
7. Once the macarons are cooked and cooled, dip the bottoms into the melted dark chocolate and place them on parchment paper to set.
8. Let the chocolate set before serving the coconut macaroons.

Slow Cooker Spiced Plum Compote

Makes: Approximately 500g Prep time: 15 minutes / Cook time: 2 hours

Ingredients:

* 500g fresh plums, pitted and sliced
* 100g granulated sugar
* 1/2 tsp ground cinnamon
* 1/4 tsp ground ginger
* 1/4 tsp ground cloves
* 1/4 tsp ground nutmeg
* Zest and juice of 1 lemon
* 1 tbsp water

Preparation instructions:

1. In the crockpot, combine the sliced fresh plums, granulated sugar, ground cinnamon, ground ginger, ground cloves, ground nutmeg, lemon zest, lemon juice, and water. Stir to combine.
2. Cover and cook on low for 2 hours or until the plums are soft and cooked down into a thick compote.
3. Stir occasionally during cooking to ensure even spicing.
4. Let the spiced plum compote cool to room temperature before transferring it to sterilised jars.
5. Store the compote in the refrigerator for up to 2 weeks or preserve it using proper canning methods for longer shelf life.
6. Serve the spiced plum compote as a topping for desserts, yoghurt, or toast.

Crockpot Blackberry Jam

Makes: Approximately 500g Prep time: 10 minutes / Cook time: 3 hours

Ingredients:

* 500g fresh blackberries
* 250g granulated sugar
* Juice of 1 lemon

Preparation instructions:

1. In the crockpot, combine the fresh blackberries, granulated sugar, and lemon juice. Stir well to coat the blackberries in sugar.
2. Cover and cook on low for 3 hours, stirring occasionally, until the blackberries break down and the mixture thickens into jam-like consistency.
3. Using a potato masher, mash the blackberries to desired consistency for a smoother jam or leave it chunky for a

textured jam.

4. Let the blackberry jam cool to room temperature before transferring it to sterilised jars.

5. Seal the jars and store the jam in the refrigerator for up to 2 weeks or preserve it using proper canning methods for longer shelf life.

6. Spread this delightful blackberry jam on toast, scones, or use it as a filling for pastries and cakes.

Slow Cooker Mango Sticky Rice

Serves: 4 Prep time: 10 minutes / Cook time: 2 hours

Ingredients:

- 200g glutinous rice, soaked in water for 1 hour and drained
- 400ml coconut milk
- 80g granulated sugar
- 1/2 tsp salt
- 2 ripe mangoes, peeled, pitted, and sliced

Preparation instructions:

1. In the crockpot, combine the soaked glutinous rice, coconut milk, granulated sugar, and salt. Stir well to combine the Ingredients.

2. Cover and cook on low for 2 hours or until the rice is tender and has absorbed the coconut milk mixture, stirring occasionally.

3. Once the rice is cooked, let it cool slightly before serving.

4. Serve the warm mango sticky rice with sliced ripe mangoes on top. Drizzle with extra coconut milk if desired.

Crockpot Caramel Apple Dip

Makes: Approximately 500g Prep time: 10 minutes / Cook time: 1.5 hours

Ingredients:

- 4 large apples, peeled, cored, and diced
- 200g soft caramels, unwrapped
- 120ml double cream
- 1/2 tsp vanilla extract
- Pinch of salt

Preparation instructions:

1. In the crockpot, combine the diced apples, unwrapped soft caramels, double cream, vanilla extract, and a pinch of salt. Stir well to combine the Ingredients.

2. Cover and cook on low for 1.5 hours or until the apples are soft and the caramel is melted and smooth, stirring occasionally.

3. Once cooked, stir the caramel apple dip well to combine all the Ingredients.

4. Serve the caramel apple dip warm with apple slices, pretzels, or cookies for dipping.

Slow Cooker Chocolate Raspberry Cake

Serves: 4 Prep time: 15 minutes / Cook time: 2.5 hours

Ingredients:

- 200g plain flour
- 50g cocoa powder
- 1 tsp baking powder
- 1/2 tsp baking soda
- 1/4 tsp salt
- 150g granulated sugar
- 2 large eggs
- 180 ml whole milk
- 80 ml vegetable oil
- 1 tsp vanilla extract
- 200g fresh raspberries

Preparation instructions:

1. Grease the base and sides of the crock pot insert.

2. In a bowl, whisk together the plain flour, cocoa powder, baking powder, baking soda, salt, and granulated sugar.

3. In another bowl, whisk the large eggs, whole milk, vegetable oil, and vanilla extract until well combined.

4. Pour the wet Ingredients into the dry Ingredients and mix until smooth.

5. Gently fold in the fresh raspberries into the batter.

6. Pour the batter into the greased crockpot insert, spreading it evenly.

7. Cover and cook on low for 2.5 hours or until a toothpick inserted into the centre of the cake comes out clean.

8. Once cooked, let the chocolate raspberry cake cool slightly before serving. Enjoy this delightful dessert warm or at room temperature.

Crockpot Lemon Curd

Makes: Approximately 400g Prep time: 10 minutes / Cook time: 2 hours

Ingredients:

- Zest of 2 lemons
- 150ml fresh lemon juice (from about 4-5 lemons)
- 200g granulated sugar
- 100g unsalted butter, melted
- 3 large eggs, beaten

Preparation instructions:

1. In the crockpot, combine the lemon zest, fresh lemon juice, granulated sugar, melted unsalted butter, and beaten eggs. Whisk until well combined.

2. Cover and cook on low for 2 hours, stirring occasionally, until the lemon curd thickens and coats the back of a spoon.

3. Once the lemon curd is thickened, remove it from the crockpot and let it cool to room temperature.

4. Transfer the lemon curd to sterilised jars and seal. Store in the refrigerator for up to 2 weeks.

5. Enjoy the vibrant and zesty lemon curd on toast, scones, or as a filling for cakes and pastries.

Slow Cooker Pistachio Pudding

Serves: 4 Prep time: 10 minutes / Cook time: 2 hours

Ingredients:

- 600ml whole milk
- 100g granulated sugar
- 40g cornstarch
- 1/4 tsp salt

- 3 large egg yolks, beaten
- 1/2 tsp vanilla extract
- 100g shelled pistachios, finely chopped

Preparation instructions:

1. In the crockpot, combine 500ml of whole milk and granulated sugar. Stir until the sugar is dissolved.
2. In a separate bowl, mix cornstarch with the remaining 100 ml of whole milk to create a slurry.
3. Gradually whisk the cornstarch slurry into the milk mixture in the crockpot. Add salt and stir well.
4. Cover and cook on low for 2 hours, stirring occasionally, until the pudding thickens.
5. Once the pudding is thickened, temper the beaten egg yolks by adding a small amount of the hot pudding mixture while whisking constantly. Then, slowly pour the tempered yolks back into the crockpot, whisking continuously.
6. Cook for an additional 10 minutes until the pudding is smooth and creamy.
7. Remove from the crockpot and stir in the vanilla extract and finely chopped pistachios.
8. Let the pistachio pudding cool slightly before serving. Garnish with extra pistachios if desired.

Crockpot Blueberry Cobbler

Serves: 4 Prep time: 10 minutes / Cook time: 2 hours

Ingredients:

- 500g fresh blueberries • 100g granulated sugar
- 1 tbsp lemon juice • 150g plain flour
- 50g granulated sugar (for the batter)
- 1 1/2 tsp baking powder
- 1/2 tsp salt • 120ml whole milk
- 60g unsalted butter, melted

Preparation instructions:

1. In the crockpot, combine the fresh blueberries, granulated sugar, and lemon juice. Stir well to coat the blueberries in sugar.
2. In a mixing bowl, whisk together the plain flour, 50g granulated sugar, baking powder, and salt.
3. Add the whole milk and melted unsalted butter to the dry Ingredients. Mix until a thick batter forms.
4. Drop spoonfuls of the batter evenly over the blueberry mixture in the crockpot.
5. Cover and cook on low for 2 hours, or until the blueberries are bubbling and the cobbler topping is cooked through.
6. Serve the warm blueberry cobbler with a scoop of vanilla ice cream or a dollop of whipped cream.

Slow Cooker Orange Marmalade

Makes: Approximately 400g Prep time: 15 minutes / Cook time: 3 hours

Ingredients:

- 4 large oranges
- 1 lemon
- 1.2 litres water
- 1kg granulated sugar

Preparation instructions:

1. Wash the oranges and lemon thoroughly. Cut them in half and squeeze out the juice. Remove and reserve the seeds.
2. Slice the orange and lemon peels into thin strips or chunks according to your preference.
3. In a large pot, combine the orange and lemon juice, sliced peels, reserved seeds, and water. Bring to a boil and let it simmer for 2 hours, stirring occasionally, until the mixture is reduced by half.
4. Strain the mixture through a fine mesh sieve, pressing down to extract as much liquid as possible. Discard the seeds.
5. Return the liquid to the pot and add the granulated sugar. Stir over low heat until the sugar is completely dissolved.
6. Transfer the mixture to the crockpot and cook on low for 3 hours or until the marmalade thickens to your desired consistency, stirring occasionally.
7. Pour the hot marmalade into sterilised jars and seal them immediately. Allow the jars to cool to room temperature before storing them in a cool, dark place.
8. Enjoy the homemade orange marmalade on toast, scones, or as a filling for pastries.

Crockpot Cherry Clafoutis

Serves: 4 Prep time: 10 minutes / Cook time: 2 hours

Ingredients:

- 400g fresh cherries, pitted and halved
- 50g granulated sugar • 3 large eggs
- 60ml whole milk • 60ml double cream
- 50g plain flour • 1/4 tsp almond extract
- Butter, for greasing

Preparation instructions:

1. Grease the crockpot with butter to prevent sticking.
2. In a bowl, toss the pitted and halved cherries with granulated sugar. Spread them evenly at the bottom of the crockpot.
3. In another bowl, whisk the eggs, whole milk, double cream, plain flour, and almond extract until smooth.
4. Pour the egg mixture over the cherries in the crockpot.
5. Cover and cook on low for 2 hours or until the clafoutis is set and golden brown around the edges.
6. Let it cool slightly before serving. Dust with icing sugar if desired.

Slow Cooker Honeycomb

Makes: Approximately 200g Prep time: 10 minutes / Cook time: 1 hour

Ingredients:

- 100g golden syrup
- 200g granulated sugar
- 1 1/2 tsp baking soda

Preparation instructions:

1. In the crockpot, combine the golden syrup and granulated sugar. Stir well.
2. Cover and cook on low for 1 hour without stirring.
3. After 1 hour, carefully add the baking soda to the mixture and quickly stir until it foams up.

4. Pour the foaming mixture onto a baking tray lined with parchment paper. Let it cool and harden.
5. Once completely cooled, break the honeycomb into chunks and store in an airtight container.

Crockpot Apricot Jam

Makes: Approximately 400g Prep time: 15 minutes / Cook time: 2 hours

Ingredients:
- 500g fresh apricots, pitted and chopped
- 200g granulated sugar
- Juice of 1 lemon

Preparation instructions:
1. In the crockpot, combine the chopped apricots, granulated sugar, and lemon juice. Stir well.
2. Cover and cook on low for 2 hours, stirring occasionally, until the apricots are soft and the mixture thickens.
3. Using a hand blender, blend the mixture to your desired consistency.
4. Pour the jam into sterilised jars and seal them immediately. Allow the jars to cool to room temperature before storing them in a cool, dark place.

Slow Cooker Almond Joy Bars

Makes: 16 bars Prep time: 15 minutes / Cook time: 2 hours

Ingredients:
- 200g sweetened condensed milk
- 200g desiccated coconut • 100g powdered sugar
- 150g whole almonds • 200g dark chocolate, melted
- 1/2 tsp almond extract

Preparation instructions:
1. In a bowl, mix the sweetened condensed milk, desiccated coconut, powdered sugar, and almond extract until well combined.
2. Press the mixture evenly into the bottom of the greased crockpot.
3. Place whole almonds on top of the coconut layer.
4. Cover and cook on low for 2 hours or until the coconut is set.
5. Once the bars are set and cooled, cut them into squares and drizzle with melted dark chocolate.
6. Let the chocolate set before serving. Store any leftovers in an airtight container.

Crockpot Cranberry Sauce

Serves: 4 Prep time: 5 minutes / Cook time: 2 hours

Ingredients:
- 300g fresh cranberries • 200g granulated sugar
- 240ml water • Zest and juice of 1 orange

Preparation instructions:
1. In the crockpot, combine the fresh cranberries, granulated sugar, water, orange zest, and orange juice. Stir well.
2. Cover and cook on low for 2 hours, stirring occasionally, until the cranberries burst and the sauce thickens.
3. Taste and adjust sweetness if necessary, adding more sugar if desired.
4. Let the cranberry sauce cool before serving. Transfer to a jar and refrigerate until ready to use.

Slow Cooker Pecan Pie

Serves: 4 Prep time: 15 minutes / Cook time: 3 hours

Ingredients:
- 200g shortcrust pastry (store-bought or homemade)
- 100g unsalted butter, melted
- 200g golden syrup • 3 large eggs, beaten
- 1 tsp vanilla extract • 200g pecan halves

Preparation instructions:
1. Roll out the shortcrust pastry and line a greased crockpot dish with it, trimming any excess.
2. In a bowl, mix the melted butter, golden syrup, beaten eggs, and vanilla extract until well combined.
3. Arrange the pecan halves evenly over the pastry base in the crockpot.
4. Pour the syrup mixture over the pecans.
5. Cover and cook on low for 3 hours or until the filling is set.
6. Let the pecan pie cool slightly before serving. Serve warm or at room temperature.

Crockpot Sticky Orange Cake

Serves: 4 Prep time: 15 minutes / Cook time: 2 hours

Ingredients:
- 200g self-raising flour
- 100g unsalted butter, softened
- 100g granulated sugar
- 2 large eggs
- Zest and juice of 2 oranges
- 100ml whole milk
- For the sticky orange glaze:
- 50g icing sugar
- 2 tbsp orange juice

Preparation instructions:
1. In a bowl, cream together the softened butter and granulated sugar until light and fluffy.
2. Beat in the eggs, one at a time, and then add the orange zest and juice.
3. Gradually fold in the self-raising flour and mix until well combined. Stir in the milk to create a smooth batter.
4. Grease the crockpot dish and pour the batter into it.
5. Cover and cook on low for 2 hours or until a toothpick inserted into the centre of the cake comes out clean.
6. While the cake is cooking, prepare the sticky orange glaze by mixing the icing sugar with the orange juice until smooth.
7. When the cake is done, poke several holes in the top with a skewer and pour the sticky orange glaze over the warm cake.
8. Let the cake cool slightly before serving. Serve slices with a dollop of whipped cream or a scoop of vanilla ice cream.

14370709R00077